EMERGENT MODELS
of GLOBAL LEADERSHIP

Nancy S. Huber and
Mark C. Walker, Editors

a volume in the International Leadership Association series
Building Leadership Bridges

THE INTERNATIONAL LEADERSHIP ASSOCIATION (ILA) is a global network for all those who practice, study, and teach leadership. The mission of the ILA is the cultivation of leadership knowledge and practice for individuals, organizations, and society. The principal means by which this mission is accomplished is through the synergy of bringing together public- and private-sector leaders, scholars, educators, and consultants from many disciplines and many nations. For more information, please visit the ILA's Web site at www.ila-net.org.

The ILA is an affiliate of The James MacGregor Burns Academy of Leadership at the University of Maryland. The Burns Academy of Leadership fosters leadership through scholarship, education, and training, with special attention to advancing the leadership of groups historically underrepresented in public life. For more information, please visit www.academy.umd.edu.

The ILA partnered with the Center for Creative Leadership (CCL®) to produce this publication. CCL is an international, nonprofit educational institution whose mission is to advance the understanding, practice, and development of leadership for the benefit of society worldwide. Based in Greensboro, North Carolina, it conducts research, produces publications and assessment tools, and offers a variety of educational programs. For more information, visit CCL's Web site at www.ccl.org.

For additional copies of this book, please contact the publisher:

THE JAMES MACGREGOR BURNS ACADEMY OF
LEADERSHIP
University of Maryland
College Park, MD 20742-7715 USA
Phone: 301-405-5218
Fax: 301-405-6402
E-mail: ila@ila-net.org
Web: www.ila-net.org

Library of Congress ISBN: 1-891464-27-2

Production: Center for Creative Leadership
Production Editor: Joanne Ferguson

Table of Contents

Introduction

Greetings and welcome to the new *Building Leadership Bridges*.

As the International Leadership Association (ILA) continues to grow and develop, we have sought to improve its publishing presence so that it not only reflects the knowledge and experience of its membership but also begins to play a more crucial role in the marketplace of ideas. We all have a stake in sharing our knowledge as well as ideas for the creative application of leadership wisdom. It is our belief that *Emergent Models of Global Leadership,* a volume in the *Building Leadership Bridges (BLB) Series,* is an excellent step in that direction.

We take great pride in the current volume in this transition year. Instead of a compendium of selected proceedings from the previous year's conference, we offer perspectives on the ILA's theme for 2005, Emergent Models of Global Leadership. This theme will be further explored at the seventh annual conference in Amsterdam. The submission process for this volume was thoughtfully separated from the conference in order to expand the opportunity for people to participate in the association.

With nearly fifty submissions to choose from, we have selected an outstanding variety of articles that will be of interest to members from all of the Global Learning Communities (GLCs) within ILA. The authors included hail from Europe, Russia, Australia, and the United States and discuss topics as diverse as shared leadership, ethics, charisma, the use of learning journals, social change, allophilia, strategic visioning, nonverbal communication, and deaf leadership. It is an impressive array.

We sincerely urge you to continue to share your work and perspectives with us. We also suggest that you visit the ILA Web site—at http://www.ila-net.org/—often to see the news and resources published there and for deadlines for the next volume of *BLB*. Our collective wisdom is our greatest resource.

In conclusion, we have many people to thank for the success of this project. Specifically, our partnership with the Center for Creative Leadership continues to provide the editing and production assistance essential to our ability to offer a high-quality publication; we are grateful for the talent and patience of Joanne Ferguson. We must also thank the ILA Board of Directors for a vision that has allowed *Building Leadership Bridges* to evolve over time as we attempt to better serve our natural constituency—those who study, practice, teach, and care about the phenomenon of leadership.

Nancy S. Huber and Mark Clarence Walker
Editors

Shared Leadership and Culture: Potential Emergence and Global Application

By Jay Carson

AS OUR WORLD SEEKS TO ADAPT TO CHANGES RESULTING FROM globalization, organizational leadership plays a heightened and more complex role in organizational success. Cultural values also have a significant impact on individual cognition (Markus, Kitayama, & Heiman, 1996; Nisbett, Peng, Choi, & Norenzayan, 2001), motivation (Earley, 1989, 1993; Erez, 1994; Iyengar & Lepper, 1999), emotion (Mesquita & Frijda, 1992), and relational understandings (Markus & Kitayama, 1991). Therefore, the intersection of organizational leadership and cultural values represents a fruitful area of understanding for those interested in improving organizational success. Whether faced with greater cultural diversity in the workforce or working with partner organizations around the world, differing cultural values can impact both the responses to and the effectiveness of different approaches to leadership (e.g., House et al., 1999).

Leadership has traditionally been viewed as a top-down influence process based on positional hierarchy. However, some researchers have begun to examine the impact of shared forms of leadership (e.g., Pearce & Conger, 2003). Leadership from this perspective is seen as a process of mutual and reciprocal influence within groups and organizations that results in leadership tasks, roles, and behaviors that are shared by multiple individuals (e.g., Barry, 1991; Pearce & Sims, 2000; Perry, Pearce, & Sims, 1999; Seers, 1996). Shared leadership has shown promise as an effective approach to maximizing worker effectiveness, particularly in team settings (Avolio, Jung, & Sivasubramaniam, 1996; Pearce & Sims, 2002; Sivasubramaniam, Murry, Avolio, & Jung, 2002).

While several studies have attempted to capture universal dimensions of cultural values, researchers are progressing toward convergence around similar value dimensions. In particular, the dimension of individualism/collectivism has emerged across studies and has been related to a wide variety of societal and organizational phenomena (Earley & Gibson, 1998; Triandis, 1995). Power distance is a second dimension that has proven to be fairly robust and has been examined in many studies as well (Brockner et al., 2001; Bruins et al., 1993). Together, these two key cultural dimensions have received the most consistent attention in the organizational literature and are of particular relevance to research involving groups and types of influence (Gibson & Zellmer-Bruhn, 2001).

Shared leadership by nature has a collective or relational orientation in that it focuses not on a single individual but instead on influence present among a group of people. Shared leadership also implies a greater degree of power at lower levels of organizational hierarchy. Thus, these two prominent dimensions of cultural values seem to be closely related to the construct of shared leadership. However, research to date has not considered whether shared leadership is likely to be discovered in certain cultural settings or how implementation of shared leadership might be affected by cultural values.

In order to explore the relationship between shared leadership and cultural values, I first consider the types of cultures in which shared leadership is more likely to emerge as a natural phenomenon by examining two important dimensions of cultural values—individualism/collectivism and power distance. Second, given the potential of shared leadership for organizational effectiveness, I consider factors that are likely to lead to successful global implementation of shared leadership in various cultures.

Shared Leadership

Shared leadership represents an emerging perspective that contrasts with traditional views of leadership. For decades, the study of leadership has centered on a focal individual and his or her traits (e.g., House, 1977; McClelland, 1961, 1975) and behaviors (e.g., Kahn & Katz, 1953; Stogdill & Coons, 1957), as well as situational contingencies (e.g., Fiedler, 1967; House, 1971; Vroom & Yetton, 1973) related to the individual's effectiveness as a leader. Leadership from this traditional perspective is seen as the responsibility of certain designated individuals for developing effective approaches to tasks (e.g., Fleishman, Harris, & Burt, 1955; Kahn & Katz, 1953), motivating and developing followers (House et al., 1999), and stimulating creativity, change, and growth within the organization (e.g., Schein, 1992). These individuals typically are positioned in higher levels of organizational hierarchy and their influence is seen as flowing in a downward direction to those followers within their span of control. Pearce and Sims (2002) have referred to this traditional type of leadership as vertical leadership.

Shared leadership, on the other hand, focuses on influence that emanates from multiple individuals within a group. The idea of leadership being shared or distributed among persons in group or team settings is not new (cf. Gibb, 1954; Katz & Kahn, 1978), although recently the idea has received much more attention (Brown & Hosking, 1986; Cox, Pearce, & Perry, 2003; Gronn, 2002). Scholars have long argued that shared leadership provides synergy, and that "those organizations in which influential acts are widely shared are most effective" (Katz & Kahn, 1978, p. 332).

" SHARED LEADERSHIP IS A *GROUP* PHENOMENON. "
IT REPRESENTS A SOCIAL PROCESS INVOLVING
INFLUENCE EXHIBITED BY MANY GROUP MEMBERS
IN THE SHAPING OF GROUP TASKS, MOTIVATION OF
GROUP MEMBERS, AND STIMULATION OF CHANGE
AND GROWTH.

Shared leadership is conceptually distinct from empowerment (Conger & Kanungo, 1988), participative decision making or problem solving (Vroom & Yetton, 1973), self-leadership (Manz & Sims, 1980), and collective vision and purpose (Klimoski & Mohammed, 1994). While these are all potential antecedents to shared leadership (Carson & Tesluk, 2005; Cox et al., 2003), none of them sufficiently captures the notion of mutual and reciprocal *influence* that is fundamental to shared leadership. Shared leadership is a *group* phenomenon. It represents a social process involving influence exhibited by many group members in the shaping of group tasks, motivation of group members, and stimulation of change and growth.

Several empirical studies have been conducted with shared leadership as an explicit source of leadership (Cox et al., 2003), and the results are quite promising. Bowers and Seashore (1966) examined "mutual leadership" among life insurance agents and found this to be predictive of the types of insurance that were sold and the cost per unit of new policies. Avolio and colleagues (1996) explored shared leadership among teams of undergraduate students and found a positive correlation with self-reported effectiveness. Pearce and Sims (2002) studied the relationship between shared leadership and change management team effectiveness at a large automotive manufacturing firm and found shared leadership to be a more useful predictor than the vertical leadership of the appointed team leader. Sivasubramaniam and colleagues (2002) found that team leadership, defined similarly to shared leadership as collective influence of members in a team on each other, was positively related to team performance and potency over time in a sample of undergraduate business students. Carson and Tesluk (2005) found that shared leadership was strongly related to consulting team performance as rated by the end users of the team's work product.

These studies all suggest that shared leadership may be a more important predictor of effectiveness in group settings than the traditional vertical leadership. However, the appropriateness of sharing leadership within organizational groups may be partly due to expectations of power distribution and the degree of group versus individual orientation present in various cultures.

Cultural Dimensions

Research on culture has shown consistently that "culture matters" as it has an influence on human cognition, emotion, motivation, and behavior (Markus & Kitayama, 1991). However, culture remains a difficult concept to define and has been suggested to be the human-made part of the environment (Herskovits, 1955), somewhat like a set of programs that control behavior or a software of the mind (Hofstede, 1980, 1991). Researchers tend to agree that culture consists of shared elements (both subjective and objective), is a result of adaptive human interactions, and is transmitted over time (Triandis, 1994). Culture can thus be thought of as a "pattern of beliefs, attitudes, self-definitions, norms, and values" that are shared by a group of people (Triandis, 1994).

Several studies have attempted to distill and organize the hundreds of values on which cultures might differ into a succinct set of dimensions that are useful for comparing nations or societies. The most well-known and influential of these is Hofstede's 1980 study of matched samples of IBM marketing and servicing employees across fifty nations which found four factors that accounted for differences in responses on questionnaires. The four dimensions of culture were named power distance, individualism/collectivism, masculinity/femininity, and uncertainty avoidance (Hofstede, 1980). *Power distance* refers to the extent to which the less powerful members of institutions and organizations within a country expect and accept that power is distributed unequally. *Individualism* refers to societies that value loose social relations in which everyone looks out for themselves and their immediate families, whereas *collectivism* refers to societies in which people are integrated into strong, cohesive ingroups which look out for them in exchange for unquestioning lifelong loyalty. *Masculinity/femininity* refers to societies in which social gender roles are clearly distinct versus those where social gender roles overlap. *Uncertainty avoidance* refers to the extent to which people in a society feel threatened by uncertain or unknown situations.

Subsequent studies have attempted to replicate and extend Hofstede's research in order to consider whether these dimensions of culture are accurate and complete. A group of researchers known as the Chinese Culture Connection (CCC), led by Michael Bond, sought to develop a set of cultural dimensions based on Eastern culture rather than Western (Chinese Culture Connection, 1987). The CCC developed an emic Chinese Values Survey (CVS) that resulted in four factors. Two of these were correlated differentially with individualism and power distance, one correlated directly with femininity, and one was unique from Hofstede's findings (referred to in the CCC study as "Confucian Work Dynamism," it was later adopted by Hofstede and renamed "Long-Term Orientation").

Schwartz employed both an emic and etic approach to understanding cultural values and found three bipolar value dimensions (Schwartz, 1994a, 1994b). The first is autonomy (person is viewed as an autonomous, bounded entity) versus conservatism (person is viewed as embedded in a collective), which is conceptually similar to individualism/collectivism. The second is hierarchy (hierarchical system of ascribed roles) versus egalitarianism (individuals as moral equals who share basic interests), which is conceptually similar to power distance. The third is mastery (people seek to assert control and exploit the natural and social world) versus harmony (people accept the world as it is and seek to preserve it).

In an attempt to find convergence among these three dimensional approaches, Bond conducted a second-order factor analysis for twelve nations that had available data from all three studies—Hofstede, CCC, and Schwartz (Bond, 1996). This yielded four factors, but only two made sense conceptually. In part, this was due to the fact that the number of nations was less than the number of dimensions. Schwartz later correlated his data directly to Hofstede's and found that autonomy and egalitarianism correlated negatively with power distance and positively with individualism, whereas conservatism and hierarchy showed an opposite pattern—correlating positively with power distance and negatively with individualism (Smith & Schwartz, 1997). The findings from all of these dimensional approaches thus seem to be showing some degree of convergence on two basic dimensions of culture: preferred cultural views of individual versus group relations (individualism/collectivism) and preferred cultural modes of enacting social roles through negotiation among equals versus acceptance of unequal, hierarchical roles (power distance).

Given the convergence on these two important cultural dimensions and the conceptual connection that each one has with shared leadership, it makes sense to consider how these two dimensions are related to one another. In Hofstede's original research, he ran correlations between the two dimensions of individualism/collectivism and power distance at the national level and found that they tend to be negatively correlated with one another (correlation coefficient of -.68). High power distance countries tend to be more collectivistic, whereas low power distance countries tend to be more individualistic. In fact, of the fifty nations included in Hofstede's study, only six deviated from this pattern. Five of these (Spain, France, Italy, Belgium, and South Africa) were of medium power distance but were strongly individualistic, suggesting a stratified form of individualism where everyone has a rank that is more imposed by traditions than the group (Hofstede, 1980). Only one country (Costa Rica) was found to have low power distance in a strongly collectivistic culture.

Potential Emergence of Shared Leadership Within Cultures

Having developed a basic understanding of shared leadership and having linked it conceptually with two important cultural dimensions, we can consider the types of cultures in which leadership might be more likely to be shared among group members as a naturally occurring phenomenon. By crossing the dimensions of individualism/collectivism and power distance, it is possible to create a two-by-two matrix representing different types of cultures on these crucial dimensions (see Figure 1).

	Low Power Distance	High Power Distance
Individualism	**Quadrant I** High Possibility of Shared Leadership	**Quadrant II** Some Possibility of Shared Leadership?
Collectivism	**Quadrant IV** Highest Possibility of Shared Leadership, But Cultural Rarity	**Quadrant III** Low Possibility of Shared Leadership

Figure 1
Potential Emergence of Shared Leadership Within Cultures

Power distance will be the more important of these two variables in predicting the emergence of shared leadership, with cultures that are lower in power distance exhibiting a higher likelihood of shared leadership. The reason for this is that shared leadership is fundamentally about involvement by multiple individuals in the leadership process. In order for shared leadership to occur, individuals must feel empowered to participate in the leadership of their group, must be involved in determining the direction and efforts of the group, and must support and inspire one another toward achievement of the group's purpose or mission. These types of processes are far less likely to occur naturally in cultures that are characterized by an unequal, often hierarchical, distribution of power and distinct social roles. On the other hand, cultures that are low in power distance are much more likely to be accepting of shared leadership processes because the culture already has an understanding of power being distributed through processes of negotiation among people of equal status. Therefore, the propensity for low power distance cultures to allow individuals at lower organizational levels to feel empowered and to become involved in mutual leadership is greater.

Whereas power distance is likely to influence the degree to which cultures will accept leadership from equals, an individualistic or collectivistic orientation is likely to influence the degree to which cultures are comfortable working on tasks that are highly interdependent versus highly independent and the nature of preferred rewards. Individualistic societies tend to emphasize looking out for yourself and your family, which often leads to an independent self-construal (Markus & Kitayama, 1991). Therefore, individualistic societies are likely to prefer working on autonomous tasks and to receive individual rewards for a job well done. On the other hand, collectivistic societies tend to emphasize embeddedness in designated groups and unwavering loyalty to those in your ingroup, which often leads to an interdependent self-construal. Therefore, collectivistic societies are likely to prefer working on interdependent tasks in teams and to receive group-based rewards for a job well done (Bond, Leung, & Wan, 1982; Kirkman & Shapiro, 2000). Since shared leadership requires some degree of interdependence, mutual involvement and inspiration, and collective support, it is more likely to emerge in collectivistic cultures than individualistic cultures.

Perhaps one reason that shared leadership has only recently been explored at any length is that cultures provide a natural impediment to shared leadership. I have just argued that shared leadership is most likely to occur in cultures that are low in power distance and in cultures that are collectivistic. However, I previously discussed Hofstede's findings that showed a strong negative correlation between these two dimensions. In fact, of the fifty countries studied by Hofstede, only one (Costa Rica) was found to be *both* collectivistic and low in power distance. Nonetheless, shared leadership has been found to operate effectively in countries other than Costa Rica, so I will consider each quadrant of the matrix in Figure 1 in turn.

The first type of culture that will be considered is one with a fairly high possibility of shared leadership occurring naturally. This can be found in Quadrant I of Figure 1 and represents cultures that are individualistic and low on power distance (I/LP). Nations that would fall into this quadrant include the United States, England, Australia, and the Nordic countries. Low power distance will facilitate the acceptance of leadership from peers, but the individualistic nature of I/LP cultures may impede the development of trust, interdependent involvement, and collective purpose. However, the cultural acceptance of negotiation among equals should enable groups to come together and agree to pursue shared forms of leadership.

> **" PERHAPS ONE REASON THAT SHARED LEADERSHIP HAS ONLY RECENTLY BEEN EXPLORED AT ANY LENGTH IS THAT CULTURES PROVIDE A NATURAL IMPEDIMENT TO SHARED LEADERSHIP. "**

The second type of culture can be found in Quadrant II of Figure 1 and represents cultures that are individualistic and relatively high on power distance (I/HP). Nations that would fall into this quadrant include France, Belgium, Italy, Spain, and South Africa. At first glance, one would expect that I/HP cultures should represent the lowest likelihood of shared leadership since low power distance and collectivism have been argued to best facilitate the emergence of shared leadership. However, I/HP nations tend to be closer to the middle in terms of power distance rather than extremely high. Thus, while the same concerns over individualism are present as noted above with I/LP cultures, the fact that power distances are imposed more by self or tradition than by others in the group (Hofstede, 1980) should allow for the possibility of discussing the potential advantages of the collective involvement and mutual influence provided by shared leadership.

The third type of culture can be found in Quadrant III of Figure 1 and represents cultures that are collectivistic and high on power distance (C/HP). Nations that would fall into this quadrant include China, much of the Middle East, and most African and Latin American countries. C/HP cultures represent the least likely areas for shared leadership to be discovered naturally. The extremely high power distance will make it very difficult for individuals to ascribe leadership to anyone who is not in a natural position of higher power. Therefore, processes of mutual influence among peers are not likely to develop without intervention.

The fourth type of culture can be found in Quadrant IV of Figure 1 and represents cultures that are collectivistic and low on power distance (C/LP). While C/LP cultures represent the highest possibility of shared leadership, they are also a cultural rarity as previously noted. Nonetheless, from a theoretical standpoint, shared leadership should be most likely to naturally emerge within this particular cultural profile.

Application of Shared Leadership Within Cultures

Despite the impediments to natural emergence of shared leadership in most cultures, it is likely to prove beneficial if these cultural barriers can be overcome. Previous research has demonstrated positive effects of shared leadership over and above that demonstrated by vertical forms of leadership (e.g., Pearce & Sims, 2002; Carson & Tesluk, 2005). Therefore, I will return to the two-by-two matrix of power distance and individualism/collectivism in order to examine factors that might be necessary for implementing shared leadership in organizations within each quadrant (see Figure 2).

	Low Power Distance	High Power Distance
Individualism	**Quadrant I** Encourage and facilitate: • Shared purpose and goals • Mutual inspiration • Social support and trust • Collective involvement	**Quadrant II** • Share leadership according to roles—maintain role boundaries • Maintain status differences —certain leadership roles are exclusive to higher status
Collectivism	**Quadrant IV** • Cultural rarity—encourage shared leadership and monitor for any potential threats	**Quadrant III** • Overcome effects of power distance—maintain buffers between team members and former supervisors • Take advantage of collectivism—maintain an interdependent team orientation

Figure 2
Application of Shared Leadership Within Cultures

Cultures in Quadrant I are I/LP cultures (e.g., United States, England, Australia, and the Nordic countries). The presence of low power distance in these cultures is likely to support shared leadership as long as the potential limitations of individualism can be overcome. There are at least four major group-level antecedent conditions for shared leadership to take place in I/LP cultures: a shared sense of purpose and goals, mutual inspiration, social support and trust among team members, and collective involvement by team members (Carson & Tesluk, 2005). Whether work groups have a designated internal leader or an external supervisor, these organizational leaders should encourage and facilitate these four conditions in order to provide an environment where shared leadership can develop.

> " THERE ARE AT LEAST FOUR MAJOR GROUP-LEVEL ANTECEDENT CONDITIONS FOR SHARED LEADERSHIP TO TAKE PLACE IN I/LP CULTURES: A SHARED SENSE OF PURPOSE AND GOALS, MUTUAL INSPIRATION, SOCIAL SUPPORT AND TRUST AMONG TEAM MEMBERS, AND COLLECTIVE INVOLVEMENT BY TEAM MEMBERS. "

First, a sense of shared purpose and collective goals is a crucial foundation for shared leadership. Avolio and colleagues (1996) argue that shared leadership can only truly and fully exist when a collection of individuals has evolved into a team such that there is a shared sense of purpose and common goals. At this point individuals become willing to sacrifice for the beliefs of the team and have a collective desire to pursue team goals. Thus, the individualistic tendency to focus primarily on autonomy and personal goals and outcomes must be overcome in I/LP cultures. This may involve participation by the group in determining the purpose and goals of the team, and may also include the use of formal routines or symbols that emphasize the importance and priority of team goals and purposes. Second is mutual inspiration, whereby team members inspire one another to pursue the shared purpose of the group by enthusiastically reminding team members of the team's purpose through both words and actions. Once again, this requires subordination of personal goals and interests to those of the group, which may be more difficult in individualistic cultures.

Third is social support and trust, whereby team members support one another through encouragement and recognition of both individual and team accomplishments. Individual accomplishments must be recognized by group members because of the importance placed on individual success in I/LP cultures, but team accomplishments must also be recognized by group members so that individuals see the importance of staying focused on team purposes and supporting one another. While this type of relational support and harmony is characteristic of ingroups in collectivistic cultures, it may or may not exist in work groups in individualistic cultures. Therefore, organizational leaders in I/LP cultures should foster a climate within teams that encourages interdependence and trust (Edmondson, 1999) if they hope to develop shared leadership.

Fourth is collective involvement, whereby team members are given input into team processes and decisions in order to mutually influence one another. If a few individuals are allowed to dominate group discussions it will be impossible for the influence of the remaining team members to emerge within the team. This is likely to be a common tendency in I/LP cultures since lower power distance leads to greater perceptions of voice and the right to speak up; however, not everyone is an extravert and some individuals may be content to let others take on leadership roles. Therefore, organizational leaders should encourage and facilitate norms that allow for collective involvement of all members in team decisions and processes.

Cultures in Quadrant II are I/HP cultures (e.g., France, Belgium, Italy, Spain, and South Africa). These cultures, as previously discussed, must overcome effects from both power distance and individualism in order to implement shared leadership, which will likely present difficulties. However, there may still be some possibility for shared leadership to develop in this quadrant. In countries that represent I/HP culture, power distances tend to be imposed more by the self or tradition than by others in the group, reflecting a stratified form of individualism where everyone has some type of rank (Hofstede, 1980). Authority for formal leaders in these cultures is typically based both on the rules describing their role or office and on their personal authority due to intelligence, experience, moral values, etc. (Fayol, 1949); there is a sense of status given implicitly to supervisory positions, but some authority might also be conferred to non-supervisory employees due to expertise or other personal influence. Implementation of shared leadership in I/HP cultures is therefore likely to depend on the presence of roles and their boundaries in groups.

In order for shared leadership to work in I/HP cultures, individuals in supervisory roles must be physically removed from the group; otherwise deference to their positional authority will prevent the emergence of influence for individuals in "lesser" roles within the group. The nature of the supervisory role should be made explicit and clear, and a clear boundary should be maintained; the exact nature of this role may differ from country to country and from organization to organization depending on the typical or traditional attributions of authority. This supervisory role will still be considered of "higher status" in the organization as evidenced by important symbols, but the role will not encompass leadership of all facets of the groups under that influence. In other words, supervisors should be followed, but their span of influence over the group should be limited by formal role descriptions. Within groups, this will allow for the influence to be ascribed to multiple members primarily based on expertise and other forms of personal influence. Thus, shared leadership in I/HP cultures is perhaps most promising for cross-functional teams where there is less overlap in the types of knowledge and experience possessed by group members.

Cultures in Quadrant III are C/HP cultures (e.g., China, much of the Middle East, and most African and Latin American countries). These cultures are likely to benefit from the presence of collectivistic values as they seek to implement shared leadership, but will find difficulty as a result of the high power distances. Power distances in these cultures seem to be somehow exacerbated by the presence of collectivism, such that people who are dependent on ingroups are often very dependent on high power individuals as well (Hofstede, 1980). Thus the primary intervention that is necessary in C/HP cultures will be to overcome the effects of power distance that are likely to inhibit the development of shared leadership within work groups at lower levels of the organization.

The first step to effective implementation of shared leadership in C/HP cultures will therefore be to provide buffers between work groups and their external leaders. Similar to I/HP cultures, this will begin with the physical removal of the external leaders or supervisors from the team. The supervisor's office should not be located in or near the team's work area, and formal meetings with the supervisor should be less frequent and conducted with a team representative rather than the team as a whole. This is due to the fact that the collective mind-set will likely reinforce the positional authority of the supervisor if meetings are conducted as a group; meetings with an individual may be less susceptible to these effects. Incentive structures for both the group and the supervisor should also reinforce the buffers between the group and the supervisor. In particular, the supervisor's reward structure should reflect elements of the group's overall performance but might be reduced if the supervisor is overstepping his or her boundary. Supervisors should assist with determining the group's purpose and should be involved in goal setting, but should leave the process and pursuit of the purpose and goals up to team members. Group rewards, on the other hand, should be based on achievement of group goals (Wageman, 1995) and might include appraisals of the degree of autonomous functioning and shared leadership exhibited by the group.

At the same time, the benefits of collectivistic values should be reinforced in order to effectively implement shared leadership in C/HP cultures. Due to the emphasis in collectivistic cultures on relational harmony, it should not be difficult for groups to develop mutual inspiration, social support, and trust—these will come quite naturally. Collective involvement may not be as natural, however. While group members are likely to be accustomed to working interdependently with one another and are focused more on group than individual outcomes, there may be a sense of reliance on the formal leader or supervisor for direction and influence. There may be a hesitancy to speak up and suggest improvements to team processes or solutions to dilemmas facing the team. Thus, training interventions in effective group processes and group decision making will likely enable these teams to begin exerting influence over one another in the direction of the team's work. In this way, members may become more actively involved and begin to share the leadership within the group. It will also be important for formal supervisors to provide ongoing encouragement and reinforcement of the importance of shared leadership in order for teams to truly feel empowered to lead themselves without usurping the authority of the formal leader.

Finally, cultures in Quadrant IV are C/LP cultures. Hofstede identified only one country that represents this particular pairing of values (Costa Rica). However, theoretically this cultural type possesses rich soil in which shared leadership might flourish and grow. Organizations would simply need to encourage the implementation of shared leadership and monitor the organizational design for any potential incompatibilities. Shared leadership should be a rather natural process for team members in these cultures and should function effectively as long as the structure of the organization is aligned with this approach to organizational leadership.

Conclusions

My purpose has been to explore the role that cultural values might play in the discovery and development of shared leadership. Since shared leadership is a group phenomenon that results in higher levels of authority at lower levels of the organization, I have argued that there are two dimensions of cultural values that should critically affect the presence or absence of shared leadership: individualism/collectivism and power distance. Power distance should have the greater impact on shared leadership due to its effects on the acceptance of leadership from peers as opposed to superiors, as well as its effects on the readiness to contribute leadership by lower-level organization members. Individualism/collectivism will also have an impact on shared leadership due to its effects on the degree to which group members possess an interdependent versus independent orientation. These two dimensions were crossed with one another to create four different types of cultures (I/LP, I/HP, C/HP, C/LP), which should differ in the degree to which shared leadership is likely to emerge naturally. Each of these cultures is also likely to present unique challenges for organizations seeking to implement shared leadership.

This research has both theoretical and practical implications. From a theoretical standpoint I have extended the ideas of emerging research on shared leadership by considering how it is likely to differ based on cultural contexts. Leadership has traditionally been examined as an exclusively top-down and individualistic phenomenon, which is partly a result of the influence of cultural values on the nature of research questions and agendas (Erez, 1994). Thus, considering shared leadership from a cross-cultural perspective holds great promise for enriching our understanding of effective leadership. Future research should seek to validate the relative impact of shared leadership in different cultural contexts. From a practical standpoint, I have suggested that the effectiveness of shared leadership is likely to be influenced by cultural context as well. Thus, managers seeking to benefit from the advantages offered by a shared leadership approach should carefully consider how organizational designs and practices should differ according to cultural context in order to enhance the likelihood that shared leadership will function well.

REFERENCES

Avolio, B. J., Jung, D. I., & Sivasubramaniam, N. (1996). Building highly developed teams: Focusing on shared leadership processes, efficacy, trust, and performance. In M. M. Beyerlein, D. A. Johnson, & S. T. Beyerlein (Eds.), *Advances in interdisciplinary study of work teams: Team leadership* (Vol. 3, pp. 173–209). Greenwich, CT: JAI Press.

Barry, D. (1991). Managing the bossless team: Lessons in distributed leadership. *Organizational Dynamics, 20*, 31–47.

Bond, M. H. (1996). Chinese values. In M. H. Bond (Ed.), *Handbook of Chinese psychology* (pp. 208–226). Hong Kong: Oxford University.

Bond, M. H., Leung, K., & Wan, K. C. (1982). How does cultural collectivism operate? The impact of task and maintenance contributions on reward distribution. *Journal of Cross-cultural Psychology, 13*, 186–200.

Bowers, D. G., & Seashore, S. E. (1966). Predicting organizational effectiveness with a four factor theory of leadership. *Administrative Science Quarterly, 11*, 238–263.

Brockner, J., Ackerman, G., Greenberg, J., Gelfand, M., Francesco, A., Chen, Z., et al. (2001). Culture and procedural justice: The influence of power distance on reactions to voice. *Journal of Experimental Social Psychology, 37*(4), 300–315.

Brown, M. H., & Hosking, D. M. (1986). Distributed leadership and skilled performance as successful organization in social movements. *Human Relations, 39*(1), 65–79.

Bruins, J., Den Ouden, M., Depret, E., Extra, J., Gornik, M., Iannaccone, A., et al. (1993). On becoming a leader: Effects of gender and cultural differences on power distance reduction. *European Journal of Social Psychology, 23*(4), 411–426.

Carson, J. B., & Tesluk, P. E. (2005). *Shared leadership in teams: An investigation of antecedent conditions and performance.* Paper presented at the 65th Annual Meeting of the Academy of Management, Honolulu, 2005.

Chinese Culture Connection. (1987). Chinese values and the search for culture-free dimensions of culture. *Journal of Cross-cultural Psychology, 18*(2), 143–164.

Conger, J. A., & Kanungo, R. N. (1988). The empowerment process: Integrating theory and practice. *Academy of Management Review, 13*(3), 471–482.

Cox, J. F., Pearce, C. L., & Perry, M. L. (2003). Toward a model of shared leadership and distributed influence in the innovation process: How shared leadership can enhance new product development team dynamics and effectiveness. In C. L. Pearce & J. A. Conger (Eds.), *Shared leadership: Reframing the hows and whys of leadership* (pp. 48–76). Thousand Oaks, CA: Sage.

Earley, P. C. (1989). Social loafing and collectivism: A comparison of the United States and the People's Republic of China. *Administrative Science Quarterly, 34*, 565–581.

Earley, P. C. (1993). East meets Midwest: Further explorations of collectivistic and individualistic work groups. *Academy of Management Journal, 36*(2), 319–348.

Earley, P. C., & Gibson, C. B. (1998). Taking stock in our progress on individualism–collectivism: 100 years of solidarity and community. *Journal of Management, 24*(3), 265–304.

Edmondson, A. (1999). Psychological safety and learning behavior in work teams. *Administrative Science Quarterly, 44*(2), 350–383.

Erez, M. (1994). Toward a model of cross-cultural industrial and organizational psychology. In H. C. Triandis, M. D. Dunnette, & L. M. Hough (Eds.), *Handbook of industrial and organizational psychology* (Vol. 4, pp. 559–607). Palo Alto, CA: Consulting Psychologists Press.

Fayol, H. (1949). *General and industrial management* (C. Storrs, Trans.). London: Pitman.

Fiedler, F. E. (1967). *A theory of leadership effectiveness.* New York: McGraw-Hill.

Fleishman, E. A., Harris, E. F., & Burt, H. E. (1955). *Leadership and supervision in industry.* Columbus: Ohio State University Press for Bureau of Educational Research.

Gibb, C. A. (1954). Leadership. In G. Lindzey (Ed.), *Handbook of social psychology* (Vol. 2, pp. 877–917). Reading, MA: Addison-Wesley.

Gibson, C. B., & Zellmer-Bruhn, M. E. (2001). Metaphors and meaning: An intercultural analysis of the concept of teamwork. *Administrative Science Quarterly, 46*(2), 274.

Gronn, P. (2002). Distributed leadership as a unit of analysis. *Leadership Quarterly, 13,* 423–451.

Herskovits, M. J. (1955). *Cultural anthropology.* Oxford, England: Knopf.

Hofstede, G. (1980). *Culture's consequences: International differences in work related values.* Beverly Hills, CA: Sage.

Hofstede, G. (1991). *Cultures and organizations: Software of the mind.* London: McGraw-Hill.

House, R. J. (1971). A path goal theory of leader effectiveness. *Administrative Science Quarterly, 16,* 321–338.

House, R. J. (1977). A 1976 theory of charismatic leadership. In J. G. Hunt & L. L. Larson (Eds.), *Leadership: The cutting edge.* Carbondale: Southern Illinois University Press.

House, R. J., Hanges, P. J., Ruiz-Quintanilla, S. A., Dorfman, P. W., Javidan, M., Dickson, M. W., et al. (1999). Cultural influences on leadership and organizations: Project GLOBE. In W. H. Mobley, M. J. Gessner, & V. Arnold (Eds.), *Advances in global leadership* (Vol. 1, pp. 171–233). Stamford, CT: JAI Press.

Iyengar, S. S., & Lepper, M. R. (1999). Rethinking the value of choice: A cultural perspective on intrinsic motivation. *Journal of Personality and Social Psychology, 76*(3), 349–366.

Kahn, R. L., & Katz, D. (1953). Leadership practices in relation to productivity and morale. In D. Cartwright & A. Zander (Eds.), *Group dynamics* (pp. 554–571). New York: Harper & Row.

Katz, D., & Kahn, R. L. (1978). *The social psychology of organizations* (2nd ed.). New York: John Wiley and Sons, Inc.

Kirkman, B. L., & Shapiro, D. L. (2000). Understanding why team members won't share: An examination of factors related to employee receptivity to team-based rewards. *Small Group Research, 31*(2), 175–209.

Klimoski, R., & Mohammed, S. (1994). Team mental model: Construct or metaphor? *Journal of Management, 20*(2), 403–437.

Manz, C. C., & Sims, H. P., Jr. (1980). Self-management as a substitute for leadership: A social learning perspective. *Academy of Management Review, 5*(3), 361–367.

Markus, H. R., & Kitayama, S. (1991). Culture and the self: Implications for cognition, emotion, and motivation. *Psychological Review, 98*(2), 224–253.

Markus, H. R., Kitayama, S., & Heiman, R. J. (1996). Culture and "basic" psychological principles. In E. T. Higgins & A. W. Kruglanski (Eds.), *Social psychology: Handbook of basic principles* (pp. 857–913). New York: Guilford.

McClelland, D. C. (1961). *The achieving society.* New York: Van Nostrand Reinhold.

McClelland, D. C. (1975). *Power: The inner experience.* New York: Irvington.

Mesquita, B., & Frijda, N. H. (1992). Cultural variations in emotion: A review. *Psychological Bulletin, 112*(2), 179–204.

Nisbett, R. E., Peng, K., Choi, I., & Norenzayan, A. (2001). Culture and systems of thought: Holistic versus analytic cognition. *Psychological Review, 108*(2), 291–310.

Pearce, C. L., & Conger, J. A. (2003). *Shared leadership: Reframing the hows and whys of leadership.* Thousand Oaks, CA: Sage.

Pearce, C. L., & Sims, H. P., Jr. (2000). Shared leadership: Toward a multi-level theory of leadership. In M. M. Beyerlein, D. A. Johnson, & S. T. Beyerlein (Eds.), *Advances in the interdisciplinary studies of work teams* (Vol. 7, pp. 115–139). New York: JAI Press.

Pearce, C. L., & Sims, H. P., Jr. (2002). The relative influence of vertical vs. shared leadership on the longitudinal effectiveness of change management teams. *Group Dynamics: Theory, Research, and Practice, 6*(2), 172–197.

Perry, M. L., Pearce, C. L., & Sims, H. P., Jr. (1999). Empowered selling teams: How shared leadership can contribute to selling team outcomes. *Journal of Personal Selling & Sales Management, 3*, 35–51.

Schein, E. H. (1992). *Organizational culture and leadership* (2nd ed.). San Francisco: Jossey-Bass.

Schwartz, S. H. (1994a). Are there universal aspects in the structure and contents of human values? *Journal of Social Issues, 50*(1), 19–45.

Schwartz, S. H. (1994b). Beyond individualism/collectivism: New cultural dimensions of values. In U. Kim, H. C. Triandis, C. Kagitcibasi, S.-C. Choi & G. Yoon (Eds.), *Individualism and collectivism: Theory, method, and applications* (Vol. 18, pp. 85–119). Thousand Oaks, CA: Sage.

Seers, A. (1996). Better leadership through chemistry: Toward a model of emergent shared team leadership. In M. M. Beyerlein, D. A. Johnson, & S. T. Beyerlein (Eds.), *Advances in the interdisciplinary study of work teams: Team leadership* (Vol. 3, pp. 145–172). Greenwich, CT: JAI Press.

Sivasubramaniam, N., Murry, W. D., Avolio, B. J., & Jung, D. I. (2002). A longitudinal model of the effects of team leadership and group potency on group performance. *Group & Organization Management, 27*(1), 66–96.

Smith, P. B., & Schwartz, S. H. (1997). Values. In J. W. Berry, Y. H. Poortinga, & J. Pandy (Eds.), *Handbook of cross-cultural psychology* (2nd ed., Vol. 3, pp. 77–118). Needham Heights, MA: Allyn & Bacon.

Stogdill, R. M., & Coons, A. E. (1957). *Leader behavior: Its description and measurement.* Columbus: Ohio State University Press for Bureau of Business Research.

Triandis, H. C. (1994). *Culture and social behavior.* New York: McGraw-Hill.

Triandis, H. C. (1995). *Individualism and collectivism.* Boulder, CO: Westview Press.

Vroom, V. H., & Yetton, P. W. (1973). *Leadership and decision-making.* Pittsburgh, PA: University of Pittsburgh Press.

Wageman, R. (1995). Interdependence and group effectiveness. *Administrative Science Quarterly, 40*(1), 145–180.

JAY CARSON is a Ph.D. candidate in the Robert H. Smith School of Business at the University of Maryland. His research interests include leadership, teams, and cross-cultural issues. His current research focuses on consulting team effectiveness, shared leadership and goal congruence in teams, and a case study on the strategic use of exemplars. Jay can be contacted at jcarson@rhsmith.umd.edu.

Emerging Leadership Ethics in an Interdependent World
Human Capabilities Development as a Global Imperative for Moral Leadership[1]

By Benjamin Paul Dean

TO AN UNPRECEDENTED DEGREE, GLOBALIZATION IS STIMULATING greater awareness of the increasing need for moral leadership at every level of civil society. An understanding of globalization and its challenges becomes vitally important as leaders attempt to cope with and manage these new and evolving worldwide interconnections (Crocker, 2002). As globalization intensifies, leaders must comprehend the moral implications of global interdependence and be prepared to deal with the problems of an increasingly interdependent world. One of the crucial intellectual and social challenges that leaders must face is the need to define ethical leadership standards that are equitable and broadly acceptable to the diverse participants in this new global environment (Kelly, 2004). Many complex relations exist among corporate and other actors who come from numerous different countries (Beyer & Nino, 1999, citing Donaldson & Dunfee, 1999). Because global expectations regarding the responsibilities of multinational enterprises and other international organizations and institutions remain in flux, their leaders need a clearer articulation of cross-culturally recognized standards of ethical business conduct.

The central theme here is that, as global leadership ethical standards are emerging, human capabilities development in particular affords an increasingly well-defined construct that has evolved through an interdisciplinary field of study known as development ethics. This construct reflects an already functioning set of cross-cultural expectations by which to evaluate and order social arrangements and thus ethical leadership attitudes and behavior, particularly at the corporate, organizational, and institutional levels. This article suggests that human capabilities development may constitute a near-universally applicable ethical standard for moral leadership that seeks to expand human capabilities and promote substantive freedoms.

Globalization, a phenomenon of increasing worldwide interdependence, involves the integration of countries and peoples worldwide. It is "the widening, deepening and speeding up of worldwide interconnectedness in all aspects of contemporary social life . . . ." (Crocker, 2002, p. 15, citing Held, McGrew, Goldblatt, & Perraton, 1999). Globalization reflects the impact of significant decreases in the cost of international transportation and communications, and reduced barriers to the flow of goods, services, capital, knowledge, and people across national borders (Stiglitz, 2003, p. 9). Multinational corporations and their rate of growth have continued to increase in recent decades due to globalization (Lozano & Boni, 2002).

The Need for Cross-Culturally Accepted Ethical Standards of Leadership

A consequence of globalization processes is that the leaders of states, multinational enterprises, and various other public and private organizations and institutions are experiencing major changes in their roles internationally. In many new ways, states, multinational corporations and other international organizations and institutions even appear vulnerable to radical changes and uncertain conditions stimulated by the intensification of globalization (Kelly, 2004). The sovereign nation-state, with its governmental institutions, traditionally has been the pivotal actor internationally, and particularly in regard to the transnational protection of the civil, political, and social rights of its citizens (Matten & Crane, 2005). However, because of globalization processes and changing international roles, states can no longer be expected to serve as the sole guarantors of such rights (ibid., citing Falk, 2000). Indeed, globalization is rewriting social expectations internationally (Batstone, 2003). Transnational activities and cross-cultural interactions among states and multinational enterprises have sharply increased (Buller, Kohls, & Anderson, 1991). Such enormous influence for multinational enterprises implies new challenges and greater responsibilities (Lozano & Boni, 2002). Increasing globalization and expanding scrutiny by nongovernmental organizations (NGOs) over corporations operating transnationally has helped to shape and heighten stakeholders' expectations and concerns regarding the ethics of an array of social and economic issues (Robertson & Crittenden, 2003). Matten and Crane (2005) are among those observers who contend that corporations are obligated to step into the arena of protecting rights in those circumstances where traditional governmental actors fail to act, particularly in developing countries. In effect, transnational corporations are increasingly being asked to take responsibility for civil society (Batstone, 2003). Leaders of multinational enterprises operating in this environment of increasing worldwide interconnectedness especially need a clearer articulation of cross-culturally recognized standards of ethical conduct. Globalization processes have highlighted a growing need for more effective moral leadership in general, but especially within organizations and institutions operating transnationally, and a need for more leaders who can engage ethical issues and reconcile cross-cultural differences in ethical norms (Buller et al., 1991).

The changes and uncertainties of globalization have generated diverse attempts to normatively evaluate globalization processes and the human consequences. David Crocker (2002) identifies three different broad normative views of globalization: (a) *hyperglobalism*, which sees globalization as the emergence of an integrated global economy and a single world market and welcomes the ascension of multinational corporations and the corresponding decline of state sovereignty and power; (b) *skepticism*, which rejects the hyperglobalist view or concedes that such trends exist, but contends that nation-states should defend their sovereignty, resist economic and market integration, and preserve their national and local identities and well-being; and (c) *transformationalism*, which views the processes of globalization as an unprecedented and powerful force that produces greater worldwide interconnectedness, resulting in advantages to some nations and peoples and disadvantages to others. The transformationalists' perspective is that worldwide interconnectedness is neither intrinsically good nor evil, but at times it may either enable or impede what Crocker refers to as "good human and communal development" (2002, p. 16).

**❝ THE CHANGES AND UNCERTAINTIES OF GLOBAL- ❞
IZATION HAVE GENERATED DIVERSE ATTEMPTS TO
NORMATIVELY EVALUATE GLOBALIZATION
PROCESSES AND THE HUMAN CONSEQUENCES.**

Writing specifically in regard to business ethics in the global context, Amartya Sen (1999) states that successful economic exchange depends on the formation of trust and on the application of behavioral norms—both explicit and implicit. When behavioral norms exist, their significance is easily overlooked, but when such norms have yet to be cultivated their absence can create major barriers to exchange (Sen, 1999). Thus, the greater the commonality of cross-cultural normative expectations, the fewer cross-cultural conflicts will likely occur as differences in ethical standards converge. Notwithstanding geopolitical and cultural trends that may be increasing cultural divergence (see, e.g., Huntington, 1996), there is evidence that global interdependence may be stimulating gradual progress in some key respects toward more universally recognized moral principles and ethical standards (see Buller et al., 1991).

The framework for an emerging global ethical system would consist of those universal or near-universal principles that tend to arise dynamically from the ethically reinforcing interactions that are ongoing internationally within and among the various major social levels (Buller et al., 1991, citing Donaldson & Dunfee, 1999). Buller et al. offer a model that depicts global ethics as involving four interrelated levels of ethical analysis: (a) the individual level, (b) the organizational or corporate level, (c) the national or societal level, and (d) the global or international level (Buller et al., 1991; see also Robertson & Crittenden, 2003). Ethical leadership standards become crucial at each of these levels of analysis.

The challenges presented by an increasingly interconnected world call for vision-driven people who "are able to transform their environment, morally elevate their followers, and chart new paths of progress and human development" (Safty, 2003, p. 84). Effectively engaging the moral issues raised by globalization requires leaders to cross-culturally define and apply normative criteria by which to ethically evaluate, and indeed perhaps re-evaluate, globalization's processes and human effects (Crocker, 2002). As Adel Safty (2003) observes, where there is a lack of organizational and governmental leaders who are truly committed to exercising moral leadership, there will be more pressure for other forms of moral leadership to emerge, mainly through civil society groups and through what Safty refers to as *people-driven moral leadership*. There remains a crucial need for greater clarity in articulating global organizing and directing principles that can transform public and private institutions so that all persons will be able to share in the benefits of an expanding global economy (Kelly, 2004).

Multinational enterprises face especially difficult practical and moral problems in operating internationally across the substantial variations in ethical standards of home and multiple host nations (Windsor, 2004). Windsor contends that the practice and study of international business ethics currently faces "conditions approaching chaos" because international business ethics do not exist (2004, p. 729, citing Donaldson, 1996). On closer examination, however, such a negative assessment of the current status of international business ethics may be unwarranted. In their efforts to facilitate the growth of transnational activities and cross-cultural interactions, leaders tend to discern and align their actions with normative principles that are emerging transnationally and are recognizable cross-culturally, a dynamic that helps to define and reinforce a discernible global ethic for leaders (see Buller et al., 1991). Indeed, even as Windsor (2004) notes, a way forward does exist through the evolutionary processes generated by the emergence of *international policy regimes*, defined as functioning and functional sets of actor expectations ordering cross-cultural expectations and behavior. An international policy regime is "a bilateral or multilateral 'concurrence' on functionally useful behavior, mutually regarded, such that reasonably reliable expectations can govern choices" (Windsor, 2004, p. 741). Moral leadership—including by leaders and managers of corporations—can be vital to the emergence of normative regimes. The result of such an evolutionary process can be normative expectations that are both functional and functioning and that serve as rules of the game—either with or without a moral grounding. Regional and global business norms may arise through the evolution of multiple, sometimes even fragmented, international policy regimes that have real-world applicability. The evolution of international public policy regimes need not involve immediate agreement on cross-cultural universals and need not involve the creation of institutions, although institutions might evolve along with and serve as evidence of the regime (Windsor, 2004, citing Bryson & Crosby, 1992).

Development Ethics and Its Emerging Standard for Evaluating Leaders

Leadership is a process whereby an individual influences a group of individuals to achieve a common goal (Northouse, 2004). In view of its inherent social context, leadership should be apprehended normatively as "a set of values dedicated to promoting human development for the common good of people" (Safty, 2003, p. 84). A fundamental issue that the world has yet to resolve at the societal and cultural level, however, is the question of what constitutes the common good, i.e, the *good* we must share as equal partners in a worldwide community (Kelly, 2004). This perspective essentially equates to the transformationalist appraisal of globalization in terms of promoting social changes that lead to *good* human and communal development (Crocker, 2002, p. 16). "'Development' is the most widely used concept for thinking about the great changes that are occurring throughout the world" (Crocker, 1991, p. 466, quoting Segal, 1986). Historically, there has been little substantive discussion in the economic and social science literature on development's meaning or any exclusive or systematic treatment of it as a concept (Clark, 2002). The narrower views of development identify development with measures of growth of gross national product, rise in personal incomes, increases in industrialization or technology, or advances in social modernization (Sen, 1999). Development in its broader scope, however, is fundamentally a process of broader social change (Crocker, 1991). Because of leadership's crucial role with respect to influencing the processes of societal and cultural change and the consequent human effects, one can readily see the importance of key leaders having a well-grounded moral view of what actually constitutes good human and communal development, and the means to achieve it.

A significant new construct for analyzing human well-being has emerged from within economics and social science through what is known as *international development ethics* (Crocker, 1991). Finding normative and empirical answers to issues relating to what ought to constitute the priorities for human well-being is the overarching goal of development ethics (Crocker, 2002). Its practical objective is to render the outcomes of development decisions and efforts to be humane and sustainable (Goulet, 1997).[2] Development ethics stimulates an interdisciplinary and cross-cultural dialogue to more fully understand and ensure genuine human development at all levels of community and in all kinds of institutions. Significantly, development ethics also has undertaken a new and pressing task in formulating an ethical evaluation of globalization and, in so doing, helps us to better deal with the social changes and moral challenges associated with global integration (Crocker, 2002).

**“ DEVELOPMENT ETHICS STIMULATES AN INTERDIS- ”
CIPLINARY AND CROSS-CULTURAL DIALOGUE TO
MORE FULLY UNDERSTAND AND ENSURE GENUINE
HUMAN DEVELOPMENT . . .**

Consistent with the transformationalist view of globalization, Sen (1999) observes that global trade can bring with it greater economic prosperity for each nation, but there can also be losers as well as winners, even when the aggregate trend is moving up. The central controversy of globalization is not globalization *per se*, but rather that the processes of globalization lead to inequalities in the overall institutional arrangements and produce unequal benefits and outcomes worldwide (Sen, 2002). Crocker also adopts the transformationalist view, but notes that regardless of how globalization is understood, development ethics must be able to evaluate it ethically. Development ethics offers reasoned normative criteria for evaluating and discerning the kinds of globalization processes most likely to benefit human beings, for encouraging everyone to share in the responsibilities for the well-being of all others in society, and for allocating duties to the various agents of social change (Crocker, 2001).

Development ethics represents an increasingly well-defined and cross-culturally recognized set of ethical principles (see, e.g., Lozano & Boni, 2002). The construct focuses on the advancement of people as the ultimate object of development, rather than merely viewing people as instrumental means to other ends. It has become increasingly important as an interdisciplinary subject of study because of this emphasis on protecting human dignity and respecting the value of all people. This supports an observation that the intended beneficiaries at least ought to perceive development ethics' objectives as being ethical and valid. Further, the principles underlying development analysis are relevant not only for decision makers in less developed countries but also for those in richer countries (Sen, 1999). One commentator, writing from the viewpoint of a person from a developing nation, affirms the importance of development ethics and states that development ethics evidences the need for a broader construct of *globalization ethics* (Villacorta, 2001).

The underlying principles of development ethics suggest a vital global role that moral leadership can play in advancing human development. Development ethics also extends our understanding of the ethical use of transactional and transformational influence processes. "Transformational leadership is concerned with the performance of followers and also with developing followers to their fullest potential" (Northouse, 2004, p. 174, citing Avolio, 1999; Bass & Avolio, 1990). The leaders and members of an organization constitute a community of persons in which human value creates a moral obligation for the leader to be responsible for the development of those members (Kanungo & Mendonca, 1996). An ethical leadership imperative therefore flows from one's concern for human value (ibid.).

Development Defined as Expanded Human Capabilities and Substantive Freedoms

The most promising ethical perspective that has evolved from the study of development ethics is the work of Amartya Sen (Crocker, 2002). Sen is the 1998 recipient of the Nobel Prize in Economic Science. His perspective has emerged as the foremost alternative to traditional development concepts of human welfare (Clark, 2002). His approach has been described as one of the "greatest contributions to the human development concept" (Lozano & Boni, 2002, p. 170). According to David Clark, Sen has "revolutionized the way in which social science understands the concept of 'development'" and also was "responsible for inspiring other social scientists to take an active interest in development ethics" (Clark, 2002, p. 832). Sen approaches human development in terms of expanding basic human *capabilities* and promoting substantive freedoms (Sen, 1990, 1999). Development's purpose is to improve human lives by expanding the range of things that one can be and do (Fukuda-Parr, 2003). According to Sen, the concept of human development is about people being able to live in freedom and dignity, and also being able to exercise choices in pursuit of a full and creative life (Sen, 1999; see also Fukuda-Parr, 2003). The capability approach proposes that social arrangements be evaluated according to the extent of freedom afforded to people in promoting or achieving the functionings that people value within the multiple, diverse aspects of their life (Sen, 1999; see also Alkire, 2005).

Sen and others who focus on human capabilities attempt to avoid the ongoing dispute between universalists[3] and particularists by evoking a cross-cultural consensus around the freedoms necessary for all members of a community to participate in the choices and priorities that affect well-being and development (Crocker, 2002; see, e.g., Nussbaum & Sen, 1993). Sen's ethical theory combines *cross-cultural moral minimums* with appropriate sensitivity to cultural differences (Crocker, 1991). Sen and Nussbaum draw on a blend or a balance of cultural immersion and cultural critique (Crocker, 2002; see Nussbaum & Sen, 1993). Sen's capability approach to human development has been augmented by some (e.g., Crocker, 1992; Nussbaum, 1995) and criticized by others (e.g., Griffin, 1986; Qizilbash, 1996), yet the capability approach has proven highly influential.

The core principles of human capabilities development are widely accepted, as demonstrated by having provided since 1990 the conceptual framework used by the United Nations Development Programme (Fukuda-Parr, 2003). Through Sen's formulations, and the annual publication of the United Nations' Human Development Reports (HDRs), a distinctive international paradigm of development has evolved. As pointed out by Sakiko Fukuda-Parr of the United Nations Development Programme, this approach is unique in assessing development by the extent to which development efforts seek to expand the capabilities of *all* people (Fukuda-Parr, 2003). Sen's human capability development perspective is also very useful because it enables ethicists to scrutinize the effects that globalization has on *everyone's* capabilities (Crocker, 2002).

Within the human development approach, there exists both an evaluative aspect and an agency aspect (Fukuda-Parr, 2003). The evaluative aspect assesses improvements in human lives and has been predominant, as indicated by the United Nations' HDRs and the establishment of a Human Development Index (HDI), a composite measurement for evaluating achievements in human development (Fukuda-Parr, 2003). The HDI's measurements incorporate "the most basic capabilities for human development"; these are "living a long and healthy life, being educated, having a decent standard of living and enjoying political and civil freedoms to participate in the life of one's community" (United Nations Development Programme, 2003, p. 28). However, the capabilities approach to human development is broader and not limited to just these capabilities (Fukuda-Parr, 2003). Combining the capabilities or *choices* identified as important by the United Nations' HDRs, we can derive the following representative list:

1. To be healthy and well nourished (i.e., to live "a long and healthy life").
2. To be knowledgeable (education).
3. To have access to the resources needed to enjoy "a decent standard of living."
4. To have equity in the delivery and distribution of basic services.
5. To have guaranteed human rights.
6. To have personal self-respect and autonomy in making decisions about one's own life.
7. To be able to participate in the life of the community (i.e., to enjoy political freedom, participation through democratic institutions, and collective agency for mobilizing social action).
8. To have a healthy and sustainable environment in which to live.

(see United Nations Development Programme, 1990, 1995; see also Fukuda-Parr, 2003).

Human Capabilities Development as a Functioning Global Ethic

Formal ethical theories can inform and guide the moral leadership initiatives that advance international policy regimes that in turn eventually generate accepted global norms (Windsor, 2004). The human capabilities' well-reasoned approach to development already has shaped an international policy regime in the interdisciplinary field of development and also would seem to constitute an ethical theory that can inform and guide global ethical leadership behavior.

Human development's focus on preserving human dignity, promoting substantive rights, and expanding human capabilities also is highly consistent with the international system of fundamental human rights. The dramatic rise in the number of major international instruments ratified on human rights, and the comprehensive set of norms on human rights embodied in these instruments, reflects an overall recognition that universal or near-universal global normative principles do exist (Fukuda-Parr, 2003). A fundamental human right recognized under international law constitutes a claim on and a responsibility of society, by imposing obligations not only on nation-states but on all persons and institutions. The international legal recognition and guarantees of fundamental human rights for individuals and the expansion of human capabilities and substantive freedoms embraced in the human development construct have become significant both in terms of their intrinsic and their instrumental worth (Fukuda-Parr, 2003). According to Lozano and Boni (2002), human rights are not culture-dependent, they are transcultural and universal.

Human rights (much like human capabilities and substantive freedoms) represent a measure of the efforts to manage or redirect the tide of globalization toward just and equitable benefits for all peoples. Human rights also provide the framework within which development, democracy, and human security become possible (Amnesty International, 2002). At the same time, the human development approach holds major implications for enhancing capabilities, development, freedom, empowerment, and human rights (Fukuda-Parr, 2003; see also Crocker, 2002). Thomas Donaldson has identified a "minimal list" of ten *fundamental international rights* that he presents "as a beginning consensus for evaluating international conduct" (Donaldson, 1989, p. 68). This list includes the following rights[4]:

1. To freedom of physical movement.

2. To ownership of property.

3. To freedom from torture.

4. To a fair trial.

5. To nondiscriminatory treatment.

6. To physical security.

7. To freedom of speech and association.

8. To minimal education.

9. To political participation.

10. To subsistence.

These internationally recognized human rights resemble and are compatible with the *choices* identified by the United Nations as constituting basic human capabilities and substantive freedoms (see United Nations Development Programme, 1990, 1995, 2003; see also Fukuda-Parr, 2003).

Windsor (2004) includes human rights in his example of how international policy regimes can evolve into accepted global business norms. He identifies the following three dimensions of global business operations: (a) international business ethics; (b) international business law; and (c) international public policy (consisting of the core concepts of global public good and global civil society) (Windsor, 2004). He also cites the United Nations' "Global Compact for the 21st Century," with its constituent U.N. declarations, as an example of how multinational corporations have been encouraged to adopt global standards for the protection of human rights, labor, and the environment. Windsor describes these international standards as examples of global business norms that are evolving by means of what he refers to as the "international regimes policy construct" (2004, p. 742). Similarly, the human capabilities development paradigm reflected in the U.N.'s HDRs appears to be comparable to the U.N.'s Global Compact as a valid international policy regime and as a substantive basis for discerning international ethical norms.

The Responsibility of Ethical Leadership for Expanding Human Capabilities

There exists within the human development approach not only the evaluative aspect but also its agency aspect (Fukuda-Parr, 2003). Leaders in particular are vital to advancing human capabilities development because leaders have the opportunity to serve as active agents of change in regard to human development. People are not consigned to merely being passive beneficiaries of economic and social progress in a society; rather, they may become active agents of change either through *individual action* or *collective action* (Fukuda-Parr, 2003). By definition, leaders hold power or influence over others and also influence and motivate others toward collective action within a social context (see Northouse, 2004). Leaders thus have significant potential for enhancing or impairing the human development of followers. Leaders are crucial as active agents of change in the human development process at every level at which leadership may be conceptually analyzed (see Buller et al., 1991).

Regarding leadership behaviors' cultural dimensions, leaders in some societies when compared to other societies may be even more influential as agents of change. This may be the case, for example, in developing countries whose specific cultural characteristics are collectivist and where leaders tend to be accorded more trust and power in their position (Hess & Dunfee, 2003, p. 266, citing Husted, 2002).

Because worldviews and moral perspectives are inherent components of culture, the socioeconomic interactions within a given nation or society also will have a significant impact on ethics at all levels of leadership (see Buller et al., 1991). Moral philosophies and ethical standards in a society also vary from culture to culture (Donaldson, 1996). Indeed, any attempt to define a conception of *development* must presuppose a normative perspective (Crocker, 1991, citing Steidlemeier, 1987). However, the principles of development ethics—and the moral reasoning that under-lies them—are basic insofar as an absence or lack of basic human capabilities would foreclose many other possibilities in life and thus these capabilities tend to be universally valued by people (Fukuda-Parr, 2003).

Although the emergence of a functioning public policy regime need not be morally grounded (Windsor, 2004), the construct of human capabilities development already is both functioning and well-grounded in normative theory. The capability approach to development ethics embraces Immanuel Kant's moral foundation to the extent that one must view people as ends and never as simply means to other ends. Sen's concept of functionings derives from Aristotle's focus on human flourishing and capacity (Sen, 1999). Sen and Nussbaum further contend that an adequate assessment of development also needs to adopt Aristotle's view that well-being must be practical and genuinely rooted in the experience of the people, "'and yet be evaluative in such a way as to help leaders structure things for the best, enabling people to live as good and flourishing a life as possible . . . .'" (Crocker, 1991, p. 465, quoting Nussbaum & Sen, 1989, p. 308).

From the Judeo-Christian ethical standpoint, a biblical mandate beginning with the creation narrative in Genesis affords substantial moral grounds for development as an ethic that is consistent with moral leadership's pursuit of human elevation and transformation. Steidlemeier, a theologian, advocated an ethical basis for development that he described as "an ecumenical tradition of Christian humanism" (Crocker, 1991, p. 465). John-Paul II observed that the realities and experience of global interdependence in its various dimensions tends to elicit a concern for the common good and a sense of responsibility for all (quoted in Kelly, 2004). This accomplishes among humans a morally virtuous level of relationality referred to as *solidarity* (ibid.). According to Kelly, it is through solidarity that individuals combine with others to achieve objectives that are beyond the capabilities of humans acting alone. The concept of solidarity therefore logically furthers our understanding of human development and also supports the moral imperative for developing the human capabilities of others. The opportunity to partner with others in moral solidarity and the need to combine human capabilities to attain objectives beyond the capabilities of any individual afford a valid entry point for the exercise of ethical leadership.

Research Strategies for Human Capabilities Development as a
Basis of Ethical Leadership

A clear need exists for the further study of ethical issues and outcomes that occur as a result of increasing global interdependence (Buller et al., 1991). Determining which ethical norms ought to have priority in understanding and ensuring human well-being and development also represent key areas for future work (Crocker, 2002). Presumably, this should be equally true regarding the need for research to determine the ethical priorities for moral leadership and to better equip ethical leaders who can serve as global change agents who can advance more effectively human capabilities and freedoms.

Research on the cross-cultural aspects of international business ethics has been growing rather slowly, despite the crucial strategic implications of universally applicable ethical norms for leaders of multinational enterprises (Robertson & Crittenden, 2003, p. 385). The inherent complexities of transnational research have limited research efforts focusing on cross-cultural ethics (ibid.), but such research efforts should continue.

Future research on ethical leadership must also attempt to further refine the operational construct of Sen's capability approach to human development (Clark, 2002). Operationalizing the capability approach needs to occur in many countries, at many institutional levels, and in respect to a variety of global issues (Alkire, 2005). As Alkire observes, Sen has provided an analytical map of important and useful variables that are sensitive and adaptive to context and that respect the agency of those who seek to employ the approach. Applying human capabilities development to the specific context of ethical leadership, we should look for effects of this emerging ethical imperative on leadership attitudes and behaviors in relation   to all four levels of analysis (individual, corporate/organizational, national/societal, and global), as iden-tified by Buller et al. (1991). Hosmer and Kiewitz (2005) state that, at the corporate and organizational level of analysis, organizational policies, decisions, and actions affirming the rights and well-being of others will over time produce benefits for the organization itself and thus promote its success (see also Sen, 1993).

> **THE OPPORTUNITY TO PARTNER WITH OTHERS IN MORAL SOLIDARITY AND THE NEED TO COMBINE HUMAN CAPABILITIES TO ATTAIN OBJECTIVES BEYOND THE CAPABILITIES OF ANY INDIVIDUAL AFFORD A VALID ENTRY POINT FOR THE EXERCISE OF ETHICAL LEADERSHIP.**

Additional studies could examine the extent to which leaders' mental models and actual theories-in-use reflect that they have either embraced or rejected, con-sciously or unconsciously, the ethical imperative of human capabilities development as an approach to ethical leadership. Hosmer (2000) acknowledges Kant's warning that we cannot actually measure the extent and sincerity with which people—and thus leaders—actually adopt ethical principles and intend that their actions be moral. However, as Hosmer suggests, we can at least seek to measure outcomes. We should be able to tie leadership outcomes to the indicators of expanded capabilities and substantive freedoms of followers in the corporate, organizational, and institutional contexts, respectively. The objective, outcomes-oriented research question that Hosmer would pose is this: "Do members of the various stakeholder groups believe that they are treated as ends, worthy of dignity and respect, not merely as means to less worthy aims?" (2000, p. 240). This approach appears consistent with Clark's suggestion of finding out "how poor people themselves perceive development" (2002, p. 834). Applying Hosmer's and Clark's suggestions to other aspects of leader-follower research, we can infer that questions regarding the perceptions of the intended beneficiaries of the human development process (i.e., the followers) are also worthy of empirical study (see Hosmer, 2000).

Conclusion

Corporate and other organizational and institutional leaders operating in today's international context should recognize that development ethics, reinforced by emerging international policy regimes, has produced a moral imperative for human development that affords a well-reasoned and well-articulated standard for ethical leadership. Leadership can and should be evaluated cross-culturally according to normative standards regarding the extent to which leadership efforts promote social arrangements and outcomes that expand human capabilities and freedoms. Leadership attitudes and behaviors embracing the ethical principles defined within Amartya Sen's human capabilities development construct would readily serve to expand human capabilities and to promote substantive freedoms and human dignity. This imperative for human capabilities development continues to emerge as a cross-culturally applicable ethical standard for moral leadership in an increasingly interdependent world.

NOTES

1. I would like to acknowledge the assistance of Bramwell Osula, Ph.D., Professional-in-Residence at Regent University, and express my sincere appreciation for his very helpful comments and suggestions in the research and initial preparation of this article.

2. The modern literature on development ethics is substantial. Luis-Joseph Lebret (1954, 1961) articulated development ethics in terms of human good and scaled needs along a *human ascent*. Denis Goulet (1971, 1997) presented additional concepts of human development identified in terms of life sustenance, self-esteem, and freedom from servitude. Goulet (1997) contends that development ethics inherently involves normative issues and ethical judgments relating to the good life, to quality of relationships, to social structures that are just, and also considers justice in society and human rights as ends rather than instrumental means.

3. Donaldson and Dunfee (1999) refer to universal or near-universal norms or global standards of conduct as global *hypernorms* (see also Windsor, 2004, p. 739). Although not articulated in terms of hypernorms, the global ethical principles of human capabilities development appear to have emerged in a form sufficiently well established to be analogous to a hypernorm.

4. Donaldson concludes that these fundamental individual rights should qualify under a basic three-part test of (a) protecting something of great importance, (b) being subject to substantial and recurrent threat of the possibility of deprivation, and (c) being associated with duties that are limited in light of their fairness and affordability. In addition, human capabilities development is also closely related to an emerging but less well-defined international right to development.

REFERENCES

Alkire, S. (2005). Why the capability approach? *Journal of Human Development, 6*(1), 115–133.

Amnesty International. (2002, May). Globalise this: Human rights. *The OECD Observer, 231/232*, 38–39. Organisation for Economic Cooperation and Development.

Avolio, B. J. (1999). *Full leadership development: Building the vital forces in organizations.* Thousand Oaks, CA: Sage.

Bass, B. M., & Avolio, B. J. (1990). The implications of transactional and transformational leadership for individual, team, and organizational development. *Research in Organizational Change and Development, 4*, 231–272.

Batstone, D. (2003). *Saving the corporate soul & (who knows) maybe your own.* San Francisco: Jossey-Bass.

Beyer, J. M., & Nino, D. (1999). Ethics and cultures in international business. *Journal of Management Inquiry, 8*(3), 287–297.

Bryson, J. M., & Crosby, B. C. (1992). *Leadership for the common good: Tackling public problems in a shared-power world.* San Francisco: Jossey-Bass.

Buller, P. F., Kohls, H. H., & Anderson, K. S. (1991, October). The challenge of global ethics. *Journal of Business Ethics, 10*, 767–775.

Clark, D. A. (2002). Development ethics: A research agenda. *International Journal of Social Economics, 29*(11), 830–848.

Crocker, D. A. (1991). Toward development ethics. *World Development, 19*(5), 457–483.

Crocker, D. A. (1992). Functioning and capability: The foundations of Sen's and Nussbaum's development ethic. *Political Theory, 20*(4), 584–612.

Crocker, D. A. (2001, April). Globalization and human development: Ethical approaches. *Globalization Ethical and Institutional Concerns* (Proceedings of the Seventh Plenary Session). Vatican City: The Pontifical Academy of Social Sciences.

Crocker, D. A. (2002). Development ethics and globalization. *Philosophy & Public Policy Quarterly, 22*(4), 13–20.

Donaldson, T. (1989). Fundamental international rights. In L. P. Hartman (Ed.), *Perspectives in business ethics* (3rd ed., 2005) (pp. 68–71). New York: McGraw-Hill/Irwin.

Donaldson, T. (1996). Values in tension: Ethics away from home. *Harvard Business Review, 75*(5), 48–58.

Donaldson, T., & Dunfee, T. W. (1999). *Ties that bind: A social contracts approach to business ethics.* Boston: Harvard Business School Press.

Falk, R. (2000). The decline of citizenship in an era of globalization. *Citizenship Studies, 4*, 5–17.

Fukuda-Parr, S. (2003). The human development paradigm: Operationalizing Sen's ideas on capabilities. *Feminist Economics, 9*(2–3), 301–317.

Goulet, D. A. (1971). *The cruel choice: A new concept in the theory of development.* New York: Atheneum.

Goulet, D. A. (1997). Development ethics: A new discipline. *International Journal of Social Economics, 24*(11), 1160–1171.

Griffin, J. P. (1986). *Well-being: Its meaning, measurement and moral importance.* Oxford: Clarendon Press.

Held, D., McGrew, A., Goldblatt, D., & Perraton, J. (1999). *Global transformations.* Palo Alto, CA: Stanford University Press.

Hess, D., & Dunfee, T. (2003). Taking responsibility for bribery: The multinational corporation's role in combating corruption. In R. Sullivan (Ed.), *Business and human rights: Dilemmas and solutions* (pp. 260–271). Sheffield, UK: Greenleaf Publishing.

Hosmer, L. T. (2000). It's time for empirical research in business ethics. *Business Ethics Quarterly, 10*(1), 233–242.

Hosmer, L. T., & Kiewitz, C. (2005). Organizational justice: A behavioral science concept with critical implications for business ethics and stakeholder theory. *Business Ethics Quarterly, 15*(1), 67–91.

Huntington, S. P. (1996). *The clash of civilizations and the remaking of world order.* New York: Touchstone.

Husted, B. (2002). Culture and international anti-corruption agreements in Latin America. *Journal of Business Ethics, 37*(1), 413–422.

Kanungo, R. N., & Mendonca, M. (1996). *Ethical dimensions of leadership.* Thousand Oaks, CA: Sage.

Kelly, J. E. (2004). Solidarity and subsidiarity: "Organizing principles" for corporate moral leadership in the new global economy. *Journal of Business Ethics, 52*, 283–295.

Lebret, L.-J. (1954). Pour une economie de besoins. *Economie et Humanisme, 84.*

Lebret, L.-J. (1961) *Dynamique concrete du developpement.* Paris: Les Editions Ouvrieres.

Lozano, J. F., & Boni, A. (2002). The impact of the multinational in the development: An ethical challenge. *Journal of Business Ethics, 39*(1/2), 169–178.

Matten, D., & Crane, A. (2005). Corporate citizenship: Toward an extended theoretical conceptualization. *Academy of Management Review, 30*(1), 166–179.

Northouse, P. G. (2004). *Leadership: Theory and practice* (3rd ed.). Thousand Oaks, CA: Sage.

Nussbaum, M. C. (1995). Human capabilities, female human beings. In M. C. Nussbaum & J. Glover (Eds.), *Women, culture and development: The capabilities approach* (pp. 61–104). Oxford: Oxford University Press.

Nussbaum, M. C., & Sen, A. (1989). Internal criticism and Indian rationalist traditions. In M. Krausz (Ed.), *Relativism: Interpretation and confrontation.* Notre Dame, IN: University of Notre Dame Press.

Nussbaum, M. C., & Sen, A. (Eds.). (1993). *The quality of life.* Oxford: Clarendon Press.

Qizilbash, M. (1996). Capabilities, well-being and human development: A survey. *The Journal of Development Studies, 33*(2), 143–162.

Robertson, C. J., & Crittenden, W. F. (2003). Mapping moral philosophies: Strategic implications for multinational firms. *Strategic Management Journal, 24*(4), 385–392.

Safty, A. (2003, Fall). Moral leadership: Beyond management and governance. *Harvard International Review, 25*(3), 84–89.

Segal, J. M. (1986, October). *What is development?* (Working Paper DN-1). College Park, MD: Institute for Philosophy and Public Policy.

Sen, A. (1990). *Development as capability expansion.* Oxford: Oxford University Press.

Sen, A. (1993). Does business ethics make economic sense? *Business Ethics Quarterly, 3*(1), 45–54.

Sen, A. (1999). *Development as freedom.* New York: First Anchor.

Sen, A. (2002). Globalization, inequality and global protest. *Development, 45*(2), 11–17.

Steidlemeier, P. (1987). *The paradox of poverty: A reappraisal of economic development policy.* Cambridge, MA: Ballinger.

Stiglitz, J. E. (2003). *Globalization and its discontents.* New York: W.W. Norton.

United Nations Development Programme. (1990). *Human development report 1990.* New York: Oxford University Press.

United Nations Development Programme. (1995). *Human development report 1995.* New York: Oxford University Press.

United Nations Development Programme. (2003). *Human development report 2003.* New York: Oxford University Press.

Villacorta, W. V. (2001, April). Globalization and disparities in Southeast Asia. *Globalization ethical and institutional concerns* (Proceedings of the Seventh Plenary Session). Vatican City: The Pontifical Academy of Social Sciences.

Windsor, D. (2004). The development of international business norms. *Business Ethics Quarterly, 14*(4), 729–754.

BENJAMIN PAUL DEAN is the Director of Global Partnerships for PIONEERS, an international outreach agency based in Orlando, Florida. He teaches on intercultural leadership development, leadership ethics, and the rule of law in developing nations. He also provides on-site consultation and training for indigenous leaders of various countries who are engaged in cross-cultural missions and community development projects. Ben is a graduate of the University of North Carolina at Chapel Hill (B.A. in International Studies, Highest Honors, 1977), the University of North Carolina School of Law (J.D., 1984), and The Judge Advocate General's School in Charlottesville, Virginia (LLM, 1988). He currently is conducting dissertation research as a candidate for a Ph.D. in organizational leadership, studying in the School of Leadership Studies at Regent University in Virginia Beach, Virginia.

Allophilia: A Framework for Intergroup Leadership[†]

By Todd L. Pittinsky

ONE OF THE MOST PRESSING CONCERNS CONFRONTING LEADERS IS intergroup conflict, often inspired or facilitated by prejudice. While the reduction of prejudice is essential to the reduction of intergroup conflict, in this chapter I argue that the necessary approach is not to replace prejudice with the neutral stance of tolerance. Something critical lies beyond the reduction of prejudice and the promotion of tolerance: the enhancement of positive intergroup attitudes, allophilia. While the academic and applied literature on intergroup relations is well supplied with terms for negative intergroup attitudes (e.g., xenophobia, sexism, racism, anti-Americanism, classism, ageism, homophobia), there are surprisingly few terms for positive inter-group attitudes. *Allophilia* is a term I coined to refer to positive intergroup attitudes. The concept of allophilia provides a powerful anchor for a new framework for understanding intergroup leadership, the focus of this chapter.

Intergroup Leadership

Leaders confront many challenges that are rooted in conflict among social identity groups. Not only might they inherit conflicts between political, religious, or organizational groups, but they may unwittingly contribute to them. When one considers ingroup leadership in the context of intergroup relations, a tradeoff quickly surfaces. Foundations of strong *intragroup* leadership, such as fostering strong group identification and cohesion, are often stepping stones to *intergroup* conflict. I refer to this as

[†] The author thanks Seth A. Rosenthal and John Elder for helpful comments on an early draft of this chapter, Katherine Chen for research assistance, and Joe Bourneuf, Head of Reference for Widener Library at Harvard College, for his help with Greek conjugations. The Center for Public Leadership at the John F. Kennedy School of Government provided financial support. Sections of this chapter are drawn from an article by the author, "Allophilia and Intergroup Leadership."

the "ingroup/outgroup leadership tradeoff." This insight of the ingroup/outgroup leadership tradeoff builds on classic work by sociologists and more recent work by psychologists, work which examines the tradeoff between internal cohesion and external conflict (e.g., Markides & Cohn, 1982) but does not focus on the perspective of groups' leaders.

Leaders whose concern is restricted to the members of their own ingroup are likely to sacrifice intergroup relations for ingroup leadership. Some make the tradeoff quite deliberately, exploiting, or in some cases creating, intergroup hostilities to rally followers and enhance ingroup cohesion in pursuit of their goals (Bekkers, 1977). In other words, while leaders can establish credibility, define constituencies, and motivate followers through ingroup identities ("we are X" and "X is good"), they can also do so through intergroup identities ("we are not Y" and "Y is bad"). Leaders whose positions are threatened may be more likely to initiate conflict and competition with another group in order to hold on to their power. Leaders will scapegoat or demonize the people of other nations to build support for war or to achieve domestic objectives (Hermann & Kegley, 1995).

For global leaders who define their sphere of concern and their constituencies more broadly than their own ingroup, balancing the ingroup/outgroup leadership tradeoff is essential but problematic. Some of the most important acts of global leadership bring mutually hostile identity groups (e.g., ethnic, national, religious, linguistic, and others) into harmony. Because the actions of the former group of leaders are so harmful and the success of the latter group is so important, the study of the intersection of leadership and intergroup attitudes is crucial to a science of leadership studies. The central questions of such a study might be "how can negative intergroup attitudes (e.g., prejudice) be reduced?" and "how can leaders promote tolerance for members of other identity groups?"

In fact, these questions are not sufficient for theory and the goals they proclaim are not sufficient for the practice of leadership to reduce and prevent conflict. Something critical lies beyond the reduction of prejudice and the promotion of tolerance. Allophilia is a term I coined, derived from the Greek words meaning "liking or love of the other".[1] The concept of allophilia provides a powerful anchor for a new framework for understanding global intergroup leadership.

This chapter introduces the framework of allophilia for understanding leader effects on intergroup attitudes. I argue that allophilia promotion, rather than prejudice reduction, is a primary and under-examined facet of leadership. To initiate the development of a framework of allophilia and leadership, I address three interrelated questions:

- What is allophilia in the context of intergroup relations?
- What role does—and might—allophilia play in intergroup leadership?
- What are the keys to further developing allophilia as a framework for intergroup leadership theory and practice?

Allophilia in Intergroup Relations

The story of intergroup relations in the world is often the story of entrenched hatred, intolerance, and violent conflict. Prejudices are often critical triggers to intergroup conflict.

Gordon Allport (1954) put forth a classic definition of prejudice: antipathy based on faulty and inflexible generalization. This definition captures the critical component of prejudice common to all definitions: negative regard for another identity group. Other definitions of prejudice have suggested that it can entail not only negative regard (dislike) but also positive regard (liking). However, when prejudice is operationalized by researchers, and when it is discussed by practitioners, only negative regard is emphasized.[2] Scant attention has been paid in scholarship or communities of practice to positive regard. I introduce the concept and term allophilia to the literature to focus attention on the lack of investigation into positive regard toward members of outgroups.

There have been numerous subsequent definitions of prejudice. Two features common to these definitions are: (a) negative behaviors and (b) overgeneralization (i.e., a prejudice not just as a negative attitude toward a group, but as the process whereby that negative attitude for the group is applied to any particular individual member of that group). Because there are many definitions of prejudice, and because they differ in the extent to which they address negative behaviors and/or overgeneralizations, I frame allophilia as positive regard for the members of another social identity group. Allophilia may (or may not) be associated with positive behaviors and/or overgeneralization. By definition, however, it is always associated with positive regard toward another social identity group.

Allophilia is theoretically fascinating and practically useful, offering a compelling anchor for a framework of intergroup leadership. Figure 1 locates allophilia vis-à-vis its related constructs of (negative) prejudice and tolerance. When leaders wish to reduce prejudice, the typical remedy they seek is to bring their groups into a state of tolerance. However, tolerance is not the logical antithesis of prejudice; it is the midpoint between negative feelings and positive feelings toward others. The introduction of allophilia, positive intergroup attitudes, as an anchor identifies a new domain for theory, research, and leader interventions beyond prejudice reduction: allophilia enhancement.

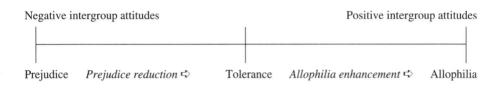

Figure 1. Prejudice, Tolerance, and Allophilia

Why have intergroup researchers overlooked the study of allophilia? Why are positive intergroup attitudes so under-theorized and under-studied? One reason is that prejudice has caused so much suffering that researchers have felt compelled to address it. A second reason is that, while prejudices are widely held throughout the world, allophilia may be less common. Negative intergroup attitudes may not only be more prevalent than positive intergroup attitudes, they may also be more natural. For example, evidence suggests that when constructing identities, people are accepting of those who are familiar and similar, but will distance themselves from those who are dissimilar and less familiar (Druckman, 1994). Social psychological research has shown that merely dividing participants into groups based on minimal and arbitrary criteria will lead individuals to prejudicial attitudes and discriminatory acts, both in favor of "their own" and at the expense of "the others" (Brewer, 1979; Brewer & Kramer, 1985; Kramer & Brewer, 1984; Messick & Mackie, 1989; Tajfel, 1982; Turner, Hogg, Oakes, Reicher, & Wetherell, 1987). Prejudicial attitudes are so rooted in individual psychology and so perpetuated by our social systems that individuals will engage in discriminatory acts even to the disadvantage of their own groups.

There is, however, at the same time evidence to suggest that allophilia may not be as rare or as unnatural as it might, on first consideration, seem. Children often express great curiosity about things and people who are novel and different. And most teachers of young children—those same teachers who have observed dislike and hatred among children for others who are different—often have also observed, in the same cohorts, great curiosity and liking for others who are novel and different, and represent the "other."

The fact that allophilia may be relatively less common than prejudice is not a valid reason for scholars and practitioners to overlook it.[3] Some of the most important human experiences occur only infrequently. In fact, allophilia's relative rarity may suggest that its occurrence is related to acts of transformational leadership.

Allophilia and Intergroup Leadership

To understand leader effects on intergroup allophilia, it is instructive to first consider the general impact of leaders on intergroup attitudes. There is little question that leaders can exert powerful influence over their followers' attitudes.[4] In a seminal study of intergroup relations, Sherif, Harvey, White, Hood, and Sherif (1961) identified leadership as a critical factor in intergroup attitudes and relations. Others (e.g., Grove, 2001) have expanded on this idea by suggesting that leadership can interact with ingroup and outgroup attitudes (e.g., nationalism) to incite nationalist mobilization (Grove, 2001). Figure 2 illustrates a range of possible feelings a follower might have for members of another social identity group under conditions of weak or strong ingroup leadership.

		Attitudes toward outgroup members		
		Prejudice	Tolerance	Allophilia
Ingroup leadership	Strong	A.	B.	C.
	Weak	D.	E.	F.

Figure 2. Follower Attitudes toward Ingroup and Outgroup Members

The "ingroup/outgroup leadership tradeoff" referenced earlier refers to the possibility that the same things a leader does to promote strong ingroup leadership (i.e., promote group cohesion and encourage strong identification) may exacerbate conflict with other groups. For some "bad" leaders (Kellerman, 2004), this may be a desirable outcome. They are content to sacrifice intergroup leadership in order to be strong ingroup leaders. This is represented by Cell A—strong ingroup leadership accompanied by prejudice toward the outgroup. Cell B, in which there is strong ingroup leadership and tolerance for the outgroup, is the focus of many analyses and popular normative interventions, and is often considered the desirable state to be achieved. However, Cell C, in which there are both strong ingroup leadership and *positive* attitudes for outgroup members, is the overlooked cell, which the allophilia and intergroup leadership framework highlights. Here are the loftiest of leadership ambitions. Because the combination of strong ingroup leadership and positive attitudes for outgroup members is uncommon and difficult to achieve, this may also be the cell where the strongest and best leadership is required. In Cells D, E, and F, ingroup leadership is weak so there is no ingroup/outgroup leadership tradeoff.

Allophilia promotion requires strong and skillful leadership for at least two reasons. First, it is likely that allophilia promotion requires that people be pushed beyond their natural predispositions to prejudice. Second, it requires leaders to abstain from some very effective strategies for consolidating their own power.

Several leadership strategies might be considered as alternatives to allophilia promotion: prejudice reduction, superordinate goals and superordinate identities, intergroup contact, and individuation. Each is intended to improve intergroup attitudes, and by extension, to improve intergroup relations. While investigating these alternative strategies, I will simultaneously explore whether allophilia enhancement is necessary for improving intergroup relations.

Prejudice Reduction

A leader can demonstrate intergroup leadership by calling on followers to feel, or at least to show, less prejudice toward members of other social identity groups; the ultimate goal is tolerance. For example, in the wake of the September 11th terrorist attacks in the United States, several American civil rights leaders pled for tolerance toward Arab-Americans. But is tolerance promotion a sufficient leadership strategy to reduce intergroup conflict? It appears not to be for at least two reasons. The first is realistic group conflict (Blake & Mouton, 1961; Diab, 1970; Sherif, 1966; Sherif et al., 1961). Groups may engage in competitive activities where one group's victory necessarily harms the other's interests. Such "real" conflict leads to frustration, antagonism, and—ultimately—prejudice. A vicious cycle occurs in which individuals on each side become more strongly identified and attached to their own group and thus become even more antagonistic toward the other. Even if intergroup relations are stabilized at the level of tolerance, they will quickly disintegrate into prejudice when real-world conflicts arise. Therefore, countervailing forces in the direction of allophilia need to be introduced. This way, when problems born of actual conflict arise, intergroup relations are likely to deteriorate to the level of tolerance but not to the level of prejudice.

The second reason is the human predisposition toward categorical thinking. The last three decades of social cognition research have demonstrated quite powerfully that humans are hard-wired and predisposed to category-based thinking. Thus, prejudices are, in part, a byproduct of the way our minds naturally organize information. Because of this, anchoring intergroup relations at the point of tolerance is not a strong enough countervailing force to keep groups from slipping back into prejudice, whereas anchoring intergroup relations in allophilia may be. Figure 3 locates the direction in which realistic conflict and categorical thinking move intergroup attitudes; it illustrates the importance of leader efforts to foster allophilia in order to counteract these influences.

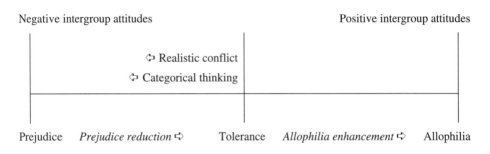

Figure 3. Realistic Conflict, Categorical Thinking, Prejudice, Tolerance, and Allophilia

Superordinate Goals and Superordinate Identities

Research suggests that recategorizing the members of a different identity group as part of one's own ingroup can reduce intergroup conflict; negative intergroup attitudes vanish as the outgroup becomes part of the ingroup. Leaders may therefore try to compel their followers to expand their view of the ingroup to encompass the outgroup. Working cooperatively is particularly effective at dissolving former subgroups into a new, inclusive group (Gaertner, Dovidio, Anastasio, Bachman, & Rust, 1993; Gaertner, Dovidio, Nier, Ward, & Banker, 1999; Gaertner, Dovidio, Rust, Nier, Mottola, et al., 1999). Nonaggression within certain groups, such as the community of liberal democratic nations, may result from leaders and citizens of these countries identifying themselves as part of a larger single ingroup, all of whose members deserve mutual support (Hermann & Kegley, 1995; Mintz & Geva, 1993). In fact, wars are less easily justified against those who are similar to us, and are more often fought between states with different political systems than between states with similar political systems (Hermann & Kegley, 1995; Maoz & Abdolali, 1989; Maoz & Russett, 1992, 1993).

Recategorization can occur through the emphasis of similarity and the de-emphasis of differences, or through the introduction of superordinate identities or superordinate goals. Superordinate identities are overarching categories, such as national identity in a nation comprising distinct ethnic populations. Superordinate goals are shared by two or more groups who rely on each other's support to achieve them. Superordinate goals change the relationship between groups, breaking the cycle of hostility and conflict. Superordinate identities and superordinate goals may occur naturally, giving leaders the opportunity to highlight them in order to make them salient, or they may be actively promoted. Indeed, leaders are often normatively advised to foster common identities (Kaufmann, 2003) such as pan-ethnic (e.g., Arab), pan-geographic (e.g., African), or pan-religious (e.g., Muslim) identities.

66   **LEADERS MUST ATTEND DIRECTLY THEIR**   **99**
FOLLOWERS' ATTITUDES TOWARD "THE OTHER"
RATHER THAN HOPING TO MAKE "THE OTHER"
VANISH INTO "US."

Nevertheless, superordinate identities and superordinate goals, and the recategorization processes they stimulate, are not sufficient leadership practices to reduce intergroup prejudice and conflict. Some differences between social identity groups are bona fide and robust. Leaders may strategically emphasize commonalities to attain shorter-term goals, but the differences are likely to reemerge over time. Bad leaders (Kellerman, 2004) will go so far as to exaggerate and even fabricate such differences in order to capitalize on them politically. For example, in the past, Serbs and Croats spoke a common language known as Serbo-Croatian. After the breakup of Yugoslavia, nationalist leaders in the two independent and hostile nations, Serbia and Croatia, each claimed to have their own languages: Serbian and Croatian. Two separate languages—which for all practical purposes do not exist—have now been constructed and two separate linguistic identity groups have been created, a powerful illustration of the ingroup/outgroup leadership tradeoff. In Rwanda, bad leaders capitalized on differences in the physical features of Tutsis and Hutus to strengthen ingroup cohesion and promote intergroup conflict in the form of a civil war culminating in genocide, undoing six hundred years of shared commerce, language, culture, and intermarriage.

Because group differences are sometimes genuine and robust and may even be desirable (Hogg & Hornsey, 2002), and because perceptions of difference can so easily be created (even without any factual basis) and manipulated, recategorization strategies such as superordinate goals and superordinate identities are not sufficient to reduce intergroup prejudice and conflict. Such strategies may work in laboratory settings, but in the real world, identity groups prove to be remarkably resilient. Superordinate groups working toward superordinate goals can quickly splinter again, with disastrous outcomes. Leaders must attend directly their followers' attitudes toward "the other" rather than hoping to make "the other" vanish into "us."

Recategorization strategies also run afoul of a level-of-analysis paradox: rather than eliminating a conflict, they may simply move it to a higher level of social organization. U.S. President Reagan (1985, p. 1434) recognized this in a description of meetings with then-General Secretary Gorbachev:

> Just think how easy his task and mine might be in these meetings that we held if suddenly there was a threat to this world from some other species, from another planet, outside in the universe. We'd forget all the little local differences that we have between our countries . . .

Hackman similarly observes: "The best way to get peace on earth is an invasion from Mars" (J. R. Hackman, lecture, fall 1999). Indeed, superordinate groups are often created in response to a threat from an outgroup. But the accompanying positive attitudes and reduced conflict are predicated on other negative attitudes and other increased conflict. Often the positive attitudes that threats promote will not outlast the threat that created them. After the rival Athenians and Spartans joined forces against a mutual enemy during the Persian Wars (500–449 B.C.), they fought each other in the Peloponnesian War (431–404 B.C.). The alliance of the United States and the Soviet Union against a mutual enemy during World War II was immediately followed by the 44-year Cold War.

Contact

Allport (1954) suggested that contact between groups under optimal conditions would effectively reduce intergroup prejudice; drawing on earlier theoretical and empirical work (e.g., Williams, 1947), he identified those conditions as equal status between groups, common goals, intergroup cooperation, and the support of authority (e.g., through laws or customs). While intergroup contact, under very specific conditions, does appear to help reduce intergroup prejudice (Pettigrew & Tropp, 2000), encouraging contact is not, however, a sufficient leadership strategy for reducing intergroup conflict for at least four reasons. First, contact has been shown to aid in prejudice reduction in very specific and limited circumstances at best, but has not been shown to foster positive attitudes. Second, contact between group members is not always possible when there is conflict. Third, Allport's four prerequisite conditions for contact to work are frequently outside a leader's control, if not downright impossible. This limitation is particularly damning because research has found that the right conditions are critical, and that contact in suboptimal conditions may actually *increase* prejudice. Fourth, contact is not the only determinant of intergroup attitudes; for example, they are also formed by the propensity to categorical thinking. Thus, while contact may influence intergroup attitudes, it is not a sufficient leadership strategy for reducing intergroup conflict.

Individuation

It is logical to ask why leadership should promote positive attitudes toward some group rather than simply encouraging followers to see members of the outgroup as individuals. However, there are three reasons why it would not be a sufficient strategy to simply think about the members of other identity groups as individuals. First, most important political and policy decisions are made about groups, not individuals. For example, immigration policies represent, to some extent, people's attitudes toward outgroups. If leaders promote *no* attitudes about outgroups, then followers are most likely to maintain their negative or neutral attitudes, with deleterious effects on policy. Second, leaders themselves operate at the group level. Leaders are defined in relation to groups of followers. In situations where conflict might arise, the identity of the conflicting leader and followers are salient as a group, not as individuals. The third and perhaps most compelling reason is, once again, the human propensity for category-based thinking. Therefore it is essential to balance negative intergroup attitudes with positive intergroup attitudes—allophilia.

Case Examples

For all of the reasons noted above, the four intergroup leadership strategies reviewed—prejudice reduction, superordinate goals and superordinate identities, contact, and individuation—are not sufficient to reduce prejudice and reduce conflict. In contrast, allophilia promotion provides a critical framework for the advancement of effective intergroup leadership. Allophilia enhancement is a rare but important intergroup leadership strategy. Allophilia may apply to many different types of leadership, including political, quasi-political, religious, organizational, and athletic leadership. One can see glimmers of it in secular and religious leaders' words and actions, particularly in some of the most widely credited and highly regarded global leaders. While a comprehensive case study is beyond the scope of the current chapter, consideration of the intergroup relations strategies of a number of transformational leaders (Bass, 1985) suggests that they were very likely motivated by allophilia—positive intergroup attitudes—above and beyond simple tolerance. At the least, these leaders were motivated to promote allophilia as a way to address or prevent conflict.

For example, Nelson Mandela, the renowned South African peacemaker, never wavered on his universal vision of a multi-ethnic South African society. To promote his vision, he learned the language and the history of the "other," the Afrikaans language and history. At the 1995 Rugby World Cup finals, he cheered for South Africa's national team, previously regarded as a powerful symbol of "white" nationalism, and sported the team captain's jersey (Lieberfeld, 2003).

Martin Luther King Jr. is widely recognized for his leadership in racial desegregation in the United States. But King also waged a war on poverty by initiating a movement known as the Poor People's Campaign. King attempted to extend the civil rights movement beyond race, and beyond championing the rights of the racial identity group to which he belonged, to include economic class. While it is difficult to infer motives from a distance, the care and attention King paid to exposing the lack of rights and care afforded the poor in the United States, a group to which he did not belong, went far beyond promoting tolerance. Indeed, King was explicit about the importance of moving beyond mere tolerance toward positive intergroup attitudes. He remarked that, while he originally felt love was in the domain of individual relationships, he later concluded that it could be a "potent instrument for social and collective transformation" (Carson, 1998, pp. 23–24).

> **" A PRELIMINARY STATISTICAL FACTOR ANALYSIS OF THESE DATA REVEALED SEVERAL FACTORS OR COMPONENTS OF ALLOPHILIA, INCLUDING: (1) RESPECTING THE GROUP, (2) BELIEVING THAT POSITIVE TRAITS CHARACTERIZE THE GROUP, (3) SEEING THE GROUP AS COMPETENT, (4) FEELING CONNECTED TO THE MEMBERS OF THE GROUP, AND (5) FEELING WARM TOWARD THE MEMBERS OF THE GROUP. "**

The allophilia framework may also help us understand the factors that led some individuals to take great personal risks during the Second World War. For example, many Danes resisted German deportation of Jews; a small number of Germans sheltered and protected Jews; and Raoul Wallenberg, the Swedish diplomat, faked documents to help establish "safe houses" to save Hungarian Jews. Tolerance—the absence of prejudice—is unlikely to fully explain these brave acts. While it is possible that social justice motives, rather than allophilia, may have motivated their first steps, love for the beneficiaries of these courageous acts may have come to sustain many of the individuals who brought them about.

A widely circulated set of images in the late 1980s showed Princess Diana hugging children with HIV, and she was often seen with children in developing countries by her side. These images surfaced in a time when people were tremendously fearful of direct social contact with those with HIV. These children were, for Western audiences, the "other," suffering from a largely misunderstood illness and separated from the Princess by economic class, ethnicity, and geography. This pairing powerfully captured the differences between the Princess and the children, and her act—a simple hug—demonstrated for the world not just tolerance for the other, but love.

Allophilia in Intergroup Leadership Theory and Practice: An Agenda

Much work remains to be done to advance a framework for intergroup leadership based on allophilia enhancement as an emergent model of leadership. A major direction for work on the allophilia and intergroup leadership framework will entail multifaceted research to understand the components and factors of allophilia. This will help us to research practical intervention strategies that leaders can use to foster allophilia.

At present, allophilia is best understood as a general, theoretical construct. However, researchers are currently developing a more nuanced and precise empirical understanding of allophilia (Pittinsky & Rosenthal, 2005). This research will enable us to identify and measure the specific factors that make up the general construct of allophilia. In order to accomplish this, over 3,500 statements describing facets of allophilia were collected from a diverse cohort of 281 respondents: 65 percent female, 35 percent male, aged 18 to 74. Thirty-three percent of the respondents were non-white; 46 percent were from outside the United States. These descriptions of allophilia were rephrased in the form of questions, redundancies were eliminated, and the 122 most compelling and relevant questions were selected for further study. These questions were then customized to measure allophilia toward a specific social identity group and administered to approximately 300 research participants. A preliminary statistical factor analysis of these data revealed several factors or components of allophilia, including: (1) respecting the group, (2) believing that positive traits characterize the group, (3) seeing the group as competent, (4) feeling connected to the members of the group, and (5) feeling warm toward the members of the group. These factors were moderately correlated, suggesting that they are conceptually related to each other, but they also each contributed independent variance, suggesting that they each offer distinct insights into allophilia.

Continued work on the factors of allophilia will yield not only theoretical knowledge but also critical insight into leadership practice. Our factor analysis will yield a measurement tool (i.e., a questionnaire) for the empirical study of allophilia in intergroup leadership; investigation of allophilia as a predictor variable, an outcome variable, and a mediator or moderator variable can then begin in earnest. Furthermore, each factor of allophilia brought to light will suggest a lens through which positive intergroup attitudes can be understood and a means by which they can be fostered by leaders.

Conclusion

One of the most pressing concerns confronting global leaders is intergroup conflict, often inspired or facilitated by prejudice. While the reduction of prejudice is essential, I argue that the necessary approach is not to replace prejudice with the neutral stance of tolerance but with positive intergroup attitudes—allophilia. A framework of intergroup leadership anchored in allophilia prompts leaders to push their societies and the world community away from the natural direction in which individuals and social system might otherwise unfold, leading them instead on a trajectory of positive intergroup relations.

NOTES

1. For example, a full text keyword search for "allophilia" in the following online databases produced no results: Academic Search Premier (EBSCOhost), PsycINFO, Sociofile, Educational Resource Information Center (EBSCOhost), JSTOR, PAIS (Public Affairs Information Service), LexisNexis, and Google Scholar.

2. Similar behavior can be observed in the literature on stereotypes. It is overwhelmingly the study of negative stereotypes, with very little theoretical or empirical work on positive stereotypes (Pittinsky, Shih, & Ambady, 2000; Shih, Pittinsky, & Ambady, 1999).

3. I am indebted to Harvard psychologist J. Richard Hackman for pointing out that Chris Argyris' work on authenticity is noteworthy in this regard. Wishing to study authenticity, Argyris was confronted with an obstacle: it occurs only infrequently. Believing authenticity was nonetheless important to study, he created laboratory conditions under which it was likely to be expressed; in those settings he began his influential research.

4. A body of work applies Social Identity Theory (SIT) to leadership. In this literature, SIT, a lynchpin construct of intergroup relations research, is often profitably applied to *intragroup* leadership dynamics. For examples, see the work of Chen and Van Velsor (1996), Hogg (2001), and Van Vugt and De Cremer (1999). For applications of SIT to *intergroup* leadership dynamics, see Duck and Fielding (1999); Hogg (1996); Jetten, Duck, Terry, and O'Brien (2002); Katz (1977); Platow, Hoar, Reid, Harley, and Morrison (1997); Sherif, Harvey, White, Hood, and Sherif (1961); and De Cremer and Van Vugt (2002).

REFERENCES

Allport, G. W. (1954). *The nature of prejudice.* Reading, MA: Addison-Wesley.

Bass, B. M. (1985). *Leadership and performance beyond expectations.* New York: The Free Press.

Bekkers, F. (1977). Threatened leadership and intergroup conflicts. *Journal of Peace Research, 14,* 223–247.

Blake, R. R., & Mouton, J. S. (1961). Comprehension of own and of outgroup positions under intergroup competition. *Journal of Conflict Resolution, 5,* 304–310.

Brewer, M. B. (1979). In-group bias in the minimal intergroup situation: A cognitive-motivational analysis. *Psychological Bulletin, 86,* 307–324.

Brewer, M. B., & Kramer, R. M. (1985). The psychology of intergroup attitudes and behavior. *Annual Review of Psychology, 36,* 219–243.

Carson, C. (Ed.). (1998). *The autobiography of Martin Luther King, Jr.* New York: Warner Books.

Chen, C. C., & Van Velsor, E. (1996). New directions for research and practice in diversity leadership. *Leadership Quarterly, 7,* 285–302.

De Cremer, D., & Van Vugt, M. (2002). Intergroup and intragroup aspects of leadership in social dilemmas: A relational model of cooperation. *Journal of Experimental Social Psychology, 38,* 126–136.

Diab, L. (1970). A study of intragroup and intergroup relations among experimentally produced small groups. *Genetic Psychology Monographs, 82,* 49–82.

Druckman, D. (1994). Nationalism, patriotism, and group loyalty: A social psychological perspective. *Mershon International Studies Review, 38,* 43–68.

Duck, J. M., & Fielding, K. S. (1999). Leaders and subgroups: One of us or one of them? *Group Processes and Intergroup Relations, 2,* 203–230.

Gaertner, S. L., Dovidio, J. F., Anastasio, P. A., Bachman, B. A., & Rust, M. C. (1993). The common ingroup identity model: Recategorization and the reduction of intergroup bias. *European Review of Social Psychology, 4,* 1–26.

Gaertner, S. L., Dovidio, J. F., Nier, J. A., Ward, C. M., & Banker, B. S. (1999). Across cultural divides: The value of superordinate identity. In D. A. Prentice & D. T. Miller (Eds.), *Cultural divides: Understanding and overcoming group conflict* (pp. 173–212). New York: Russell Sage Foundation.

Gaertner, S. L., Dovidio, J. F., Rust, M. C., Nier, J., Mottola, G. R., Banker, B., Ward, C. M., & Houlette, M. (1999). Reducing intergroup bias: Elements of intergroup cooperation. *Journal of Personality and Social Psychology, 76,* 388–402.

Grove, A. (2001). Theory, perception, and leadership agency: A multiple processing model of nationalist mobilization. *Nationalism and Ethnic Politics, 7,* 1–32.

Hermann, M. G., & Kegley, C. W., Jr. (1995). Rethinking democracy and international peace: Perspectives from political psychology. *International Studies Quarterly, 39,* 511–534.

Hogg, M. A. (1996). Intragroup processes, group structure, and social identity. In W. Robinson (Ed.), *Social groups and identities: Developing the legacy of Henri Tajfel* (pp. 65–93). Oxford, England: Butterworth-Heinemann.

Hogg, M. A. (2001). A social identity theory of leadership. *Personality and Social Psychology Review, 5,* 184–200.

Hogg, M. A., & Hornsey, M. J. (2002). Assimilation and diversity: An integrative model of subgroup relations. *Personality and Social Psychology Review, 4,* 143–158.

Jetten, J., Duck, J., Terry, D. J., & O'Brien, A. (2002). Being attuned to intergroup differences in mergers: The role of aligned leaders for low status groups. *Personality and Social Psychology Bulletin, 28,* 1194–1201.

Katz, R. (1977). The influence of group conflict in leadership effectiveness. *Organizational Behavior and Human Performance, 20,* 265–286.

Kaufmann, K. M. (2003). Cracks in the rainbow: Growing commonality as a basis for Latino and African-American political coalitions. *Political Research Quarterly, 56,* 199–210.

Kellerman, B. (2004). *Bad leadership: What it is, how it happens, why it matters.* Boston: Harvard Business School Press.

Kelman, H. C. (1986). Interactive problem solving: A social psychological approach to conflict resolution. In W. Klassen (Ed.), *Dialogue toward inter-faith understanding* (pp. 293–314). Tantur/ Jerusalem: Ecumenical Institute for Theological Research.

Kramer, R. M., & Brewer, M. B. (1984). Effects of group identity on resource use in a simulated commons dilemma. *Journal of Personality & Social Psychology, 46*(5), 1044–1057.

Lieberfeld, D. (2003). Nelson Mandela: Partisan and peacemaker. *Negotiation Journal, 19,* 229–250.

Maoz, Z., & Abdolali, N. (1989). Regime types and international conflict, 1816–1976. *Journal of Conflict Resolution, 33,* 3–35.

Maoz, Z., & Russett, B. (1992). Alliance, contiguity, wealth, and political stability: Is the lack of conflict among democracies a statistical artifact? *International Interaction, 17,* 245–267.

Maoz, Z., & Russett, B. (1993). Normative and structural causes of democratic peace, 1946–1986. *American Political Science Review, 87,* 624–638.

Markides, K., & Cohn, S. F. (1982). Eternal conflict/internal cohesion: A reevaluation of an old theory. *American Sociological Review, 47,* 88–98.

Messick, D. M., & Mackie, D. M. (1989). Intergroup relations. *Annual Review of Psychology, 40,* 45–81.

Mintz, A., & Geva, N. (1993). Why don't democracies fight each other? An experimental assessment of the "political incentive" explanation. *Journal of Conflict Resolution, 37,* 484–503.

Montville, J. V. (1989). *Conflict and peacemaking in multi-ethnic societies.* Lexington, MA: Lexington Books.

Pettigrew, T. F., & Tropp, L. R. (2000). Does intergroup contact reduce prejudice? Recent meta-analytic findings. In S. Oskamp (Ed.), *Reducing prejudice and discrimination: The Claremont symposium* (pp. 93–114). Mahwah, NJ: Erlbaum.

Pittinsky, T. L., & Rosenthal, S. (2005). *The measurement of positive intergroup attitudes: The Allophilia Scale.* Unpublished manuscript.

Pittinsky, T. L., Shih, M., & Ambady, N. (2000). Will a category cue affect you? Category cues, positive stereotypes and recall for applicants. *Social Psychology of Education, 4,* 53–65.

Platow, M. J., Hoar, S., Reid, S., Harley, K., & Morrison, D. (1997). Endorsement of distributively fair and unfair leaders in interpersonal and intergroup situations. *European Journal of Social Psychology, 27,* 465–494.

Reagan, R. (1985). *Public papers of the presidents of the United States. Ronald Reagan. Book II. June 29 to December 31, 1985.* Washington, DC: Federal Register Division, National Archives and Records Service, General Services Administration.

Sherif, M. (1966). *In common predicament.* Boston: Houghton Mifflin.

Sherif, M., Harvey, O. J., White, B. J., Hood, W. R., & Sherif, C. W. (1961). *Intergroup cooperation and competition: The Robbers Cave experiment.* Norman, OK: University Book Exchange.

Shih, M., Pittinsky, T. L., & Ambady, N. (1999). Stereotype susceptibility: Identity salience and shifts in quantitative performance. *Psychological Science, 10,* 81–84.

Tajfel, H. (1982). Social psychology of intergroup relations. *Annual Review of Psychology, 33,* 1–39.

Turner, J. C., Hogg, M. A., Oakes, P. J., Reicher, S. D., & Wetherell, M. S. (1987). *Rediscovering the social group: A self-categorization theory.* Oxford and New York: Basil Blackwell.

Van Vugt, M., & De Cremer, D. (1999). Leadership in social dilemmas: The effects of group identification on collective actions to provide public goods. *Journal of Personality and Social Psychology, 76,* 587–599.

Williams, R. J. (1947). *The reduction of intergroup tensions.* New York: Social Science Research Council.

TODD L. PITTINSKY is an Assistant Professor of Public Policy and a core faculty member of Harvard's Center for Public Leadership. Todd's research lab focuses on the psychological science of leadership and the nature of allophilia (love of the other) in intergroup relations. He uses quantitative and qualitative research methods in the laboratory and the field. He earned his B.A. in psychology from Yale University, his M.A. in psychology from Harvard, and his Ph.D. in organizational behavior from the Harvard Graduate School of Arts and Sciences. In 2002 he was selected to represent Harvard in the Young Faculty Leaders Forum, a working group of faculty members selected from America's leading universities. Todd can be contacted at todd_pittinsky@harvard.edu.

Leadership Coherence: An Emerging Model from Interviews with Leaders Around the Globe

By Nancy Stanford-Blair and Michael H. Dickmann

INSIGHTS DRAWN FROM INTERVIEWS WITH THIRTY-SIX EXEMPLARY leaders describe a natural and potent relationship between leadership formation, performance, and sustainability. Through sharing their leadership stories, leaders of acknowledged reputation in diverse contexts across the globe revealed prominent themes about: (a) how leaders are formed to the role of influencing others toward the achievement of goals, (b) how leaders perform such influence on others, and (c) how leaders sustain themselves and their leadership influence over time and adversity. The collective insight of the storytellers ultimately frames a model of coherent leadership—a model that facilitates understanding about how aligned values, character, behavior, and dispositions expand the consequence of leadership influence on organizational growth and achievement.

Leadership has intrigued humanity over the millennia, yet as a formal field of study it is relatively young and—while theories and formulas abound—conclusive understanding of the phenomenon is less accessible (Antonakis, Cianciolo, & Sternberg, 2004). The quest for deeper understanding nevertheless continues at the beginning of this new century. It is a quest fueled by concern as the quality of local, national, and international leadership is increasingly called into question.

Wheatley (2002) has observed that we are in a time of increasing economic and political instability, growing divisiveness, and fear of failing systems. With that sense that we have painted ourselves into some very serious corners comes the awareness that leadership is in demand. Fullan (2001) captured this sentiment in observing that the requisite "effective leadership is in very short supply." Indeed, at a time that our need is greatest, many perceive that the supply of quality leaders has peaked—or perhaps diminished (Ferrandino & Tirozzi, 2000). It is a shortage that confronts a board of directors searching for a CEO, a nation seeking to elect a prime minister or president, or a school system hunting for a new principal or superintendent. Good leaders, it would appear, are increasingly hard to come by. Such perceptions of a leadership shortage might merely reflect the anxiety endured by every generation when facing their particular challenges. It is a perception, nonetheless, that encourages the pursuit of further knowledge about the nature and nurture of leadership.

**❝ THE PARTICIPATING LEADERS WERE PURPOSE- ❞
FULLY SELECTED TO REPRESENT DIVERSITY IN
CULTURE, GENDER, AND EXPERIENCE.**

Participants in this ongoing quest for better understanding of the phenomenon quickly come to the understanding that leadership is complex and contextual. Leadership is a concept that is often deconstructed and examined in parts and from different perspectives in the interest of gaining greater understanding of the whole. Recent efforts—*Connecting Leadership to the Brain* (Dickmann & Stanford-Blair, 2002) and *Leading with the Brain in Mind* (Dickmann, Stanford-Blair, & Rosati-Bojar, 2004)— focused on the nature of human capacity and how leaders might best influence such capacity toward the achievement of goals. This study examined how leaders are formed to the task of influencing the capacity of others, how they perform such influence, and how they sustain their influence over time.

To that end, this project engaged thirty-six exemplary leaders in reflective conversation about their work. Specifically, it employed an interview protocol to structure reflection about: (a) how leaders are formed, (b) how leaders perform to influence others, and (c) how leaders sustain themselves and their leadership influence. The participating leaders were purposefully selected to represent diversity in culture, gender, and experience. With faith in others' ability to recognize effective leadership when they encountered it, credible contacts (i.e., individuals who had backgrounds in the formal study of leadership and/or were acknowledged leaders in their own right) from around the world were asked to nominate candidates for participation in this study. In order to increase the likelihood that nominated leaders would be worth the interview, the following criteria were applied to the nomination process:

1. Nominees were to be individuals who fulfilled a basic definition of leadership as: *a process of influencing others toward the achievement of a goal* (Dickmann & Stanford-Blair, 2002).

2. Nominees were to be leaders who were widely respected in their field, office, organization, or country—by both external and internal observers of their leadership.

3. Nominees were to be leaders who were known for successful results and goal achievements.

Taken independently, each criterion was important. Nominated candidates were either currently or recently involved in influential relationships with others for the purpose of achieving specific goals. Respect garnered from both within and outside of their leadership context brought forward candidates who were acknowledged by distant observers, as well as those who directly experienced their leadership (i.e., while reputations can be built on the outside of an organization, the "proof in the pudding" is often the ability to earn respect within as well). This is important, as studies have found that organizations in which members rate their leaders positively are more productive and more financially viable (Denison, 1997; Zipkin, 2000). Additionally, the nominated leaders had all demonstrated that they could accomplish results, close the deal, realize goals, or otherwise fulfill a purpose. Research has frequently defined leadership success based on outcomes achieved and accounted for by tangible results, as well as reputation garnered (Day, 2001). It was not that the nominated leaders were not vulnerable to criticism and human failing. All leaders suffer that reality. Rather, the point is that they had earned leadership credibility.

The purposeful selection of a credible pool of exemplary leaders was further influenced by an interest in discovering universal leadership perspectives and practices across diverse contexts. The Global Leadership and Organizational Behavior Effectiveness (GLOBE) Project assesses the similarities and differences in the cultural semantic definition of leadership in sixty participating countries. Similar to the definition employed in this study, GLOBE researchers have defined leadership as the ability of an individual to influence, motivate, and enable others to contribute toward the effectiveness and success of the organization of which they are members (Den Hartog et al.,1999). Since comparative leadership research is somewhat uncommon, it was the intention of this investigation to advance the understanding of leadership across diverse contexts. Accordingly, thirty-six storytellers were purposefully selected to represent a diverse population of leaders. The intent was to portray leadership across its many and diverse manifestations—from the leadership represented by prominent politicians and corporate executives to representatives of the preponderance of leadership influence exerted more quietly and subtly in everyday relationships (Burns, 1978). As a result, nominated leaders were screened toward the selection of a rich cross-section of individuals who represented diversity in:

- context and experience
- knowledge and expertise
- roles and stations
- culture and gender

The talented, articulate and diverse group of storytellers that emerged from the selection process included leaders in government, law, business, education, health, recreation, professional associations, and the arts. Figures 1-10 present the thirty-six storytellers with descriptions of their leadership context by geographical location and positions at the time they shared their stories.

> " THE TALENTED, ARTICULATE AND DIVERSE GROUP OF STORYTELLERS THAT EMERGED FROM THE SELECTION PROCESS INCLUDED LEADERS IN GOVERNMENT, LAW, BUSINESS, EDUCATION, HEALTH, RECREATION, PROFESSIONAL ASSOCIATIONS, AND THE ARTS. "

Figure 1. Government Leaders

Name	Location	Position/Role
Michael Barber	Great Britain	Director, Prime Minister's Policy Delivery Unit
Chet Bradley	Wisconsin, USA	State Supervisor for Health Education
Helen Clark	New Zealand	Prime Minister of New Zealand
Fanny Law	Hong Kong	Minister of Education and Development

Michael Barber, Chet Bradley, Prime Minister Helen Clark, and Fanny Law were influential reform-minded government officials. They were widely recognized for making an impact on their state or country's policies in a manner that enriched the quality of life for the populations they represented.

Figure 2. Nonprofit Organization Leaders

Name	Location	Position/Role
Margo De'Vai	Hungary	Head of Comprehensive Health Education Foundation, Hungary
Gabor Halmai	Hungary	President of Soros Foundation, Hungary
CJ Nickerson	Washington, USA	President/founder, Comprehensive Health Education Foundation, USA
Mechai Viraviadya	Thailand	CEO, Population Development Association, former Minister of Health and Welfare

Margo De'vai, Gabor Halmai, CJ Nickerson, and Mechai Viraviadya lead nonprofit organizations that were mostly self-created. They worked on changing systems from the outside—with all the freedom and inventiveness that their outsider status allowed.

Figure 3. K-12 Education Leaders

Name	Location	Position/Role
Tim Brighouse	Great Britain	CEO of Birmingham Schools
Rod Chamberlain	Hawaii, USA	Headmaster, Kamehameha School
Jeanne Dukes	California, USA	Director of Special Services and Alternative Education, Paso Robles School District
Ian Fox	New Zealand	New Zealand Middle School Principal of the Year
Nola Hambleton	New Zealand	Principal and President of International Principal's Association
Mandy Mcleod	Belgium	Principal, St. John's International School
Gary Rasmussen	Hong Kong	Business Manager, Hong Kong International School
Patrick Sayne	California, USA	Superintendent of Schools

Tim Brighouse, Rod Chamberlain, Jeanne Dukes, Ian Fox, Nola Hambleton, Mandy Macleod, Gary Rasmussen, and Patrick Sayne were inventive educators committed to the success of all students, and the teachers who serve them. They worked in public, private, and international schools with a common mission of building human capacity.

Figure 4. Public Health Leaders

Name	Location	Position/Role
Alex Banful	Ghana	Managing Director, GSMF International
Donald Gwira	Ghana	Communications Director, West African Division of Sight Savers International
Beth Stevenson	Georgia, USA	Director of Youth Development and Education, American Cancer Society

Alex Banful, Donald Gwira, and Beth Stevenson served organizations dedicated to the promotion of public health. They each pursued their work as leaders of nonprofit agencies dedicated to health education and discovery of effective treatment and cures.

Figure 5. Foreign Service Leaders

Name	Location	Position/Role
Roger Harmon	Thailand	Director of Peace Corps, Thailand
Brenda Schoonover	Belgium	Former U.S. Ambassador to Togo and Chief of Mission, Brussels

Brenda Schoonover served as a foreign diplomat, building bridges of understanding across cultures and amidst conflict. Similarly, Roger Harmon served his country as Director of the Peace Corps in Thailand, with the intent of reinforcing adherence to the original Peace Corps philosophy.

Figure 6. Justice System Leaders

Name	Location	Position/Role
Richard Bissen	Hawaii, USA	District Attorney, Maui, Kauai, Molokai
Denise Henare	New Zealand	Lawyer, activist, and expert in constitutional law and Maori tradition

Richard Bissen defended and protected the public safety of his county with a gentle but firm administration of the law. As a civil rights attorney, Denise Henare committed her career to securing equal rights for native Maori in New Zealand.

Figure 7. Hospitality Industry Leaders

Name	Location	Position/Role
Julianne Lowe	New Zealand	Tour Director, AAT Kings
Leotis Watson	Georgia, USA	Head Concierge, Emory Conference Center

Julianne Lowe and Leotis Watson literally lead to serve in the hospitality industry, giving care and attention to the weary tourist and harried traveler. Julianne believed in creating community among strangers and Leotis rebounded from homelessness to a position of leadership driven by a positive disposition and commitment to excellence.

Figure 8. Higher Education Leaders

Name	Location	Position/Role
Ross Gilbert	Australia	Associate Dean, Sydney Conservatory
John Hood	New Zealand	Vice-chancellor, Oxford University; former Vice-chancellor, Auckland University

Ross Gilbert and John Hood provided leadership in the most intransigent of all institutions, higher education—and they did so with remarkable success and aplomb. John has since been named as the first non-Oxford alum to the venerable position of Vice-chancellor of Oxford University.

Figure 9. Business Leaders

Name	Location	Position/Role
Boon Yoon Chiang	Singapore	CEO, Jardine-Matheson, Singapore
Bob Knight	Florida, USA	CFO, Paul Homes Construction
Ulice Payne	Wisconsin, USA	General Manager, Milwaukee Brewers
Kuami Pianim	Ghana	CEO, New World Investments Limited
Christine Rodriquez	Wisconsin, USA	Vice President, Rockwell Automation
Richard Teerlink	Wisconsin, USA	Former CEO, Harley-Davidson Corp.

Business sector leaders included Boon Yoon Chiang, Bob Knight, Ulice Payne, Christine Rodriquez, Kuami Pianim, and Rich Teerlink. As a whole, they believed that investment in people was their priority bottom line and that profits resulted as the icing on the cake.

Figure 10. Fine and Applied Arts Leaders

Name	Location	Position/Role
Gavan Flick	Australia	Owner and operator of Gevalia aboriginal art gallery
Don Hazelwood	Australia	Concertmaster for the Sydney Symphony, Sydney Opera House and First Violinist
Frank Lukasavitz	Wisconsin, USA	Industrial designer and founding father of the Milwaukee Institute of Art and Design

Three gentlemen of diverse interests and experiences represented the arts. Don Hazelwood was a gifted violinist who rose to the status of concertmaster for the Sydney Symphony. Gavan Flick, also from Australia, was an art dealer who created and operated the first and only Aborigine-owned art gallery in Sydney. Frank Lukasavitz was an industrial designer and founder of a premier post-secondary art school in Milwaukee, Wisconsin.

To engage these leaders in reflection about how they influenced others toward the achievement of goals—and what formed and sustained their leadership capacity to do so—an interview protocol was established as detailed in Figure 11. Siedman

(1998) suggests that "At the root of in-depth interviewing is an interest in understanding the experiences of other people and the meaning they make of that experience" (p. 3). To that end, each of the participating leaders was asked to make meaning of their leadership experience in an interview that lasted from one and one half to two hours.

Figure 11. Interview Protocol: Leadership Formation, Performance, and Sustainability

1. Leadership Formation: How did you come to leadership?

   Prompts:

   - What significant relationships, events, or other experiences influenced your journey to leadership?
   - What formal and/or informal preparation was valuable to your leadership development?

2. Leadership Performance: How do you conduct your leadership?

   Prompts:

   - What motivates/drives your leadership?
   - How do you see yourself as a leader?
   - What does your leadership look like to others?
   - How do you influence others toward the achievement of goals?

3. Leadership Sustainability: How do you sustain your leadership?

   Prompts:

   - How do you sustain results?
   - How do you sustain yourself?

Coherent Leadership Model

All interviews were recorded, transcribed, and aligned to field notes kept during the interview sessions. Both the transcriptions and field notes were then analyzed to discern salient themes about leadership formation, performance, and sustainability. A resulting model of leadership coherence emerged (Figure 12) that has implications for both understanding and facilitating the relationships between formation, performance, and sustainability within effective leadership. It is a model that interprets a dynamic and reciprocal relationship between clarity about value and purpose, congruent character and behavior, compounded capacity, and a resulting expansion of consequence.

Figure 12. A Model of Coherent Leadership

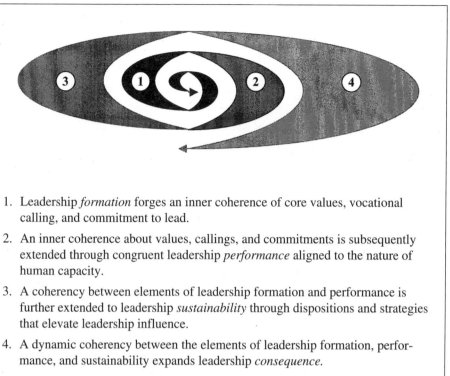

1. Leadership *formation* forges an inner coherence of core values, vocational calling, and commitment to lead.
2. An inner coherence about values, callings, and commitments is subsequently extended through congruent leadership *performance* aligned to the nature of human capacity.
3. A coherency between elements of leadership formation and performance is further extended to leadership *sustainability* through dispositions and strategies that elevate leadership influence.
4. A dynamic coherency between the elements of leadership formation, performance, and sustainability expands leadership *consequence*.

Four themes underlie the model of coherent leadership. That is, the coherent leader will advisedly: (a) know and nurture core values, (b) lead congruently, (c) compound capacity, and (d) expand consequence.

Know and Nurture Core Values

The profiled leaders described leadership formation as a process that evolved across four integrated stages.

1. Leaders build and test their values through interactions with their environment and significant others. As Michael Barber, Director of the Prime Minister's Policy Delivery Unit in Great Britain, noted, "My parents were very clear that you were put on this planet to make a difference."

2. Leaders further define and articulate their values through exploration of vocational callings and by making the most of challenges, experimenting with work, and finding opportunities to spread their wings. Such experimentation helped to define what they didn't desire as well, as Denise Henare, a Maori rights lawyer in New Zealand, found: "I worked in corporate law, but it didn't satisfy my soul."

3. Leaders commit to their values and calling by building competence and seeing the results of their efforts. As Boon Yoon Chiang, CEO of Jardin-Matheson in Singapore, put it, "It's not just about words, or espoused values, it's about action and results."

4. Leaders are compelled to accept the mantle of leadership, often through necessity, to fulfill their values and commitments. Kuami Pianim, a political activist, economic reformer, and former political prisoner in Ghana, acknowledged, "I was given the opportunity to lead. People who are given some talent have to share it. In this part of Africa we are communalistic—we are supposed to be there for one another."

The thirty-six interviewed leaders made a case for core values as the wellspring that both motivates and aligns leadership performance and sustainability. Their observations additionally suggest that the exercise of value-aligned elements of leadership performance and sustainability continually validate and reenergize commitments to compelling purpose. Being aware of and regularly reflecting about one's values and their relationship to one's conduct appears to be well advised. Such reflection cuts to the literal center of leadership. Whatever the challenge, status, or context, the referencing of core values is useful when assessing the need for and conduct of leadership, particularly when the going gets tough. This orientation is also compatible with the conceptualization of transformational leadership—leadership that is purpose driven, inducing both leaders and followers to transcend personal interests in favor of the greater good (Bryman, 1992; Burns, 1978).

In effect, core values represent the fundamental element of a coherent leadership universe. They form the primal thread of an inner leadership coherence about purpose and commitment which—when established—invites a natural and logical weaving-in of leadership performance and sustainability. Further, as the core of values is progressively wound tighter, the foundation that supports and energizes leadership becomes increasingly solid and more powerful.

Lead Congruently

Wheatley and Kellner-Rogers (1996) noted that living systems are self-organizing and that organizations act in much the same way. From that perspective, they postulated that leaders must act from "intention, not a set of plans (p. 7)." Centered by their core values, the thirty-six interviewed leaders enjoyed clarity about their intentions. Inner coherency about commitment and purpose, in turn, led them to perform their leadership roles in a naturally congruent manner. That harmony between values and performance was most notably expressed in the form of character traits and behaviors aligned to the social, emotional, and cognitive nature of human capacity.

Harmony between leadership practice and core values and commitments holds advantage in its potential for realizing unity and integration of effect. The opposite circumstance would be necessarily true for leaders who are "out of alignment" with a belief system, resulting in incongruent leadership performance and fragmented outcomes. Goleman, Boyatzis, and McKee (2002) have suggested that when such lack of congruence exists, a dissonance occurs that is detrimental to the emotional health of an organization.

The other important element within this assessment of leadership congruency is that harmony between values and performance—while valuable and desirable in itself—must also extend to a harmonious relationship with the very nature of human capacity. That is, given leaders who are clear about their values and purpose, as well as congruent character and behavior, it remains that their character and behavior must effectively connect to how human systems best learn and achieve. In effect then, leaders must get three things right—and in congruent alignment. They must be clear about values and commitments, congruent in character and behavior, and congruent in character and behavior that effectively engages the nature of human capacity. Beth Stevenson, Director of Youth Development and Education for the American Cancer Society, realized this connection as she noted, "Values are the core of the organization and become the touchstone for decision making."

As it happened, the interviewed leaders described congruency within their leadership experience that was marked by character traits and behaviors that were prominently aligned to social, emotional, and reflective dimensions of human capacity for growth and achievement. It must be emphasized, however, that the particular values, traits, and behaviors advocated by the thirty-six leaders—regardless of how attractive and universal they might appear to be—are not *the* values, traits, and behaviors to be adopted and exercised by leaders. More simply put, Mandy Macleod, Headmistress of St. John's International Intermediate School, described that "leaders must know the way, show the way and go the way." It is also important to acknowledge that leaders undoubtedly connect to human capacity in dimensions and ways beyond those described in the conversations we have examined in this chapter. The point that can be made is that there was such congruency and alignment across the leadership experience of a diverse group of exemplary leaders. Is such congruency important? One might best answer that question by reflecting upon the success prospects of thirty-six leaders had they not established such congruency between what they valued, their character and behavior, and how they connected to those they aspired to influence.

Compound Capacity

Beyond nurturing core values and leading congruently, the reflections of thirty-six leaders suggest that there is wisdom in adopting dispositions and strategies that compound capacity and sustain leadership over time.

Collins (2001) observed that great companies are headed by great leaders who are able to take their organizations to a new state of being. They do so in part by consistently encouraging solution seeking, innovation, continuous learning, and systemic thinking aligned to organizational mission. Such perception of what makes the leadership difference was also evident within the stories of the interviewed leaders. They described themselves as being particularly disposed toward being:

1. Centered on compelling purpose
2. Analytic in assessing problems and options
3. Creative in generating alternatives and opportunities
4. Positive in outlook
5. Persistent in pursuit of goals
6. Curious about new information and possibilities
7. Invested in developing the capacity of others

Such dispositions represented what the leaders perceived to be the essence of their leadership character and behavior. More important, it was how they established an enduring effect on the culture of their organization. Dispositions in thinking and behavior were the means by which the leaders moved beyond leadership of the moment to sustainable leadership. They aspired to promote organizational cultures that were focused on purpose and disposed toward analytic and creative thinking, collaboration, positive persistence in effort, and the pursuit of new knowledge and challenge. It was through the cultivation and exercise of productive dispositions of thinking and behavior, both in self and in others, that the leaders elevated the sustainability to their leadership influence on the achievement of goals. Such cultivation of capacity was consistent with Bennis's (2004) observation that gifted leaders see their primary responsibility as that of unleashing the talents of others so that a collective vision might be realized. John Hood, Vice-chancellor of Oxford University, said it so well: "What is the satisfaction of leadership? For me, it is always seeing others, for whom one has an organizational responsibility, flourish and succeed at the things they are here to pursue and do. That's really how I get my thrill out of this role, in seeing others do very, very well, and to create the environment where they can."

The interviewed leaders also adopted strategies for maintaining their personal viability and endurance within leadership roles that were physically, mentally, and emotionally demanding—strategies that sustained the leader behind the leadership. Fanny Law, Secretary of Education and Manpower in Hong Kong, realistically cautioned, "you don't die of hard work, but you might die because you are unhappy or frustrated with your work . . . You have to relax and control yourself." Specifically, the leaders collectively aspired to:

1. Stay physically fit

2. Manage emotion to their mental and physical advantage

3. Value counsel from family, friends, and colleagues

4. Create space for maintaining clarity and perspective

5. Get juiced on the challenges and results associated with their commitments

6. Seek intellectual stimulation

7. Welcome inspiration from connection to higher purpose

The valuable advice about compounding capacity, then, is that sustaining dispositions and strategies collectively elevate leadership to enduring influence and legacy. For Alex Banful, head of a public health NGO in Africa, such influence was evident. "It's not money that drives me, but people. It's the little things that bring such complete change in their lives. It feels good when you can help make that change. For me, it's a religion." Congruent leadership will get a leader into the game, but the compounding of capacity in self and others is a product of leadership sustainability. It is a matter of staying in the game and developing enduring influence through productive habits that ultimately make the leadership difference.

Expand Consequence

Mihaly Csikzentmihalyi (1991) describes happiness as the state of flow, a state where our ability is matched with our interest to such an extent that we are operating in *kairos* (natural) rather than *chronos* (precise) time. We become totally immersed in whatever we are doing in a flow state such that time seems to stand still. You look up from an engaging book and find that it is 2:00 A.M., you are working on an intriguing problem and hours disappear, or you are conversing with a dear friend and miss an appointment.

The concept of flow is useful to understanding the idea of coherent leadership. For the coherent leader, a flow emerges from an inner coherence about values and purpose, moves on through aligned character and behavior to bond with capacity, and then to the compounding of capacity through sustaining dispositions and strategies. It is the culminating effect of this flow—a natural and logical relationship between leadership purpose, performance, and sustainability—that leadership consequence is enhanced by a coherency that is both efficient and cyclical (see Figure 13).

Leadership formation, as previously noted, provides the foundation from which the alignment of leadership coherency flows. Such alignment, moreover, appears to be iterative in nature. The interviewed leaders described how they developed greater certainty about their purpose, performance, and sustaining dispositions and strategies

Figure 13. The Cyclical Flow of Leadership Coherence

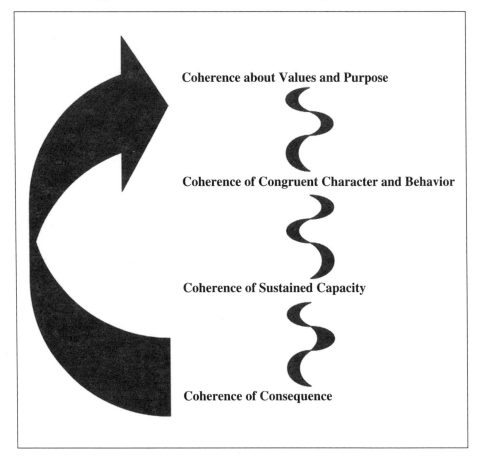

by revisiting their value base often in light of experience. Consequently, core values were strengthened and grew more powerful in their influence on leadership practice.

Hawking (2001) notes that from the density of a singularity comes the energy to not only create a universe, but to also maintain an ever-expanding ripple. Thus, it would appear to be the case with coherent leadership. A dense core of values and commitments forged in leadership formation brings forth coherency about compelling purpose, and then continues to ripple through leadership performance and sustainability with the ultimate effect of ever-expanding leadership consequence.

Within any research effort, planning is required, but by its defining alignment to the inductive process, qualitative research must remain open to possibilities. Thus, this inquiry was guided by a plan to interview an eclectic group of exemplary leaders from diverse contexts around the world about leadership formation, performance, and sustainability. The leaders were interviewed according to a set protocol to prompt a collective reflection and, thereby, discover salient patterns about how they came to leadership, performed as leaders, and sustained their leadership influence over time and challenge. Given this research approach, the expected happened. That is, the leaders did reveal prominent patterns of experience, value orientation, character, behavior, disposition, and strategy. The unanticipated insight also emerged, however, as the leaders' reflections progressively told a story that described a larger pattern of leadership coherency. It was a pattern, as has been described in prior sections of this chapter, that could be observed as moving from the internalization of core goals and commitments during formative life experience toward a congruency with leadership performance and sustainability—and back again. It was not only a pattern of natural and logical connections that moved from formation to performance to sustainability. It was also a pattern that observed a reciprocal relationship in that what the leaders did to sustain their leadership reinforced their performance, and performance, in turn, reinforced core values nested at the heart of the leaders' formative experience.

In other words, it became evident that the process of leadership formation was inextricably linked to how the leaders performed and maintained their ability to do so over time. It also appeared that within this tight pattern of coherence from formation through sustainability lies a key as to how leaders realize an expanded consequence of their leadership influence and achievement. Perhaps the most important lesson here is that a commitment to lead and lead well requires a parallel commitment to pursue leadership coherence—to continually reflect on who you are, where you are going, and how your are conducting yourself as a leader. As Ulice Payne, former manager of the Milwaukee Brewers baseball team said, "I am who I am. It's me. Its what I do. You have to believe it and live the commitment. If you don't have it, it won't last . . . it has to come from within."

REFERENCES

Antonakis, J., Cianciolo, A. T., & Sternberg, R. J. (2004). *The nature of leadership.* Thousand Oaks, CA: Sage

Bennis, W. (2004). The crucibles of authentic leadership. In J. Antonakis, A. T. Cianciolo, & R. J. Sternberg (Eds.), *The nature of leadership* (pp. 331–342). Thousand Oaks, CA: Sage.

Bryman, A. (1992). *Charisma and leadership in organizations.* London: Sage.

Burns, J. M. (1978). *Leadership.* New York: Harper & Row.

Collins, J. (2001). *Good to great.* New York: HarperCollins.

Csikzentmihalyi, M. (1991). *Flow: The psychology of optimal experience.* New York: Perennial Publishing.

Day, D. V. (2001). Assessment of leadership outcomes. In S. J. Zaccaro & R. J. Klimoski (Eds.), *The nature of organizational leadership* (pp. 384–409). San Francisco: Jossey-Bass.

Den Hartog, D. N., House, R. J., Hanges, P. J., Ruiz-Quintanilla, S. A., Dorfman, P. W., Koopman, P. L., et al. (1999). Culture specific and cross-culturally generalizable implicit leadership theories: Are attributes of charismatic/transformational leadership universally endorsed? *The Leadership Quarterly, 10,* 219–256.

Denison, D. R. (1997). *Corporate culture and organizational effectiveness.* Ann Arbor, MI: Author.

Dickmann, M. H., & Stanford-Blair, N. (2002). *Connecting leadership to the brain.* Thousand Oaks, CA: Corwin Press.

Dickmann, M. H., Stanford-Blair, N., & Rosati-Bojar, A. (2004). *Leading with the brain in mind: 101 brain-compatible practices for leaders.* Thousand Oaks, CA: Corwin Press.

Ferrandino, V., & Tirozzi, G. (2000, October 18). The shortage of principals continues. *Education Week.*

Fullan, M. (2001). *Leading in a culture of change.* San Francisco: Jossey-Bass.

Goleman, D., Boyatzis, R. E., & McKee, A. (2002). *Primal leadership: Realizing the power of emotional intelligence.* Cambridge, MA: Harvard Business School Press.

Hawking, S. (2001). *The universe in a nutshell.* New York: Bantam Books.

Siedman, I. (1998). *Interviewing as qualitative research: A guide for researchers in education and the social science.* New York: Teacher's College Press.

Wheatley, M. J. (2002). *Turning to one another: Simple conversations to restore hope to the future.* San Francisco: Berrett-Koehler.

Wheatley, M. J., & Kellner-Rogers, M. (1996). *A simpler way.* San Francisco: Berrett-Koehler.

Zipkin, A. (2000, May 31). The wisdom of thoughtfulness. *New York Times,* pp. C1, C10.

NANCY STANFORD-BLAIR is Professor of Leadership Studies at Cardinal Stritch University in Milwaukee, Wisconsin. A former teacher and administrator, Nancy currently teaches and consults in the areas of leadership formation and sustainability, organizational development and culture building, and the creation of learning organizations. She teaches at the master's and doctoral levels and consults locally, nationally, and internationally with schools, nonprofits, and businesses. Nancy has coauthored (with Michael H. Dickmann) several books on leadership, including *Connecting Leadership to the Brain* and *Leading with the Brain in Mind*, published by Corwin Press. Her research interests lie in the area of leadership formation and sustainability and coherent leadership behavior. Her latest collaboration, and the topic of this chapter, is *Leading Coherently: Reflections from Leaders Around the World*, published by Sage. Nancy can be contacted at NSBlair@aol.com.

MICHAEL H. DICKMANN, Ph.D., is Professor of Leadership Studies at Cardinal Stritch University in Milwaukee, Wisconsin. He is also an associate of the Leadership Center at Cardinal Stritch University. In his university roles, Michael teaches, advises, and conducts research in the areas of leadership, learning, and service. He is also a consultant to education, business, and service organizations in matters of leadership, learning, and organizational development. His recent publications include *Connecting Leadership to the Brain, Leading with the Brain in Mind,* and *Leading Coherently: Reflections from Leaders Around the World,* all coauthored with Nancy Stanford-Blair. Michael can be contacted at mhdickmann@stritch.edu.

Living Life Out Loud[1]
A Case Study Looking at Deaf Leadership Styles in a Production of Eugene O'Neil's *Emperor Jones*

BY LUANE RUTH DAVIS HAGGERTY

IN THE PAST DEAF PEOPLE[2] WERE THOUGHT TO HAVE SIMPLY AN audiological disability, but contemporary research into deafness illuminates a perspective that deaf people should be regarded as a cultural and language minority group (Paranis, 1996). This implies that much is to be gained by examining leadership from this point of view.

Deaf identity and cultural norms emerge almost organically from the needs of a more complex communication style. Many deaf people see themselves in the context of a community while the mainstream American culture views deaf people as isolated (Bragg, 2001). In this case study I will show the development of leadership skills in individual actors as we negotiate the trials and tribulations of a college production of Eugene O'Neil's *Emperor Jones*. This study used theater as a holding environment, which allowed Deaf leadership to evidence itself. The structure of a theatrical production naturally brings out leadership qualities similar to those mentioned in cognitive approaches to the study of parallels between storytelling and leadership.

> The ultimate impact of the leader depends most significantly on the particular story that he or she relates or embodies, and the receptions to that story on the part of audiences. (Gardner, 1995, p. 9)

Theater in mainstream hearing culture is simply the most refined developmental level of storytelling (Alberts, 1997). But storytelling takes on even greater significance in the Deaf community. Storytelling as an ordinary form of leadership is particularly effective in Deaf culture as storytelling is embedded in the American Sign Language (ASL) linguistic base (Larson, 1984). A metaphor for communicating in American Sign Language would be a series of movie shorts. Even everyday language or common communication requires the ability to create a visual story. For example, in

English one might say "I'm going to the store." In American Sign Language you begin with "store I go" adding the visual of walking there, how far it is, what the store looks like when you arrive, what you will buy, etc. The information conveyed is detailed and in a visual story form.

> 66 **THE STRUCTURE OF A THEATRICAL PRODUCTION NATURALLY BRINGS OUT LEADERSHIP QUALITIES SIMILAR TO THOSE MENTIONED IN COGNITIVE APPROACHES TO THE STUDY OF PARALLELS BETWEEN STORYTELLING AND LEADERSHIP.** 99

When individual actors or Deaf representatives decide to go it alone and portray an individual apart from the community, they are often chastised by members of the Deaf community. The Deaf community expresses response to individual Deaf characters in popular media similarly to how other minority groups respond when they see an individual from their community portraying an inaccurate or even stereotypic caricature. It is disappointing and hard to appreciate the individual's struggle (Meath-Lang, 2002). This inability to see an individual's struggle is often pointed to as a reflection of "crab-like leadership" (Schuchman, 1988), meaning that the community pulls individuals who try to "escape the pot" back into the community. Generally, this metaphor gives an image of an individual who tries to escape as trying to live and the efforts of the community to pull that person back into the pot as a certain death. I observed this tendency in the cast of actors of *Emperor Jones,* but I saw it as an attempt to keep the group whole, a way to prevent fragmentation and to ensure that the group could rise to success as a whole.

Most recently, popular media images of the Deaf allow the individual characters to be in respectable positions of power, but they are still isolated from their own community. This creates an image of a "leader-less" Deaf community as evidenced by a solitary and isolated individual character who surfaces on popular television programs such as the series *Pacific Blue* (Brown, 1998) and the miniseries *Stephen King's "The Stand"* (King & Garris, 1994). Even in the more recent portrayals on television's *West Wing* (2005) or *Sue Taylor FBI* (2004), these television portrayals make it appear that most capable deaf people leave their community and accept the daily struggle without need of common or shared experiences and without the need for signed communication. For a community that leads collectively, this leader-less image gives no discernable role models.

Leadership Literature

Although my clinical subjectivity as an artist, educator, and interpreter living in the Deaf community for many years revealed a natural Deaf leadership style, examples in the literature were hard to find. My intention in creating this study was to use what I had observed, as a foundation for how I would hold rehearsals for a college production of Eugene O'Neil's *Emperor Jones*. My directorial approach accommodated an ethnographic research model. I used participant observation as a strategy for listening and watching the cast in a natural theatrical setting. Being fluent in American Sign Language and being a member of the Deaf community granted me insights to the active participation of the actors in the creation of media images. Although I am white, hearing, and nearly twenty years older than the members in the cast of *Emperor Jones*, I was still seen as "family" by virtue of being a part of the Deaf community. I used my observations as well as informants' own comments about the process as documentation of various inferences in relation to Deaf leadership. I used my extensive knowledge[3] of improvisational theater techniques to run the rehearsal process in a pattern similar to the Deaf social club meetings I had observed. Length of time and structure of each rehearsal was predetermined, but the process left space for the actors to feel empowered to take on leadership roles. In my twenty-five years of experience in professional theater, I can attest that a cooperative environment in the rehearsal process does not always lead to the encouragement of cooperation on an individual level.

I had hoped that using the structure of a regular theater rehearsal pattern would create a secure environment and that allowing room for collaboration would free natural leaders to express themselves in their own style. These goals are consistent with the outline for making leaders as in Daniel Goleman's theories of emotional intelligence (Goleman, 2002). Goleman believes, and I agree, that leadership development should be self-directed learning, which he defines as "intentionally developing or strengthening an aspect of who you are or who you want to be or both" (2002, p. 109). By using a pattern that honored the deaf individuals' natural way of leading I hoped to reinforce the cast's sense of who they are, by giving the group a voice with which to determine how the images they would play would be presented. I hoped to encourage each cast member to develop an ideal self. I also tried to remain conscious of the way that Deaf-run organizations like Deaf social clubs are organized in order to heighten the comfort level. I planned, then, to use rehearsal as a structure to practice leadership skills that are consistent with Deaf cultural norms.

My approach for finding Deaf leaders wasn't guided by clear examples of Deaf leaders in historical references to leadership. Much of what we know of classical leaders comes from biographies, myth, tradition, or legend. Classical leaders were

Elements in the Daily Rehearsal

Greetings

Explaining the purpose of the show and warm-up using foundations of Del-Sign

2.1 – Breathing exercises – standing in a circle we breathe together as a group with the imagery that as we breathe in, positive energy is brought in and we purge negative energy in the exhale. We then share the breath. One person begins by making eye contact and exhaling; the person who receives the breath inhales, changes eye contact; and the process continues until all participants have shared the breath.

2.2 – Handshape handoff – standing in a circle a single handshape (for example, the ASL number one: index finger pointing up, all other fingers curled) is used gesturally in a different way by each person.

2.3 – Bonding energy – standing in a circle all participants allow their palms to nearly touch each other and focus on the feeling of warmth and tingles that suggests a transfer of energy around the circle.

Asking questions

3.1 – What did people notice from the warm-up?

3.2 – How should we begin the rehearsal?

3.3 – Discussion of material

Group improvisation on the material (asymmetrical turn taking)

Shaping the work (expressing interest in the actors' ideas)

Expressing cultural ignorance (encouraging the actors to explain their perspective)

Repeating what was discussed and then repeating the physical work on the material

Keeping the language that the actors used naturally in documenting the dialogue for the script. This was done using Director's rehearsal notes as well as Stage Manager and Assistant Stage Manager rehearsal notes.

Using the actor's linguistic choices in further discussions on the material

Creating hypothetical audience response to the work

Taking breaks for ten minutes every hour allowing for friendly and informal interaction

Coming together for "notes" before taking leave

perceived as either born to lead or they were exceptional physical specimens. Deaf history shows that the deaf have been removed from these categories by arbitrary laws and social mores. Before 1575 ca. it was illegal for a deaf married couple to have children. It was thought that they would have deaf children. So should a positional leader have a deaf child, it would not be expected that the deaf child would inherit the throne since the royal lineage would be stopped with them. In 1575 ca., Lasso, a Spanish lawyer, determined that deaf people can be taught to speak and should have the right to progeniture (Gannon, 1981, p. xxv). This allowed for a deaf leader to be born into power, but they were still not accepted as an exceptional physical specimen. Aristotle is quoted in 355 B.C. as saying "those born deaf become senseless and incapable of reason" (Gannon, 1981, p. xxv). His perception was shared by many well into the last century. Thus, finding a deaf leader in the classic era would be difficult.

Northouse (2001) did a more contemporary look at traits and behaviors. He compared personality traits such as gender, charisma, and vision with behavioral styles in action in different situations. For my purposes of looking at traits in Deaf leaders, Northouse's work bridges into areas of interest. The idea of communication and relationship being integral to a leader's traits directly relates to what I can see in the Deaf community. Until very recently, the deaf have used their adaptive ability at emergent or influential power to succeed. A wonderful example of Northouse's theory in the Deaf community is the student uprising at Gallaudet University. Those in positions of power had hired a hearing, non-signing President for the University and a small group of five deaf students acquired support from the media and built the support of followers to create a successful change in the policy of the University. It is now hard to conceive of a deaf organization without deaf members in the administration.

Heifetz and Laurie (1997) also discuss how important relationships are in leadership. Not only should leaders themselves analyze their abilities, they should also be aware of forming strong relationships with other people who can shore up their weaknesses. For Deaf leadership this concept takes on a whole new dimension allowing for a relationship between many leaders, managers, experts, positional leaders, and influential people.

Gardner's (1995) idea of ordinary, innovative, and visionary leaders all establishing effectiveness in their leadership styles through the use of the stories they relate can be directly married with the deaf perspective on refinement of storytelling in the American Sign Language linguistic base (Lane, 1992). As I pointed out earlier, every native speaker of American Sign Language has a highly developed sense of storytelling due to the nature of the language. If, as Gardner claims, great leaders achieve power through the stories they tell, Gardner's theory should certainly be considered in the development of deaf leadership styles.

After reviewing the various theories on leadership, I found it necessary to introduce some of these concepts into the rehearsal process for *Emperor Jones*. I maintained a consciousness to my directorial perspective that allowed for the cast to have discussions centering on how they would portray the characters and what the central message of the play should be. In analysis of theater and in the process of creating a vision with which to direct a play, it is general practice for the director to determine the central message and tailor script cuts, character analysis, and visual support elements to enhance that vision. Even a very well-known published script can be presented in a seeming limitless variety of ways. The average audience member recognizes this vision in the obvious choices of style: contemporary, fantasy, historical. But they may not realize that the theme that they leave the theater commenting on is only partially based on the plotline and dialogue in the playwright's control; it is also shaped by the image created by the director and shared by the artistic staff— set design, costume design, lighting design. For the rehearsal of *Emperor Jones* to have the leadership impact I wanted, I needed to relax my control of the vision of the production and open myself to what the actors would bring. I also had to convince the artistic staff to allow for this flexibility. This matches Greenleaf's theories on servant leadership. I became the person he describes with the positional leadership who removes herself in order to serve the greater good.

> One follows the steps of the creative process, which requires that one stay with conscious analysis as far as it will carry one, and then withdraw, release the analytical pressure, if only for a moment, in full confidence that a resolving insight will come. (Greenleaf, 2002, p. 313)

Most exciting to me was the concept Stewart (2001) proposed—a new leadership style emerging due to the changes in communication caused by computers, a networking style. The more he discussed his theory the more parallels I could see in the Deaf community. Their communication style has always required a similar structure to the electronic limitations of the computer, which has logically led to a difference in their style of leadership. Almost everyone can relate to the benefits and failures of the e-mail aspect of computer function. We are all aware of the benefit of quick connections and casual communication style. The need to talk one at a time can seem to slow things down and is often seen as a failing.

This can be compared to the Deaf community's "gossip-network" (Meath-Lang, 2002) that spreads news and information in the Deaf community quickly. Sign language also requires deeper concentration, and so a person is allowed to finish thoughts before the next person speaks. In a meeting, speaking one at a time may seem to slow the process down, but it also ensures that full thoughts are expressed without interruption.

Stewart's idea of a networking type of leadership suggests that strong leaders build trust and work through a collaborative style in order to motivate (Stewart, 2001). By having a shared sense of purpose, participatory decision-making structures are set in place. There is also a recognition that leadership exists at many levels and that the work of the whole community is required to achieve success. Once these basic assumptions are accepted one can begin to see a common thread of relational leadership that supports the concepts that apply to the use of theater as a tool to develop leadership skills. Once one accepts the notion that leadership exists at many levels and the work of the whole community is required to achieve success, one can see the common thread of a relational form of leadership that is inclusive—transformational, positional, influential, servant leadership, and even New Science theories of leadership.

Deaf Leadership Research

Deaf leadership specifically has received very little attention in the research literature. This lack of research has been previously mentioned: Sutcliffe (1980) noted that there is not much literature directly connected to deaf leaders in administrative roles. There are two dissertations (Balk, 1997; Singleton, 1994) and a handful of articles in the *American Annals of the Deaf* that look closely at deaf administrators. Unfortunately this research tends to focus on communication ability rather than leadership attributes or characteristics. In these pieces of literature, it seems that the most important trait that gets a person hired in a leadership position, from the researcher's perspective, is whether the deaf leader is orally proficient. This leads to the idea that if deaf persons can "pass" in a mainstream hearing setting they are more likely to be hired in a leadership position. Of interest to me is the lack of references to successful Deaf leaders who are superior at signed communication or mime/gestural forms.

Sutcliffe (1980) studied leadership behavior differences between deaf and hearing supervisors. Using the Leader Behavior Description Questionnaire (LBDQ) he found that there were no important differences in leadership behavior between deaf and hearing supervisors. This is contrasted with Mangrubang (1993) who studied models that deaf administrators or managers used for effective management/leadership in business. He found that deaf administrators tend to predominantly use a democratic/participatory leadership style. An autocratic leadership style tends to be a backup leadership style that is used when the prevailing style does not work in a particular situation. He also found that his research served to refute the earlier findings of Adler (1970) and Crammatte (1987); deaf supervisors tended to receive their promotions from long experience in the business, company, or organization rather than from a recognition of superior skills. Mangrubang found that the ability to do the job and background experiences in the specific area of the job task were of more value than speech skills. "Deaf leaders tend toward more relational forms of leadership partnering positional leadership with influence" (Mangrubang, 1993, p. 134).

Case Study—*Emperor Jones* by Eugene O'Neil

In this case study I used three approaches. First, I used my reflective and intuitive skills to relate the story. Second, I considered the participants' perspectives through excerpts from the rehearsal journals that the cast members were required to keep during the process. Third, I applied leadership theory to explain why events produced the result. I will be using more than one voice from the leadership literature since the relational form of leadership we used is a common theme that runs through several established leadership theories.

MacLeod-Gallinger (1993) has reported that, within the deaf population, members of ethnic minority groups experience educational and employment barriers that result in a higher unemployment level compared to deaf white men. For this production I focused on involving participants from the Ebony Club, a deaf, African-American social club. From the students' perspective, discrimination as a double minority can be hard to prove. I hoped that a side effect of this experiment might be an increase in cultural awareness and sensitivity.

After accepting my overtures to perform in this piece of theater, the Ebony Club leadership invited various African- and Caribbean-American leaders in the Rochester area to come and discuss the script with them. Their process mirrors the community form of leadership outlined in Manis' *A Fire You Can't Put Out* (1999). The Reverend Shuttlesworth had been raising awareness and confronting racial issues in Selma for many years, but he needed more visibility and clout. Thus, when Martin Luther King Jr. joined him and took over the leadership on the movement, Reverend Shuttlesworth was willing to change his position to that of a follower. In our situation, the Ebony Club had taken the lead on getting the production up and running, but when they interpreted the administration's concern about carefully presenting a sensitive play with inflammatory language as resistance, they believed they needed more support. They went to the local African-, Caribbean-, and Dominican-American community organizations and changed their position from lead organization to collaboration.

Due to the inflammatory nature of the language of the play (the word "nigger" is used frequently as is era-appropriate to the writing) and the involvement of a white faculty member in what was perceived to be an African-American project, the college community showed concern. Administration asked for reassurances that the project would be carried out in a sensitive manner. The students reacted strongly to this concern (labeling it adult mistrust) and they worked to get the project accepted. Although the work involved in getting the production into rehearsal was not part of my design for leadership training through theater, it was actually of more benefit than anything I could have manufactured. The cast had defined themselves as individuals and as a group before we had even gotten into the theater. As Shuttlesworth said, "If you can't take it, you can't make it." The participants in the show took perceived opposition to their project and made their response to that opposition a common goal. This bonded the group and further enhanced an environment that supports natural Deaf leadership development.

Emperor Jones in Production

As we began rehearsal, I saw the strange attractors that I had expected from Wheatley's (1999) theories. I had seen them before while watching the Ebony Club meetings. Leaders emerged as they were needed depending on the skills required for a particular section of rehearsals. The actors had a focused awareness of media image and an emphasis on teamwork. We conducted every rehearsal with the established rehearsal process structure, but ownership of the process belonged to the group. The elements of connective leadership (Lipman-Blumen, 2000), organic leadership (Wheatley, 1999), and networking (Stewart, 2001) were still in use.

> ❝ ALTHOUGH THE WORK INVOLVED IN GETTING THE PRODUCTION INTO REHEARSAL WAS NOT PART OF MY DESIGN FOR LEADERSHIP TRAINING THROUGH THEATER, IT WAS ACTUALLY OF MORE BENEFIT THAN ANYTHING I COULD HAVE MANUFACTURED. ❞

Our experience evidenced that a theatrical holding environment is an effective tool in leadership training and is consistent with a Deaf cultural style of leadership. Deaf culture emerges from a community effort. Theater is, by its very nature, a creative community. By peppering the rehearsal process with elements from several leadership theorists, I began to notice a common theme. The relational aspect of Goleman's (2002) emotional intelligence theory fits with Burns's (1978) thoughts on how followers grow in transformational leadership. The influential leadership of the students trumped the positional leadership of the administration (Northouse, 2001) or there wouldn't have been a production. Watching the order of rehearsal that emerged from what appeared to be the chaos of Ebony Club leadership seemed to also be congruent with Wheatley's (1999) ideas.

No established leadership theorist can fully explain the success of the *Emperor Jones* production in creating Deaf leadership training. I am drawing on a number of them to help explain how I came to the conclusion that there is a unique Deaf cultural leadership style that is collaborative, nearly communal—a style that honors the strengths as well as the weaknesses of the individual. I see it as a type of collective individualism. Recent leadership studies reveal more examples of democratic or participatory leadership styles. Even still these studies do not describe a style that I believe is an exact match for Deaf leadership style. As Deaf leadership functions, the idea that a deaf individual is a part of a whole community, not simply an outsider in a mainstream world, is crucial to understanding the development of this approach to leading. Deaf culture is best appreciated in its proper context, in a community. A theatrical production with its sense of ensemble replicates community. Theater also has the clear goal of a run of performances and, when the production has a message that reflects the actors' own beliefs, it can be a vehicle for leadership development.

66 **DEAF CULTURE IS BEST APPRECIATED IN ITS PROPER CONTEXT, IN A COMMUNITY.** 99

The Artistic Application and Results

The plotline of *Emperor Jones* can be seen as an example of black on black oppression and how despotic leaders take advantage of their own communities. The group took some time to explore their own feelings about the use of language in the script and made connections with the Caribbean community in Rochester (the setting of the play is 1930s Haiti). We invited seven children from this community to join the production. Two of these children were also members of the Deaf community and could use ASL. Group discussions resulted in a message that the script would support. The idea that if you disengage from your own community you will not survive became the theme for our production. I began to shape the direction of the piece with this message in mind. For example, I staged the ensemble to be partially hidden by the forest, continuously. The artistic precedent for this is the Aristotelian Greek chorus, but it symbolized the continual presence of the community as witnesses for Emperor Jones' journey.

Kouzes and Posner (1999) have noticed that a leader's primary contributions are the recognition of good ideas, the support of those ideas, and the willingness to challenge the system in order to get those ideas adopted. This theme supports Greenleaf's (2002) theories on servant leadership, in that the leader needs to get out of the way of the followers once the path is set. Thus, my own leadership style was affected by this process, causing a change in my approach as well as a change in the participants.

Now, not only was the particular story able to have the desired impact, the reception of the story by the audiences became important. I allowed the cast to invite friends to come into rehearsal. I instructed the non-participants that being invited to watch was an honor and that there would be time for them to give feedback, but that laughing, being distracting or rude would result in them being asked to leave. The friends took their roles very seriously, came to rehearsal on time, and sat quietly until they were asked to participate. They played a significant role in spreading by word of mouth that the show was going to be an important show to see. As Wheatley (1999) pointed out, the real power and energy in organizations is generated through relationships. Goleman (2002) also emphasizes that relationship skill allows leaders to put their emotional intelligence to work.

The people involved in this production had become an empathetic team (Goleman, 2002) by using a new acting technique developed at Interborough Repertory Theater (IRT), a small New York City–based theater company. This acting technique is called Del-Sign. As I developed this physical approach to acting, I combined parts of François Delsarte's codified movement studies with the linguistic foundations of American Sign Language. I then asked that deaf and hearing actors work together to create the characters. The cast had formed an emotionally intelligent team with collective empathy, which is the basis of all relationship skills. The *Emperor Jones* cast had become a highly effective team, which could respectfully share insights and were sensitive to their audience. The sense of community was extended past the footlights and embraced the audience members as well. This broadened the team, encouraging self-reflection and the beginnings of leadership development for everyone the production touched.

The cast enhanced their personal power by practicing emergent leadership (Northouse, 2001). As an individual felt the impulse to step forward and lead in the daily warm-up exercises before the show, the group reinforced their behavior by becoming unquestioning followers. When the next individual wished to step forward, the original leader stepped back to allow them the room and respect to emerge as a leader. This behavior was not a new skill acquired in rehearsal, but a much older habit developed as a member of the Deaf community. This could be used as a physical metaphor for how the leadership is shared in the process of production.

When we moved this production of *Emperor Jones* to Manhattan's 42nd Street for a two-week limited run, it was awarded the Off Off Broadway Review's (OOBR) award for Best Overall Showcase in 2002. Clearly the reception to the story on the part of the audience was positive. The structure of a theatrical production can naturally bring out leadership qualities. Those qualities are expressed in Deaf culture in a relational theme that is consistent across several different theories of leadership. I would propose that further studies into a unique Deaf leadership style utilize a theatrical environment. I believe theater is particularly useful for Deaf leadership enhancement since it is consistent with cultural norms. As Deaf leadership becomes a valued part of the discussion on leadership, it creates a spark of hope that can build a flame illuminating the fact that living in a world of silence does not stop anyone from living their life out loud.

NOTES

1. "If you ask me what I have come to do in this world, I who am an artist, I will reply, I am here to live my life out loud." (Emile Zola)

2. The lowercase "deaf" is used to refer to the audiological condition of deafness, or to the community. The capitalized "Deaf" is used to refer to people who have a language (American Sign Language) and a cultural awareness different from hearing society (Padden, 1980).

3. I am Artistic Director of Interborough Repertory Theater (IRT), a 20-year-old not-for-profit theater company in New York City, and have found work as a performer on Broadway and regional stages.

REFERENCES

Adler, J. (1970). Communication in the workplace. *American Annals of the Deaf, 58,* 11–20.

Alberts, D. (1997). *The expressive body: Physical characterization for the actor.* Portsmouth, NH: Heinemann.

Balk, J. W. (1997). *Leadership practices of superintendents at residential schools for the deaf.* Doctoral dissertation, University of Nebraska-Lincoln.

Bragg, L. (Ed.). (2001). *Deaf world.* New York: New York University Press.

Brown, P. (1998). Broken dreams (S. Lautanen, Director). In S. Ecclestone (Producer), *Pacific Blue.* New York: USA Network.

Burns, J. M. (1978). *Leadership.* New York: Harper & Row.

Crammatte, A. B. (1987). *Meeting the challenge: Hearing-impaired professionals in the workplace.* Washington, DC: Gallaudet University Press.

Gannon, J. R. (1981). *Deaf heritage, A narrative history of Deaf America.* Washington, DC: National Association of the Deaf.

Gardner, H. (1995). *Leading minds: An anatomy of leadership.* New York: Basic Books.

Goleman, D. (2002). *Primal leadership: Realizing the power of emotional intelligence.* Boston, MA: Harvard Business School Publishing.

Greenleaf, R. K. (2002). *Servant leadership: A journey into the nature of legitimate power and greatness* (25th Anniversary Edition). Mahwah, NJ: Paulist Press.

Heifetz, R. A., & Laurie, D. L. (1997). The work of leadership. *Harvard Business Review, 75*(1), 124–134.

King, S. (Writer) & Garris, M. (Director). (1994). *Stephen King's "The Stand."* Studio City, CA: Republic Studios.

Kouzes, J. A., & Posner, B. (1999). *Bringing leadership lessons from the past into the future.* New York: Bard Press.

Lane, H. L. (1992). *The mask of benevolence: Disabling the Deaf community.* New York: Alfred A. Knopf.

Larson, M. (1984). *Meaning-based translation: A guide to cross-language equivalence.* Lanham, MD: University Press of America.

Lipman-Blumen, J. (2000). *Connective leadership: Learning to manage in a changing world.* New York: Oxford University Press.

MacLeod-Gallinger, J. (1993). *Deaf ethnic minorities: Have they a double liability?* Paper presented at the Annual Meeting of the American Educational Research Association, Atlanta, GA.

Mangrubang, F. R. (1993). *Characteristics of leaders: Deaf administrators and managers in employment.* Doctoral dissertation, University of Maryland, College Park, MD.

Manis, A. M. (1999). *A fire you can't put out: The civil rights life of Birmingham's Reverend Fred Shuttlesworth.* Tuscaloosa: University of Alabama Press.

Meath-Lang, B. (2002). Dramatic interactions: Theater work and the formation of learning communities. *American Annals of the Deaf, 142*(2), 99–100.

Northouse, P. G. (2001). *Leadership theory and practice* (2nd ed.). Thousand Oaks, CA: Sage.

Paranis, I. (1996). *Cultural and language diversity and the deaf experience.* New York: Cambridge Press.

Schuchman, J. (1988). *Hollywood speaks: Deafness and the film entertainment industry.* Champaign-Urbana: University of Illinois Press.

Singleton, P. E. M. (1994). *Leadership style, personality type and demographic profiles of deaf female administrators.* Doctoral dissertation, Gallaudet University, Washington, DC.

Stewart, T. A. (2001). Trust me on this: Organizational support for trust in a world without hierarchies. In W. Bennis & T. G. Cummings (Eds.), *The future of leadership* (pp. 67–81). San Francisco: Jossey-Bass.

Sutcliffe, R. E. (1980). A comparative study of leader behavior among deaf and hard of hearing supervisors. *Business.* Ann Arbor: University of Michigan.

Wheatley, M. J. (1999). *Leadership and the new science: Discovering order in a chaotic world.* San Francisco: Berrett-Koehler.

LUANE DAVIS HAGGERTY is co-founder of the Interborough Repertory Theater (IRT), a nonprofit AEA Off-Off Broadway Company dedicated to inclusion and outreach to women, the disabled, and other minorities. She is also the creator of the Del-Sign acting technique most recently profiled in *Theatre Week, Village Voice,* and *Time Out* magazines. She has directed many productions in this technique, garnering a feature article in the *Chronicle of Higher Education* and winning the Theater Industry's Off Off Broadway Review (OOBR) Award. While developing the Del-Sign acting technique she accepted a position as an assistant professor at the National Technical Institute for the Deaf (NTID) at Rochester Institute of Technology in the Department of Creative and Cultural Studies.

A First Look at the Role of Receptive Nonverbal Communication in Leadership Assessment

By William A. Gentry and Karl W. Kuhnert

HAPPINESS, SADNESS, ANGER, FEAR, SURPRISE, AND DISGUST—THESE six universal emotions are cross-culturally recognizable (Ekman, 1999; Ekman, Sorenson, & Friesen, 1969). Emotions are an integral part of communication, interpersonal relationships, and leadership. The realm of leadership has overlooked the ability to accurately recognize, understand, and interpret the nonverbal behaviors of people, termed "receptive nonverbal communication" (R-NVC; Nowicki & Duke, 1992, 2001) in successful leadership; the nonverbal communication literature does not cover the importance of R-NVC specifically in leaders. The purpose of this chapter is to bridge these two domains that do not "talk" to each other very much, to make the case that R-NVC is important and should be regarded in leadership assessment. This is especially pertinent with the present trend toward globalization and global leadership, toward an interdependency among people, toward respecting other people's needs, toward finding a deeper understanding with people, and toward communicating effectively (Ayman, Kreicker, & Masztal, 1994).

The leadership literature has concluded that successful leaders are skilled in interpersonal relationships (e.g., the Ohio State and Michigan studies), and leaders display proper and effective nonverbal behaviors (Brooks, Church, & Fraser, 1986; Butler & Geis, 1990; Richmond & McCroskey, 2000). The nonverbal communication literature identified successful interpersonal relationships are predicated not only on successful verbal communication (DeVito, 1993, 2001; Giles & Street, 1994; Knapp, 1999; Wright, 1998) but also nonverbal communication (NVC), especially R-NVC (Guerrero, DeVito, & Hecht, 1999; Nowicki & Duke, 1992, 2001). However, there may be a missing link that could connect the two separate domains, namely the importance of R-NVC. Leaders frequently interact and communicate face-to-face with their followers. Those most effective demonstrate proper verbal *and* nonverbal communication (Miller, 2000). People in general, and leaders specifically, must be skilled at interpersonal relationships to be effective. Those proficient at interpersonal relationships must be adept at communication, particularly nonverbal communication, especially the ability to read nonverbal behaviors accurately, or receptive nonverbal communication.

Leadership

Several leadership theories state the importance of interpersonal relationships. Studies from Ohio State and Michigan are two examples based on the style theory of leadership. According to the Ohio State studies, an important dimension in leadership is consideration "defined in terms of behaviors oriented toward concern with employee feelings, mutual trust, open communication, and respect" (Jewell & Siegall, 1990, pp. 415–416). The Michigan studies have a comparable communication and interpersonal relationships dimension, namely "employee-oriented" behaviors.

Other leadership theories reiterate the importance of interpersonal relationships. Some trait theorists believe a characteristic central to successful and effective leadership is sociability, where leaders use their interpersonal skills for showing sensitivity and concern, and building quality social relationships with others (Northouse, 2001). Fiedler's contingency theory and House's path-goal theory both have a focus on the interpersonal needs and relationships between leader and follower. Summing up the importance of leaders' interpersonal skill in the leader-follower relationship, Riggio (2001) concluded:

> In summary, research on leadership has historically noted the contributions of sensitivity-related constructs to successful and effective leaders. Modern leadership theories seem to be putting even more emphasis on interpersonal skills, consistent with the trend toward more relationships-based theories of leadership. . . . This should be a fertile area of research as measures of interpersonal sensitivity are refined and as leadership researchers become more aware of developments in interpersonal sensitivity research. (p. 309)

To sustain interpersonal relationships, communication is paramount (DeVito, 1993, 2001; Giles & Street, 1994; Knapp, 1999; Wright, 1998). Since an estimated 66–75 percent of a manager's time is spent in interpersonal communication (Hyman, 1980), successful interpersonal interaction in relationships between leaders and followers is vital to organizational achievement and success (Jewell & Siegall, 1990). However, interpersonal relationships are contingent upon strong communication skills (Brock, 1997; Orpen, 1997).

However, verbal communication is but a small portion of total interpersonal interaction; the total amount of NVC in emotional interaction and interpersonal communication has been postulated to be anywhere from 65 percent (Birdwhistell, 1970) to 93 percent (Mehrabian, 1968). St. John (1985) revealed people spend twenty-five minutes of the day talking to others in words; the rest of communication is NVC. A review of the literature revealed a limited number of studies involving effective leadership based on NVC. Therefore, it is justified to evaluate NVC in leadership assessment. The foundation of this research question rests with Nowicki and Duke (1994), concluding "skill in nonverbal communication is assumed to be a necessary ability for effective social interaction" (p. 10). Successful leaders must be skillful at face-to-face communication and social interaction, accurately interpreting and understanding the nonverbal expressions of their followers (Bray, 1982; Cascio, 1998; Muchinsky, 1997). If this is accomplished, leaders will then have richer communication with others, more successful interpersonal relationships, and in turn, the organization will grow and prosper.

> **“ SUCCESSFUL LEADERS MUST BE SKILLFUL AT FACE- ”
> TO-FACE COMMUNICATION AND SOCIAL
> INTERACTION, ACCURATELY INTERPRETING AND
> UNDERSTANDING THE NONVERBAL EXPRESSIONS
> OF THEIR FOLLOWERS.**

Nonverbal Communication

Leaders must be effective communicators (Brock, 1997; Geddes, 1992; Hyman, 1980; Orpen, 1997) and skilled at interpersonal interactions (Northouse, 2001; Riggio, 2001). For instance, transformational leadership explains leaders must be sensitive to followers' social and emotional needs, which "requires general ability to decode emotions and attitudes" (Riggio, 2001, p. 308). Moreover, the first quality visionary leaders must possess is proper communication skills, both verbal and nonverbal, in their words and in their behavior, to effectively communicate their vision (Robbins, 2000). However, to be skilled at interpersonal reactions, one must be skilled at communication, both verbal and nonverbal (DeVito, 2001; Knapp, 1999; Nowicki & Duke, 1994).

Communicators receive, decode, and respond not only to words, but also to nonverbal behaviors. NVC has been used in association with expressive nonverbal communication (E-NVC) defined as one person expressing, producing, and sending any or all nonverbal behaviors to a specified target audience (Nowicki & Duke, 1992). On the other hand, there are few studies based on receptive nonverbal communication (R-NVC), previously defined as recognizing, understanding, and interpreting the nonverbal behaviors of the target audience (Nowicki & Duke, 1992). Effective communicators have accurate E-NVC and R-NVC (Burgoon, 1994; Nowicki & Duke, 1992). However, one must realize that there are individual differences in E-NVC and R-NVC; some people in general express and/or read nonverbal behaviors more effectively than others. People more successful in E-NVC and R-NVC are better communicators and are better at social and emotional interactions, relationships, and social adjustment (Carton, Kessler, & Pape, 1999; Nowicki & Duke, 1994).

Applications of E-NVC and R-NVC

Some studies have connected E-NVC and success in evaluating leadership. Eye contact has been shown to be important in the perceptions of leaders (Brooks, Church, & Fraser, 1986; Butler & Geis, 1990), along with clear, fluent, and articulate words (the NVC channel of paralanguage; Richmond & McCroskey, 2000). Personnel representatives in the McGovern and Tinsley (1978) study appraised actors displaying "high" E-NVC (steady eye contact, varied voice modulation, appropriate affect, high energy level with hand gestures, smiles, body movement) as better communicators with more leadership potential, than those expressing "low" nonverbal behavior. Participants in Gitter, Black, and Fishman (1975), Gitter, Black, and Goldman (1975), and Gitter, Black, and Walkley (1976) all rated actors delivering a message in a "strong" E-NVC condition (based on voice, gesture, and grimace) as having "leadership" qualities. Unfortunately, these studies used E-NVC to judge who were leaders, and not leadership effectiveness. Stein (1975) concluded there was "direct evidence that nonverbal behaviors are useful in perceiving and choosing leaders (a finding significant for the social perception and nonverbal communications literatures as well as the leadership literature)" (p. 134). This quote established a strong basis for using NVC in leadership assessment. However, two things should be noted. First, despite Stein's emphatic quote, thirty years have passed, and not much has been attempted to connect nonverbal behaviors and leadership. More important with concerns to the present study, the Stein study, as all the others, neglects the role of receptive nonverbal communication, or R-NVC, in leadership assessment.

There are relatively few studies linking R-NVC with leadership. Kay and Christophel (1995) concluded that interactions of managers with subordinates are crucial to successful companies or organizations, with nonverbal behaviors promoting openness. The NVC of managers and leaders are integral parts of communication openness, thereby aiding in the motivation of, and interaction with employees. This is a key ingredient for organizational success. Lamude, Daniels, and Smilowitz (1995) addressed the manner in which "a manager communicates with the subordinate may be more important than the content" (p. 467). Thomson (1996) amplified this sentiment, stating managers must have superior skill in NVC not only to express their messages (E-NVC), but also to gauge and realize subordinates' feelings (R-NVC). In order to display proper E-NVC, leaders, managers, and supervisors, first and foremost, must accurately "read" the nonverbal behavior of their subordinates or followers. As Hall, Gaul, and Kent (1999) suggested, "If the receiver of the nonverbal message misperceives the intent of the receiver but feels he [*sic*] is accurate, then this suggests some very important ramifications for everyday interactions" (p. 769). Reiterating the importance of R-NVC, Nowicki and Duke (2001) concluded "individuals need to be proficient in identifying the emotional communications of others [R-NVC] in order to be able to interact with them successfully" (p. 183).

Effective communicators, managers, and leaders need to understand and correctly judge the nonverbal behaviors of others (Knippen & Green, 1994). In order to maintain successful interpersonal relationships (such as those between leaders and followers), the ability to successfully interpret correct nonverbal behavior is essential (Andersen, 1999; Guerrero, et al., 1999; Lancelot & Nowicki, 1997; Noller, 1984; Nowicki & Duke, 1992, 1994; Spitzberg, 1999). As previously mentioned, successful leaders and managers of organizations and companies should be adept at R-NVC. Consequently, those proficient at R-NVC will have a necessary skill to prosper as managers and leaders in companies and organizations. The present study attempts to estimate the importance of NVC or, more specifically, R-NVC, in evaluating leadership effectiveness. Because of the apparent disregard for R-NVC in assessing leadership, this study has great potential in possibly discovering a new skill to evaluate leadership potential in individuals.

Individual differences in R-NVC should be related to leadership potential, especially leadership dimensions subsumed in interpersonal relationships. Therefore, it is hypothesized that those who can accurately identify the emotions of faces and tones of voices should be more effective at interpersonal interactions than other leadership dimensions (like task-oriented behaviors). The Student Leadership Practices Inventory (SLPI; Posner & Brodsky, 1992) contains five leadership dimensions, three of which are believed to be related to success in R-NVC skill since those three leadership dimensions are believed to encompass interpersonal relationships ("Inspiring a Shared Vision," "Enabling Others to Act," and "Encouraging the Heart"). Consequently, those with higher self ratings on the three aforementioned SLPI dimensions involving interpersonal relationships should also be more successful (commit fewer errors) at recognizing nonverbal emotions. On the surface, interpersonal relationships are not part of the other two dimensions of the SLPI ("Challenging the Process" and "Modeling the Way").

Finally, it is not known whether total successful recognition, recognition based on separate emotions, or recognition based on the intensities of the emotions are important in terms of successful nonverbal behavior and interpersonal relationships. The nonverbal accuracy test used in this study gives a unique opportunity to determine, in an exploratory manner, the predictive ability of nonverbal accuracy based on different emotions, and different intensity of emotions, on leadership effectiveness.

Method

Participants

Participants ($N = 224$; 159 females, 65 males) were incoming first-year students to a large southeastern university. They were administered the SLPI and the DANVA while they attended a weekend college orientation program. Because of incomplete data, two data records were excluded, leaving data for 222 participants to be analyzed.

Materials

Measure of Leadership Assessment.

Since students were the participants, the Student Leadership Practices Inventory (SLPI; Posner & Brodsky, 1992) was used. Posner and Brodsky interviewed students in constructing the SLPI. The results were similar to those found in the creation of the Leadership Practices Inventory (LPI; Kouzes & Posner, 1988). The SLPI is a 30-item questionnaire using a 5-point Likert scale for each question (seldom or rarely, once in a while, sometimes, fairly often, and very frequently). The inventory contains six questions for each leadership practice. Scores range from 6 to 30 for each leadership practice. The authors believed effective leaders would score higher than ineffective leaders on all five dimensions. The SLPI has been used in a wide variety of areas for various groups, including fraternity presidents (Posner & Brodsky, 1992), sorority chapter presidents (Posner & Brodsky, 1994), resident advisers (Posner & Brodsky, 1993), and orientation leaders (Posner & Rosenberger, 1997). In all instances, those students with higher ratings on the SLPI were more effective leaders, hence showing its validity. According to Posner and Brodsky (1992), indices of internal scale reliability are relatively high as well, with internal reliability above .60 and test-retest reliability ranging from .91 to .96 (Kouzes & Posner, 1998).

The discussion below briefly highlights the five leadership practices of the SLPI (Kouzes & Posner, 1998), giving reasons why the dimensions may involve or may not encompass interpersonal relationships. The researchers recommend reading Kouzes and Posner (1987, 1988, 1998) for more information about the five practices.

1. Challenging the Process involves searching for opportunities and experimenting and taking risks. Leaders are symbolized as pioneers, experimenters, and risk-takers. "Challenging the Process" deals more with the internal disposition or traits of a leader than with interpersonal relationships and does not directly entail communicating with others. For these reasons, "Challenging the Process" is hypothesized not to be a leadership dimension concerning interpersonal relationships.

2. Inspiring a Shared Vision demands envisioning an uplifting future and enlisting others in a common vision. Leaders need a vision to lead followers and the organization through unknown territories. The vision must be communicated to others. Only by knowing others, their needs and their interests, can these dreams become reality. It is believed that interpersonal relationships have a hand in the leadership dimension "Inspiring a Shared Vision."

3. Enabling Others to Act concerns the ability to strengthen others, foster collaboration, and empower others. The only way leaders can empower others, give responsibilities, and recognize achievements is to know and relate with others on a personal level. Because of this personal involvement, "Enabling Others to Act" may be a leadership dimension encompassing interpersonal relationships and interaction.

4. Modeling the Way includes setting examples and achieving small wins, and being role models. "Modeling the Way" revolves more around the personal disposition of a leader and the task at hand. On the surface, being a good role model and focusing on task-oriented behaviors are not representative of interpersonal relationships and is hypothesized not to be a leadership dimension ensconced in interpersonal relationships.

5. Encouraging the Heart encompasses recognition of individual contributions and celebrating team accomplishments. Leaders must visibly recognize hard work and successfully completed projects. Interpersonal relationships are a hallmark of the leadership dimension "Encouraging the Heart." Kouzes and Posner (1998) amplify leaders exemplary at "Encouraging the Heart" as those cultivating high quality interpersonal relationships and promoting productivity.

Measure of Receptive Nonverbal Communication.

The tool measuring the effectiveness and success of R-NVC is Nowicki and Duke's (1994) Diagnostic Analysis of Nonverbal Accuracy Scale 2 (DANVA2). The DANVA2 subtests for adults are made up of "happy," "sad," "angry," and "fearful" faces (DANVA2-AF) and paralanguage or tones of voices (DANVA2-AP). For each subtest, there are a total of twenty-four stimuli, six of each emotion. Also, each emotion is composed of three high intensities and three low intensities, for a total of twelve high intensities and twelve low intensities. There is an adult faces test and an adult paralanguage (tone-of-voice) test. Higher scores for both subtests reflect more skill in correctly identifying the emotions of the face or paralanguage.

The DANVA2-AF (Nowicki & Carton, 1993) consists of twenty-four photographs with an equal number of "happy," "sad," "angry," and "fearful" facial expressions of twelve men and twelve women, and in twelve high and twelve low intensities. Only facial expressions with at least 80 percent agreement on the given emotion are used for the DANVA2-AF. Nowicki and Carton (1993) reported internal consistency of items on the DANVA2-AF as .77 ($N = 104$ college students) and test-retest reliabilities over a two-month period as $r = .84$ ($N = 45$).

The DANVA2-AP (Baum & Nowicki, 1998) focuses on paralanguage, assessing the ability to identify happy, sad, angry, and fearful emotions based on voice tone and volume of the sentence "I'm going out of the room now but I'll be back later." The final twenty-four stimuli were chosen based on 70 percent agreement. Similar to the DANVA2-AF, the DANVA2-AP consists of an equal number of "happy," "sad," "angry," and "fearful" tones of voices, twelve male and twelve female, and twelve high and low intensities. A study reported coefficient alpha for the DANVA2-AP as .78 and test-retest reliability for the DANVA2-AP as .83 over a six-week period with college students (Nowicki, 1995).

Procedure

On the first evening of the orientation weekend, each participant completed the self-report form of the SLPI in a large room. This activity lasted between fifteen and twenty-five minutes. The next morning in the same room, participants took the DANVA2-AF and DANVA2-AP subtests, each taking approximately ten minutes to complete. For the DANVA2-AF, faces were projected onto a screen one at a time, with a three-second pause between each stimuli. For the DANVA2-AP, a cassette tape of the twenty-four voices was played over a sound system with a three-second pause between each stimuli.

Results

Correlations examined relationships between nonverbal accuracy and leadership assessment. Because of the directional nature of the hypotheses, one-tailed tests were used and alpha was set at .05. Table 1 (see page 90) displays these correlational results.

As one can see, four of the ten correlations were significant according to the .05 level. A significant positive correlation was found between the SLPI score on "Challenging the Process" and the overall score on the DANVA2-AP, $r(220) = .146$, $p < .05$ and between the SLPI score on "Inspiring a Shared Vision" and total score on the DANVA2-AP, $r\ (220) = .128$, $p < .05$. Also, positive correlations were found between "Encouraging the Heart" and both the results from the DANVA2-AP, $r\ (220) = .131$, $p < .05$, and DANVA2-AF, $r\ (220) = .161$, $p < .01$.

Regression analyses were run in an exploratory manner to determine the predictive ability of each: (a) total scores on the DANVA2-AF and DANVA2-AP, (b) total scores based on each of the emotions of the DANVA2-AF and DANVA2-AP, and (c) total scores based on intensity of the DANVA2-AF and DANVA2-AP on all five leadership practices of the SLPI. In this exploratory manner, the use of statistical significance tests of models, based on the .05 level through the "Max R-Square" method, was not the sole criteria for choosing the "best" model, for as Pedhazur (1997) explained, these values are not the true significance values, especially with multiple predictors. Therefore, high Adjusted R-squares values, and low C(p) and MSE values, were also used to determine the "best" model.

Because of the exploratory nature of these analyses, and because no prior research had been conducted to determine the predictive ability of emotions and intensity of R-NVC on leadership, a summary of certain patterns of R-NVC predictors on leadership will conclude this section. Results of the DANVA2-AP seem to be a good predictor for "Challenging the Process" (Table 2; see page 91) and "Inspiring a Shared Vision" (Table 3; see page 92). The total high intensity score from the DANVA2-AP may be a significant predictor for "Challenging the Process" (Table 2), "Inspiring a Shared Vision" (Table 3), and "Encouraging the Heart" (Table 4; see page 93). Finally, facial fear may be a significant predictor for "Challenging the Process" (Table 2) and "Encouraging the Heart" (Table 4). An angry tone of voice could predict scores on "Challenging the Process" (Table 2), "Inspiring a Shared Vision" (Table 3), and "Encouraging the Heart" (Table 4).

Discussion

Students with higher ratings on the SLPI leadership dimension "Encouraging the Heart" were more able to correctly identify "happy," "sad," "angry," and "fearful" faces and tones of voices. In fact, correlations between this leadership dimension and scores on both the DANVA2-AF and DANVA2-AP were among the highest of all correlations in the present study. This is no surprise, since "Encouraging the Heart" mainly involves interpersonal relationships, namely recognizing individuals and their contributions to the organization, and commemorating accomplishments.

On the surface, "Challenging the Process" involves internal dispositions and task-oriented behaviors like risk-taking (Kouzes & Posner, 1998). However, looking deeper into the thoughts Kouzes and Posner (1987) proposed about "Challenging the Process," leaders not only must find challenges and opportunities for their followers, but also must personally know the strengths, weaknesses, special skills, and challenges of their followers, for maximum performance. Leaders must also listen to advice from peers, superiors, or customers. Communication is imperative for creativity to prosper. It is impossible for leaders to know the strengths, weaknesses, and capabilities of their followers unless they personally interact with and personally know them. This is part of interpersonal relationships and communication, a link between effective leadership and nonverbal communication.

If interpersonal relationships and communication is so important for this dimension, one may wonder why only results from the DANVA2-AP were significantly correlated with "Challenging the Process" and not results from the facial subtest. Mehrabian (1968) postulated 93 percent of the total emotional interaction between two people is NVC, with the biggest and most important part in tone of voice, or paralanguage—the exact ability the DANVA2-AP measures. Leaders in "Challenging the Process" must listen, communicate, and establish relationships to change the status quo (Kouzes & Posner, 1987). In order to listen, to communicate, and to establish relationships, leaders must be able to correctly identify what a person is conveying through the tone of voice, for the ability to recognize tone of voice is through hearing, and tone of voice is the biggest part of interpersonal communication and, in turn, effective leadership.

Because paralanguage plays such a big part in interpersonal communication, it may overshadow and may be more important than other nonverbal channels. This could be the reason why results from the DANVA2-AP were significantly correlated with ratings from the leadership dimension "Inspiring a Shared Vision" while results from the DANVA2-AF were not significant. While both correlations were positive, only the correlation between "Inspiring a Shared Vision" and DANVA2-AP results was statistically significant. Proficiency in interpersonal relationships is dependent upon communication, especially R-NVC, with the biggest portion being paralanguage, so much so that it may transcend other channels in importance.

The only hypothesis fully disconfirmed was concerning the SLPI leadership dimension "Enabling Others to Act." Interpersonal relationships were thought to be part of this leadership dimension, but upon further review, task-oriented behaviors like delegating power, allocating work to others, and allowing independence also describe leaders "Enabling Others to Act" (Kouzes & Posner, 1987). Therefore these task-oriented behaviors may overshadow the interpersonal relationships piece to this leadership practice.

Regression used for prediction in an exploratory basis was the final statistical analysis completed. While Table 2 reveals a summary of the parameter estimates, adjusted R2, C(p), and MSE statistics for predicting "Challenging the Process,"

Table 3 is for the leadership dimension "Inspiring a Shared Vision" and Table 4 is for "Encouraging the Heart."

> ❝ **PEOPLE MAY BE FEARFUL OF GIVING OPINIONS ON HOW TO BETTER AN ORGANIZATION AND CHANGE THE STATUS QUO. SUCCESSFUL LEADERS NEED TO RECOGNIZE THOSE FEELINGS.** ❞

It seems not only will the DANVA2-AP be a good predictor for two of three leadership dimensions ("Challenging the Process" and "Inspiring a Shared Vision") but also the total high intensity score from the DANAV2-AP may be seen as a predictor for "Challenging the Process," "Inspiring a Shared Vision," and "Encouraging the Heart." This makes logical sense because of the importance of tone of voice, or paralanguage (Banse & Scherer, 1996; Mehrabian, 1968). Additionally, looking at the total *high intensity* scores from the DANVA2-AP, leaders may not have to attend to characteristics of paralanguage that are subtle, but they may have to accurately recognize the more obvious, high intensity stimuli of paralanguage to be successful.

Leaders attuned to the emotions of others can enhance the organization (Daft, 1999). These regression analyses indicate recognizing fearful faces and angry tones of voices can predict leader effectiveness. People may be fearful of giving opinions on how to better an organization and change the status quo. Successful leaders need to recognize those feelings.

The second emotion important for leaders to recognize is anger, especially in the tone of voice of others. The importance of tone of voice in interpersonal interactions has already been stated. Those who are angry may show rage, animosity, hostility, resentment, or may be violent (Daft, 1999). People in an organization may be angry with how things are (the status quo), which can be shown through their tone of voice. Differences in visions may cause anger. Also, angry people in an organization may exhibit dissatisfaction with another co-worker, may be frustrated with a difficult problem, or may be angry in a lack of recognition for their hard work. Leaders also need to be aware of these emotions.

There may be some criticisms to the study. For instance, self-presentation bias in the results could alter findings. Future research should consider using not only a self-questionnaire, but also utilizing a "360 degree" format, with peers, subordinates, and supervisors of organizations or mentors rating students to give an unbiased estimation of leadership in students. Generalizability may also be an issue; research with college students on their leadership ability is not as important as researching adults in organizations. However, studying the leadership skills of students should be of interest. According to Hirschorn (as cited in Posner & Brodsky, 1992), numerous colleges and universities believe leadership can be learned and promoted, and therefore hold a leadership education program for their students. Now knowing the ramifications of inept skill at R-NVC in an organizational context, college students should prepare themselves as future leaders in those same organizational contexts. The issue therefore rests with expanding these results to older adults in a workplace setting.

A final criticism revolves around what some may think are low magnitude findings. In other words, some may think the results may be statistically significant but may not be meaningfully significant. However, the low correlations are not out of the ordinary when looking at the leadership or the NVC literature. For instance, with Judge, Colbert, and Ilies (2004), if one looks at the relationship between an individual concept and leadership, the relationship of any one trait with leadership will most likely be low because there are a multitude of different attributes related to effective leaders (e.g., personality, cognitive ability). Though some of the results were significant at the .05 level, the correlations were all very low; results may be statistically significant, but may not be meaningfully significant. Because these results are so low, some may think that the results are not significant and meaningful for the leadership or nonverbal literature, and in the world we live in and work. The authors agree to some extent. These results are not meant to change the course of leadership, nor should these results suggest that skill in R-NVC is the most crucial in assessing leaders. However, the authors believe these results should give R-NVC its rightful place in the leadership literature, and should add an extra dimension to leadership in the nonverbal literature, since positive, significant correlations were found between variables that were never coupled before.

Moreover, globalization is becoming a trend in the world in which we work and live. With so many different people and different ideas in the workplace, leaders must be able to communicate well. The differences in culture and in ways of thinking can easily be bridged with effective communication. Everyone cross-culturally recognizes emotions like happiness, sadness, anger, and fear. Effective leaders must recognize those emotions in everyone, and act accordingly.

In conclusion, R-NVC may not be the most important dimension in assessing leaders, but may give people something novel and new to think about when assessing leadership. These results should open the door to more research examining how R-NVC may possibly be linked to leadership. Companies and organizations looking for future leaders from colleges and universities may need to look at R-NVC skill, for it has been shown to some extent that people in general, and leaders specifically, must be skilled at interpersonal relationships to be effective. Those proficient at interpersonal relationships must be adept at communication, particularly nonverbal communication, and especially receptive nonverbal communication.

Table 1
Intercorrelations Based on the Information from the
Five Hypotheses to Be Tested

SLPI Dimension	1	2
Challenging the Process		
Score from Self-rating	.107	.146*
Inspiring a Shared Vision		
Score from Self-rating	.048	.128*
Enabling Others to Act		
Score from Self-rating	.037	.082
Modeling the Way		
Score from Self-rating	.066	.045
Encouraging the Heart		
Score from Self-rating	.161**	.131*

Note. 1 = Overall Score on DANVA2-AF; 2 = Overall Score on DANVA2-AP.
  *$p < .05$
 **$p < .01$

Table 2

Summary of Regression Analyses for Variables Predicting
"Challenging the Process"

$(N = 222)$

Variable	B	$Adj\ R^2$	$C(p)$	MSE
Total Scores from DANVA2		.02	2.23	11.45
APTOTAL	.21*			
Total Emotion Score from DANVA2		.07	4.29	10.82
AFSAD	-.27			
AFFEAR	.48**			
APSAD	.35			
APANGRY	.58*			
APFEAR	-.39*			
Total Intensity Score from DANVA2		.04	1.32	11.17
APHIGH	.49**			

Note. AP = Adult Paralanguage; AF = Adult Face; HIGH = High Intensity.

*$p < .05$

**$p < .01$

Table 3
Summary of Regression Analyses for Variables Predicting
"Inspiring a Shared Vision"
(N = 222)

Variable	B	Adj R^2	C(p)	MSE
Total Scores from DANVA2		.01	1.03	13.70
APTOTAL	.19			
Total Emotion Score from DANVA2		.01	-.32	13.67
APANGRY	.50*			
Total Intensity Score from DANVA2		.02	-.82	13.53
APHIGH	.17*			

Note. AP = Adult Paralanguage; AF = Adult Face; HIGH = High Intensity.
 *p < .05
**p < .01

Table 4
Summary of Regression Analyses for Variables Predicting
"Encouraging the Heart"
(*N* = 222)

Variable	*B*	*Adj R²*	*C(p)*	*MSE*
Total Scores from DANVA2		.02	1.61	11.04
AFTOTAL	.18*			
Total Emotion Score from DANVA2		.05	1.97	10.72
AFHAPPY	.46			
AFFEAR	.34*			
APHAPPY	-.24			
APANGRY	.47*			
Total Intensity Score from DANVA2		.04	2.51	10.81
AFLOW	.21			
APHIGH	.39**			

Note. AP = Adult Paralanguage; AF = Adult Face; HIGH = High Intensity; LOW = Low Intensity.

*p < .05

**p < .01

REFERENCES

Andersen, P. A. (1999). Creating close relationships through nonverbal communication: A cognitive valence approach. In L. K. Guerrero, J. A. DeVito, & M. L. Hecht (Eds.), *The nonverbal communication reader* (2nd ed.). Prospect Heights, IL: Waveland Press, Inc.

Ayman, R., Kreicker, N. A., & Masztal, J. J. (1994). Defining global leadership in business environments. *Consulting Psychology Journal, 46,* 64–77.

Banse, R., & Scherer, K. R. (1996). Acoustic profiles in vocal emotion expression. *Journal of Personality and Social Psychology, 70,* 614–636.

Baum, K. M., & Nowicki, S., Jr. (1998). Perception of emotion: Measuring decoding accuracy of adult prosodic cues varying in intensity. *Journal of Nonverbal Behavior, 22,* 89–107.

Birdwhistell, R. L. (1970). *Kinesics and context: Essays on body motion communication.* Philadelphia: University of Pennsylvania Press.

Bray, D. W. (1982). The assessment center and the study of lives. *American Psychologist, 37,* 180–189.

Brock, S. A. (1997). Strategies for using psychological type to enhance leaders' communication. In C. Fitzgerald & L. K. Kirby (Eds.), *Developing leaders* (pp. 465–486). Palo Alto, CA: Davies-Black Publishing.

Brooks, C. I., Church, M. A., & Fraser, L. (1986). Effects of duration of eye contact on judgments of personality characteristics. *The Journal of Social Psychology, 126,* 71–78.

Burgoon, J. K. (1994). Nonverbal signals. In M. L. Knapp & G. R. Miller (Eds.), *Handbook of interpersonal communication* (pp. 229–285). Thousand Oaks, CA: Sage.

Butler, D., & Geis, F. L. (1990). Nonverbal affect responses to male and female leaders: Implications for leadership evaluations. *Journal of Personality and Social Psychology, 58,* 48–59.

Carton, J. S., Kessler, E. A., & Pape, C. L. (1999). Nonverbal decoding skills and relationships well-being in adults. *Journal of Nonverbal Behavior, 23,* 91–100.

Cascio, W. F. (1998). *Applied psychology in human resources management* (5th ed.). Upper Saddle River, NJ: Prentice Hall.

Daft, R. L. (1999). *Leadership: Theory and practice.* Fort Worth, TX: Harcourt Brace College Publishers.

DeVito, J. A. (1993). *Essentials of human communication.* New York: HarperCollins College Publishers.

DeVito, J. A. (2001). *The interpersonal communication book* (9th ed.). New York: Addison Wesley Longman, Inc.

Ekman, P. (1999). Facial expression. In T. Dalgleish & T. Power (Eds.), *The handbook of cognition and emotion* (pp. 301–320). Sussex, U.K.: John Wiley & Sons, Ltd.

Ekman, P., Sorenson, E. R., & Friesen, W. V. (1969). Pan-cultural elements in facial displays of emotion. *Science, 164,* 86–88.

Geddes, D. (1992). Sex roles in management: The impact of varying power of speech style on union members' perception of satisfaction and effectiveness. *The Journal of Psychology, 126,* 589–607.

Giles, H., & Street, R. L., Jr. (1994). Communicator characteristics and behavior. In M. L. Knapp & G. R. Miller (Eds.), *Handbook of interpersonal communication* (pp. 103–161). Thousand Oaks, CA: Sage.

Gitter, A. G., Black, H., & Fishman, J. E. (1975). Effect of race, sex, nonverbal communication and verbal communication on perception of leadership. *Sociology and Social Research, 60,* 46–57.

Gitter, A. G., Black, H., & Goldman, A. (1975). Role of nonverbal communication in the perception of leadership. *Perceptual and Motor Skills, 40,* 463–466.

Gitter, A. G., Black, H., & Walkley, J. (1976). Nonverbal communication and the judgment of leadership. *Psychological Reports, 39,* 1117–1118.

Guerrero, L. K., DeVito, J. A., & Hecht, M. L. (Eds.). (1999). *The nonverbal communication reader* (2nd ed.). Prospect Heights, IL: Waveland Press, Inc.

Hall, C. W., Gaul, L., & Kent, M. (1999). College students' perception of facial expressions. *Perceptual and Motor Skills, 89,* 763–770.

Hyman, B. (1980). Responsive leadership: The woman manager—Asset or liability? *Supervisory Management, 25,* 40–43.

Jewell, L. N., & Siegall, M. (1990). *Contemporary industrial/organizational psychology* (2nd ed.). St. Paul, MN: West Publishing Company.

Judge, T. A., Colbert, A. E., & Ilies, R. (2004). Intelligence and leadership: A quantitative review and test of theoretical propositions. *Journal of Applied Psychology, 89,* 542–552.

Kay, B., & Christophel, D. M. (1995). The relationships among manager communication openness, nonverbal immediacy, and subordinate motivation. *Communication Research Reports, 12,* 200–205.

Knapp, M. L. (1999). Nonverbal communication in developing and deteriorating relations: A conceptual framework. In L. K. Guerrero, J. A. DeVito, & M. L. Hecht (Eds.), *The nonverbal communication reader* (2nd ed., pp. 305–313). Prospect Heights, IL: Waveland Press, Inc.

Knippen, J. T., & Green, T. B. (1994). How the manager can use active listening. *Public Personnel Management, 23,* 357–359.

Kouzes, J. M., & Posner, B. Z. (1987). *The leadership challenge: How to get extraordinary things done in organizations.* San Francisco: Jossey-Bass.

Kouzes, J. M., & Posner, B. Z. (1988). *Leadership Practices Inventory (LPI): A self-assessment and analysis.* San Diego, CA: University Associates.

Kouzes, J. M., & Posner, B. Z. (1998). *Student Leadership Practices Inventory: Facilitator's guide.* San Francisco: Jossey-Bass.

Lamude, K. G., Daniels, T. D., & Smilowitz, M. (1995). Subordinates' satisfaction with communication and managers' relational messages. *Perceptual and Motor Skills, 81,* 467–471.

Lancelot, C., & Nowicki, S. (1997). The association between receptive nonverbal processing abilities and internalizing/externalizing problems in girls and boys. *Journal of Genetic Psychology, 158,* 297–302.

McGovern, T. V., & Tinsley, H. E. (1978). Interviewer evaluations of interviewee nonverbal behavior. *Journal of Vocational Behavior, 13,* 163–171.

Mehrabian, A. (1968). Communication without words. *Psychology Today, 2*(4), 52–55.

Miller, P. W. (2000). *Nonverbal communication in the workplace.* Author.

Muchinsky, P. M. (1997). *Psychology applied to work* (5th ed.). Pacific Grove, CA: Brooks/Cole Publishing Company.

Noller, P. (1984). *Nonverbal communication and marital interaction.* Oxford, U.K.: Pergamon.

Northouse, P. G. (2001). *Leadership: Theory and practice.* Thousand Oaks, CA: Sage.

Nowicki, S., Jr. (1995). *A study of the DANVA-AP in college students.* Unpublished manuscript. Department of Psychology, Emory University, Atlanta, GA.

Nowicki, S., Jr., & Carton, J. (1993). The measurement of emotional intensity from facial expressions: The DANVA FACES 2. *Journal of Social Psychology, 133,* 749–750.

Nowicki, S., Jr., & Duke, M. P. (1992). *Helping the child who doesn't fit in.* Atlanta: Peachtree Publishers.

Nowicki, S., Jr., & Duke, M. P. (1994). Individual differences in the nonverbal communication of affect: The diagnostic analysis of nonverbal accuracy scale. *Journal of Nonverbal Behavior, 18,* 1994.

Nowicki, S., Jr., & Duke, M. P. (2001). Nonverbal receptivity: The diagnostic analysis of nonverbal accuracy (DANVA). In J. A. Hall & F. J. Bernieri (Eds.), *Interpersonal sensitivity: Theory and measurement* (pp. 183–198). Mahwah, NJ: Lawrence Erlbaum Associates.

Orpen, C. (1997). The interactive effects of communication quality and job involvement on managerial job satisfaction and work motivation. *The Journal of Psychology, 131,* 519–522.

Pedhazur, E. J. (1997). *Multiple regression in behavioral research: Explanation and prediction* (3rd ed.). Fort Worth, TX: Harcourt Brace and Company.

Posner, B. Z., & Brodsky, B. (1992). A leadership development instrument for college students. *Journal of College Student Development, 33,* 231–237.

Posner, B. Z., & Brodsky, B. (1993). The leadership practices of effective RAs. *Journal of College Student Development, 34,* 300–304.

Posner, B. Z., & Brodsky, B. (1994). Leadership practices of effective student leaders: Gender makes no difference. *NASPA Journal, 31,* 113–120.

Posner, B. Z., & Rosenberger, J. R. (1997). Effective orientation advisors are leaders too. *NASPA Journal, 35,* 46–56.

Richmond, V. P., & McCroskey, J. C. (2000). *Nonverbal behavior in interpersonal relations* (4th ed.). Boston: Allyn and Bacon.

Riggio, R. E. (2001). Interpersonal sensitivity research and organizational psychology: Theoretical and methodological applications. In J. A. Hall & F. J. Bernieri (Eds.), *Interpersonal sensitivity: Theory and measurement* (pp. 305–317). Mahwah, NJ: Lawrence Erlbaum Associates.

Robbins, S. P. (2000). *Essentials of organizational behavior* (6th ed.). Upper Saddle River, NJ: Prentice Hall.

Spitzberg, B. H. (1999). Perspectives on nonverbal communication skills. In L. K. Guerrero, J. A. DeVito, & M. L. Hecht (Eds.), *The nonverbal communication reader* (2nd ed., pp. 19–23). Prospect Heights, IL: Waveland Press, Inc.

Stein, R. T. (1975). Identifying emergent leaders from verbal and nonverbal communications. *Journal of Personality and Social Psychology, 32,* 125–135.

St. John, W. D. (1985). You are what you communicate. *Personnel Journal, 64,* 40–43.

Thomson, R. (1996). Actions speak louder than words. In J. Billsberry (Ed.), *The effective manager: Perspectives and illustrations* (pp. 276–286). London: Sage Publications.

Wright, D. E. (1998). *Personal relationships: An interdisciplinary approach.* Mountain View, CA: Mayfield Publishing Company.

WILLIAM A. GENTRY is currently a Postdoctoral Fellow at the Center for Creative Leadership. His current interests are in survey development and analysis, leadership research, and leadership development. Bill graduated summa cum laude from Emory University in psychology and also majored in political science. He received his M.S. and his Ph.D. in industrial/organizational psychology from The University of Georgia. Bill can be contacted at gentryb@leaders.ccl.org.

KARL W. KUHNERT is an associate professor and Chair of the Applied Psychology Program at The University of Georgia. He received his Ph.D. in industrial and organizational psychology from Kansas State University. His teaching and research interests are in the areas of leadership development and organizational change. Karl can be contacted at kkuhnert@uga.edu.

"Lifting the Pall of Fear": Leadership and Collective Depression

By William W. Bostock

"LIFTING THE PALL OF FEAR" WAS A PHRASE USED BY NEHRU TO describe Gandhi's strategy toward achieving independence for India, and it is common to many leaders who have had to deal with the problem of large-scale depression and isolation based on fear. The need to remove a pall, or cloth covering a coffin, is an appropriate metaphor. *Depression* is a normal, familiar mental condition—a sense of isolation, inadequacy, despondency, lack of vitality, pessimism, sadness, and fear—but can also be a serious life-threatening illness. The etiology of depression is not fully known but could be (1) biochemical, (2) endocrinological, or (3) psychodynamic—often actuated by the death of someone close or other forms of profound loss and is therefore a product of grief (Haig, 1990, pp. 7–11). In the Freudian view, depression mirrors bereavement, but the loss can be an object and not simply a person (Collier, Longmore, & Harvey, 1991, p. 336). Another view is that *learned helplessness*, the hallmark of depression, results when a painfully adverse situation is experienced without being contingent upon the actions of the individual (ibid.). Depression can also be related to illness, pain, prolonged fatigue, and lack of human contact—deep areas of causality possibly best understood by imaginative artists, especially literary people who often analyze it under the term *melancholia*.

Depression among individuals is a vast worldwide problem affecting literally millions of people, but it is not untreatable. The major treatments are the self-administration of mind-altering substances such as alcohol in its many forms and other substances such as cannabis, beetle nut, belladonna, kava-kava, and countless other agents whose effects range from the mildly narcotic to the highly lethal, as in the practices of inhaling hydrocarbons such as glue and petrol. To these must be added the many pharmaceutical drugs legally and legitimately administered by physicians, particularly in Western countries, to large numbers of their patients. There are also many proven psychological techniques, from counseling to different types of psycho-therapy, psychodrama, and psychoanalysis, though this is strictly contraindicated if psychosis is suspected (Gillett, 1988, p. 148). But there is another type of depression which is socially systemic in origin and which requires a completely different mode of treatment. This type of depression can be called *collective depression*.

Collective Depression

With *collective depression*, the concept is much vaguer but clearly is another case of *learned helplessness*. It is also the subject of conjecture because of its association with the concept of a *collective mind*, as proposed by Le Bon in 1895 (Le Bon, 1960/1895), and developed by Durkheim as *collective consciousness* (Durkheim, 1964). Le Bon advanced a *contagion theory*—that crowd behavior takes over from individual behavior through the infectious spread of emotion and action. This view has been contested by those who argue for an emergent-norms theory that sees group unanimity as an illusion created by common action based on prevailing norms (Robertson, 1987, pp. 358–359). The methodological difficulty of assessing any concept of *group mind* has meant that it is not part of mainstream social science discussion, with the result that there is very little research currently being undertaken (Varvoglis, 1997).

Even if one does not accept the concept of a group mind, it is possible to state that *collective depression* can exist: it is when a large proportion of the members of a society are depressed, that is, are displaying signs of inadequacy, despondency, lack of vitality, pessimism, sadness and dependency upon substance ingestion. However, many authoritative writers do go further and assert the existence of the transcendent collective mental state. Michel Rocard, a former prime minister of France, for example, has written of a *dépression nerveuse collective* (collective nervous break-down) presently confronting France, Europe, and the world (Rocard, 2000). The psychologist and theologian José Maria Vigil has investigated the psychological well-being of the Latin American continent and diagnosed a state of *collective depression*, that is, as having actually the same symptomatology as for individual depression: disappointment, loss of self-esteem, self-accusation, demobilization, disorientation, depoliticisation, escape into spiritualism, loss of memory, withdrawal, and psychoso-matic problems (Vigil, 1996).

Collective depression can be related to defeat in war, slavery, colonialism, extreme dictatorship of left or right, or any other type of oppressive regime including economic depression and prolonged poverty. All of these conditions can create collective depression, either in a direct way or by a more insidious process of gradual accretion, always with the emotion of *fear* involved. *Collective fear* can also result in aggression and has been isolated as a causal factor in genocide (Lake & Rothchild,

1996), and *collective paranoia* has been identified as being at the basis of ethnic cleansing (Kis, 1996), while Kiev (1973) hypothesized a *collective anxiety neurosis* as being at the basis of many disturbances.

It would seem comprehensible that depression can be passed between individuals by contagion, but does research give any confirmation? Forsyth reviewed the literature and concluded that ". . . the bridge between social psychology and mental health can still not be traversed" (Forsyth, 1996, p. 5) but suggested some areas of enquiry, such as the causal power of the group to change individuals when they become part of a group. Leadership is important among the group processes that require research in the view of Forsyth (ibid.).

❝   **THE STRATEGY OF LEADERSHIP IN TREATING COLLECTIVE DEPRESSION IN THIS TYPE OF SITUATION IS TO DEMONSTRATE THAT THE SITUATIONAL FACTORS CAUSING DEPRESSION CAN BE CHANGED THROUGH THE BUILDING OF BRIDGES BETWEEN GROUPS OF PEOPLE WHO ARE DIVIDED.**   **❞**

Individual depression can be successfully treated by a range of therapies, but *collective depression*, being a different order of problem, cannot be treated by therapies for individuals. However, as noted above, it can be treated by leadership. Vigil (1996) also notes that although the Latin American continent has a state of collective depression, there are individuals standing outside this mental state and therefore placing themselves in a position to assist in its removal.

The strategy of leadership in treating collective depression in this type of situation is to demonstrate that the situational factors causing depression can be changed through the building of bridges between groups of people who are divided. The causes of division will be a result of whatever painful past experience they may have undergone, whether it is related to colonialism, social class, race, language, culture or ideology, or any other factor which may have left a legacy of resentment, hatred, or fear. But it must be noted that bad leadership can also be the cause of heightened collective depression. Hirschhorn confirms this proposition with the conclusion that poor leadership can have "toxic effects" on organizational motivation (Hirschhorn, 1990, p. 533).

As with individual depression, positive practical action to neutralize fear seems to be an initial step. Nehru wrote of Gandhi

The essence of his teaching was fearlessness and truth and action allied to these. ... So, suddenly as it were, that black pall of fear was lifted from the people's shoulders, not wholly, of course, but to an amazing degree ... It was a psychological change, almost as if an expert in psychoanalytic method had probed deep into the patient's past, found out the origins of his complexes, exposed them to his view, and thus rid him of that burden. (Nehru, 1946, pp. 361–362, cited in Rudolph & Rudolph, 1983, p. 6)

As well as dealing with fear, there are numerous other activities, no matter how seemingly small in comparison with the magnitude of the task, that can lead to a lifting of the condition, as shown with the work of some members of a Peace Institute in a village in war-torn Georgia (Rueffler, 2000). No matter how valuable steps taken at the local level may be, major collective depression will require action at the level of the political system.

The relationship between leadership and politics is clearly apparent, but between academic political science and leadership studies, the relationship is implicit rather than explicit: one that has been described as "... a surprising lack of disciplinary focus" (Paige, 1977, chap. 2). The contributions of many distinguished political scientists notwithstanding, the analysis of the role of leaders in the political process has been dominated mainly by historians and psychologists (Kets de Vries, 1990). As the following case studies in leadership will reveal, the common factor is the lifting of fear, and the common technique is the building of bridges or alliances between people. In many cases, the new alliances may include traditional enemies or people whose differences were emphasized for the purposes of political control, as with the Hindus and Muslims of India who Gandhi united in the struggle for independence.

Case Studies in Bridge-Building Leadership

The following case studies will show the determining role played by leadership in resolving problems of immense magnitude, and some concepts from leadership studies will be shown to be useful. A major conceptual distinction in leadership types is between *transformational* and *transactional* types (Burns, 1978). Another key concept is the *legitimacy to lead* (Walters, 1999), which can also be seen from the obverse face as *leadership without authority* (Heifetz, 1994). These four concepts of leadership type—transformational, transactional, legitimate, and non-legitimate—are of great value in understanding the roles of the following leaders chosen as examples of solvers of the problem of collective depression through leadership.

Bridging Colonial History and Class: George VI

As with most relationships where there is a history of colonialism, Britain's relationship with America is long and complex. An additional source of complication is provided by the history of Britain's long presence in Ireland, where there is also the dimension of a religious cleavage between Protestant and Catholic.

In the years leading up to World War II, Britain's future King, Edward VIII, had been forced to abdicate from the throne because of the matter of his impending marriage to an American lady, Mrs. Wallis Simpson, which was considered by the prime minister and other influential persons to be unacceptable, officially on grounds of her legal status as a divorced woman but unofficially on grounds of her perceived character, behavior, and nationality.

To the future Prime Minister Winston Churchill and a few others, it was clear that America's help would be needed in the coming war with Nazi Germany and Fascist Italy, and the fact that Anglo-American relations had entered a new low because of the abdication crisis was quite apparent.

When Edward's brother Albert acceded to the throne in 1936 (taking the name of George VI), he was seen as possibly even more unsuited to the role of kingship than his brother, though for completely different reasons. Albert had been afflicted with poor health, pathological shyness, and a very bad stammer, and within elite circles, was portrayed as slightly intellectually handicapped.

King George VI was thus a most unlikely candidate for the role of symbolic leader of a country at war, but he accepted this role with a deep and absolute commitment. Well aware of the need to repair and rebuild relations with the United States, George VI visited President Roosevelt at the White House in 1939. There, in secret discussions, they analyzed the magnitude of the likely consequences of Axis victory in Europe, and laid the foundations for future Anglo-American cooperation.

An additional complication was the position of the United States Ambassador to Britain, Mr. Joseph Kennedy, who was of Irish descent and who was openly defeatist, strongly anti-Roosevelt, and opposed to all aid to Britain. This background and these opinions led him to subsequently strongly advise the King to surrender. On receiving this advice, King George VI wrote in a letter to Mr. Kennedy

> We stand on the threshold of we know what not. Misery and suffering of War we know. But what of the future? The British mind is made up. I shall leave it at that. (Stevenson, 1976, p. 67)

In this statement one can see a clear affirmation of the concept of the *group mind*, and an assertion of collective willpower in resisting the onset of depression based on fear of defeat.

In addition to his transatlantic bridge building, George VI also saw the need to unify Britain's population, which was traditionally divided by social class. In this he may well have been responding to a perception of the role of internal divisions of class and ideology as certainly contributing to the collapse of morale in France (Maurois, 1941, p. 53).

In the 1920s, George had been president of the Industrial Welfare Society, and had sought to improve the conditions of workers through canteens, medical centers, and other benefits, to the extent that the comment had been made that no one in a comparable position had done so much to "establish and maintain harmonious relationships between employers and workmen" (*Digger History*, 2005). The quality of leadership through unification was no more clearly shown than when George and his family remained at Buckingham Palace throughout the war, even though it was a major target for the Luftwaffe. George VI's reign could therefore be interpreted as transformational legitimate leadership realized through the building of bridges internationally and domestically. His transformation was also personal, from a severely inhibited and depressed individual who, with the help of his Australian speech therapist Lionel Logue, went on to become a powerfully compelling leader who worked in perfect tandem with another powerfully compelling leader, Churchill (who was himself fighting personal depression), to resolve an immense problem.

Bridging Race, Language, and Culture: Mandela, Tutu, and de Klerk

Writing of apartheid in South Africa (1948–1994), one observer wrote "... (a)s an exercise in ambitious and brutal social engineering, it had few parallels in human history" (McLean, 1999, p. 12). Yet, the system was ended, without violence and with astonishing speed, by the leadership of three major interacting players.

It is possible to interpret South African policy under minority rule as an attempt to influence collective mental state by division into a multiplicity of separate collective mental states, with an overall aim of securing and enhancing the future of one group at the expense of the others, to a major or minor degree. For blacks it sought through the "mother tongue education" and the non-offering of English to create a collective mental state of insecurity, depression, dampened sense of realism, exclusion, and habituation to violence. For South Africans of British background it aimed to create some feelings of insecurity, depression and, through the hint of the likelihood of violence, it offered the possibility of inclusion in the Afrikaner collectivity as a shelter. Among Afrikaners, it sought to create a mental state of a secure future, and a mood of elation through the delusion of a God-given destiny based on an unrealistic belief in the sustainable viability of a policy of exclusion of Africans, underlaid with a habituation to a putative ever-present threat of violence.

An explanation of the highly complex political process that has been called "surrender without defeat" must include the role of the major players: de Klerk, Mandela, and Tutu. De Klerk's role, after what has been described as his "remarkable change of heart" (Lake & Rothchild, 1996, p. 16), was one of bringing to the Afrikaner mental state some acceptance of the reality of an untenable situation, though he was not entirely successful in this. It is reported that in a meeting one of his ministers angrily hurled at him the words "What have you done?! You have given South Africa away!!" (Giliomee, 1997, p. 140).

Mandela's contribution was to see the new South Africa as a larger collectivity through the inclusion of all groups in the new collective mental state where there would be a place and a role even for his former persecutors. It has been said of leadership that "... the fundamental process is a more elusive one; it is, in large part, *to make conscious what lies unconscious among followers*" (Burns, 1978, p. 40). On this last point, one commentator has noted that former president Mandela has been "highly sensitive to the language issue" (Schiff, 1996, p. 221), which was troubling many Afrikaners who saw their language as the keystone of their identity, and went on to cite as further evidence the opposition of Mandela to the elimination of the use of Afrikaans in the South African military (Schiff, 1996, p. 221).

The third major player was Archbishop Tutu, whose promotion of *ubuntu*, a traditional African communal belief in and practice of common humanity (Jaffrey, 1998), as embodied in the proposed and now realized Truth and Reconciliation Commission, provided a mechanism for the grief work necessary before the possibility of inclusion in the new collective mental state.

Bridging Ideology: Kohl

To take a final example, the aftermath of Hitler's war was a Germany divided by a wall about which in January 1989 the East German leader Honecker stated "... (it will) still be there 50, 100 years from now." Yet on November 8 of the same year it was breached by between fifty and seventy thousand people on foot who met no attempt to stop them by military or police. Three weeks later West German Chancellor Helmut Kohl presented a Ten Point Plan to create a confederation of both German states, and on March 15, 1991, a Two Plus Four Treaty came into being, creating a unified German state with unrestricted sovereignty.

The precise causality of this event may never be fully known, but the leadership of Kohl was undoubtedly crucial. This was achieved by a skillful exploitation of the ideological ambivalence of the Soviet leader and the staunch anticommunism of the three major Western leaders. It is now known from several observers that Kohl's Ten

Point Plan initially angered Gorbachev and was deeply opposed by the three main Western leaders: Mitterrand, who perceived it as a "surprise attack"; Thatcher, who was aggravated and stated bluntly that German unification was "not on the agenda"; and Bush (senior), who was taken completely by surprise but then decided to back it while pretending to have prior knowledge, which he did not, according to observers present during the process (Elbe & Kiessler, 1996, pp. 48–54). But the USSR was gravely weakened by its costly and unsuccessful engagement in Afghanistan and also the impact of postmodern thinking and the appeal of market-driven economics, which lay at the basis of liberalization throughout the Eastern bloc including the German Democratic Republic (GDR).

Attempts by the GDR regime to justify the Tiananmen massacre in China further heightened the hostility of the country's population. In 1990 a conference of NATO and Warsaw Pact states reached agreement that discussion between the two Germanys and the four Occupying Powers (Britain, France, USA, and USSR) should commence on the subject of German unification. The main points of contention were membership of NATO by reunified Germany, the presence of foreign troops on German soil, and the border with Poland. In late 1990 the United States ratified the treaty, followed by Britain, and in 1991 by France and then the Soviet Union, which was fearful of a reunited Germany's presence in NATO. The Italian newspaper *Corriere della Sera* wrote ". . . the balance needs to be freshly adjusted, not only in Europe but in the whole world" (Elbe & Kiessler, 1996, p. 204).

The difficult decision to make Berlin and not Bonn the capital of reunified Germany was another example of Kohl's leadership. Opposition was strong, mainly because of Berlin's association with Germany's criminal past, but in the Bundestag Chancellor Kohl emphasized the need for the inhabitants of the former GDR to have a sense of belonging in the new state. When the final vote was taken in the Bundestag on June 20, 1991, a small majority of 337 to 320 deputies agreed to move parliament and government from Bonn to Berlin.

Kohl was right to see former GDR citizens as being in need of support, but his seemingly generous offer of exchange of one Deutschmark for one GDR Mark was in fact a death-sentence for GDR businesses whose products instantly became grossly overvalued. Kohl's realism saw that a politically and psychologically unified Germany would come at an economic cost. Kohl remains a controversial figure, not only for his methods in achieving reunification, such as with the breaking of his promise to raise no further taxes, but also over allegations concerning the misappropriation of party funds. His leadership was transactional and may be found to be lacking in legitimacy, but his achievement in removing the cause of over four decades of collective depression was great.

Conclusion

The collective depression of isolation, demotivation, and fear is a very widespread condition, easily recognizable by its effects, even if its precise logical status may never be determined. Mostly it is treated with symptom-relieving practices and strategies which help in short-term survival but which do not provide a long-term solution. Lasting resolution requires removal of the causes of collective depression such as, for example, fear of impending invasion and defeat, as in Britain during World War II, the institutionalized system of discrimination which existed in South Africa, or the internal separation of Germany through partition over Cold War ideology—in each case a hugely depression-inducing situation. In all three cases, the solution was through leadership: in Britain, through the symbolic leadership of a King; in South Africa, through the transforming leadership of Mandela and Tutu, though with legitimacy questioned by the system, and de Klerk, whose leadership was transactional but with legitimacy insofar as it came from within the system. In the case of Germany, solution to the depressive problem of partition was also by leadership. Here Kohl, whose leadership was transactional and legitimate though flawed, enabled a successful coordination of other leadership roles toward a successful outcome. The common theme among these diverse leadership styles was removal of the sense of fear, the basis of collective depression, which was the same need also identified by Gandhi.

REFERENCES

Burns, J. M. (1978). *Leadership*. New York: Harper and Row.

Collier, J. A. B., Longmore, J. M., & Harvey, J. H. (1991). *Oxford handbook of clinical specialties* (3rd ed.). Oxford, New York, Tokyo: Oxford University Press.

Digger History: An unofficial history of the Australian and New Zealand Armed Forces. (2005). Retrieved July 20, 2005, from http://www.diggerhistory.info/pages-leaders/ww2/king_george_vi.htm.

Durkheim, E. (1964). *The rules of sociological method* (2nd ed.). London: Collier-Macmillan.

Elbe, F., & Kiessler, R. (1996). *A round table with sharp corners: The diplomatic path to German unity*. Baden-Baden: Nomos Verlagsgesellschaft.

Forsyth, D. R. (1996). *Interfacing social and clinical approaches to mental health*. Virginia Commonwealth University, Grand Rounds Presentation, February 9. Retrieved August 30, 2000, from http://www.vcu.edu/hasweb/pzy/faculty/fors/grand.html.

Gillett, R. (1988). *Overcoming depression*. Melbourne, Sydney, Auckland: Lothian.

Giliomee, H. (1997). Surrender without defeat: Afrikaners and the South African "miracle." *Daedalus*, *126*(2), 113–134.

Haig, R. A. (1990). *The anatomy of grief, biopsychosocial and therapeutic perspectives*. Springfield, IL: Charles Thomas.

Heifetz, R. A. (1994). *Leadership without easy answers*. Boston: Belknap/Harvard University Press.

Hirschhorn, L. (1990). Leaders and followers in a post-industrial age: A psychodynamic view: *Journal of Applied Behavioural Science*, *26*(4), 529–542.

Jaffrey, Z. (1998, February). Desmond Tutu. (Interview). *The Progressive, 62*(2), 18.

Kiev, A. (1973). Psychiatric disorders in minority groups. In P. Watson (Ed.), *Psychology and race* (pp. 416–431). Chicago: Aldine.

Kets de Vries, M. F. R. (1990). Leaders on the couch. *Journal of Applied Behavioral Science, 26*(4), 423–431.

Kis, D. (1996). On nationalism. *Performing Arts Journal, 53*(18.2), 13–16. Retrieved July 14, 1999, from http://muse.jhu.edu/demo/performing_arts_journal/18.2kis.html.

Lake, D. A., & Rothchild, D. (1996). Containing fear: The origins and management of ethnic conflict. *International Security, 21*(2), 41–75. Retrieved June 19, 1999, from http://web2.searchbank.com?itw/session/927/3865981w3/32/cnb_61_80.

Le Bon, G. (1960/1895). *The mind of the crowd.* New York: Viking.

Maurois, A. (1941). *Why France fell.* London: John Lane, The Bodley Head.

McLean, D. (1999). Neocolonizing the mind? Emergent trends in language policy for South African education. *International Journal of the Sociology of Language, 136,* 7–26.

Nehru, J. (1946). *The discovery of India.* Calcutta, India: The Signet Press. Quoted in L. I. Rudolph & S. H. Rudolph, *Gandhi, the traditional roots of charisma* (Chicago: University of Chicago Press, 1983), 6.

Paige, G. D. (1977). *The scientific study of political leadership.* New York: Free Press.

Robertson, I. (1987). *Sociology* (3rd ed.). New York: Worth.

Rocard, M. (2000). *La dépression nerveuse collective.* Retrieved August 30, 2000, from http://www.sante.cc/stress/articles/Rocard.html.

Rueffler, M. (2000). Healing a collective. *Association for the Advancement of Psychosynthesis.* Retrieved August 30, 2000, from http://www.aap-psychosynthesis.org/collective.html.

Schiff, B. (1996). The Afrikaners after apartheid. *Current History, 95,* 216–221.

Stevenson, W. (1976). *A man called Intrepid, the secret war.* London: Macmillan.

Varvoglis, M. P. (1997, January). Conceptual frameworks for the study of transpersonal consciousness. *World Futures, 48,* 105–114.

Vigil, J. M. (1996). The present state of Latin America's psychological well-being. *Tlahui-Politic, 2/11*(2). Retrieved August 30, 2000, from http://www.Glahui.com/horapsi.htm.

Walters, R. (1999). *The legitimacy to lead.* In "Meeting of the Minds—Between Those Who Study Leadership and Those Who Practice It." Selected Proceedings, 1998 Annual Meeting, Leaders/Scholars Association. College Park, MD: James MacGregor Burns Academy of Leadership. Retrieved February 10, 2000, from http://academy.umd.edu/ILA/publications.htm.

WILLIAM W. BOSTOCK, Ph.D., is a political scientist with a special interest in collective mental states and their management, especially through leadership, and has an extensive published research record in this and other fields. He is currently Senior Lecturer in Government at the University of Tasmania, Australia. William can be contacted at bostock@utas.edu.au.

The Challenge of Improving the Integrity and Effectiveness of Strategic Visioning

By Kuldip S. Reyatt

"Because of our obsession with how leaders behave and with the interactions of leaders and followers, we forget that in its essence, leadership is about learning how to shape the future . . . Ultimately leadership is about creating new realities."

Peter Senge's introduction to
Synchronicity: The Inner Path of Leadership
by J. Jaworski (1996, p. 3)

MANY LEADERSHIP SCHOLARS AND PRACTITIONERS STATE THAT they expect *change* to be one of the few constants for most organisations in the twenty-first century. This is already evident in today's rapidly changing and turbulent business environment, which is driven by technological advancement and increasing competitive pressures in the global economy. Consequently, there is and will continue to be a growing need for ongoing and effective strategic visioning, the process that facilitates strategic leaders to *see*, construct a compelling vision, and chart a new course with integrity. As a result, this challenging strategic leadership process, which is often the antecedent of strategic change, becomes even more critical for the leadership of organisations, whether entrepreneurs or leaders of global corporations, government institutions, and local communities.

Although applicable to many different organisational contexts, strategic visioning is often viewed as an elusive and confusing concept. This is primarily due to the myriad of leadership theories and ever-increasing pile of literature contending for the mind of the leadership practitioner. Yet too often, the literature highlights the significance of strategic vision without answering the critical question of *how* to effectively navigate this complex and sometimes treacherous strategic leadership process. Accordingly, existing, new, and developing leaders raise concerns regarding the paucity of informative research and applicable theory.

Because of the current state of fragmented knowledge, this research was initiated to develop new theory through exploring the strategic visioning experiences of the key actors—the strategic leaders themselves. At a micro level, new knowledge will contribute to the leader's, leadership group's, and other stakeholders' understanding of a critical aspect of the strategic leadership process. At the grandest scale, the aim is for leaders from a variety of organisations to consider and enhance the integrity of their strategic visioning.

This paper provides a brief overview of the research and some preliminary findings concerned with the underpinning strategic leadership theoretical perspective. These observations are drawn from analysis of the first handful of the fifty-two U.K. interviews. Implications are outlined for leadership theory and the study of strategic visioning / strategic leadership. In addition, some strategic leadership considerations are highlighted for improving the integrity and effectiveness of strategic visioning.

Strategic Visioning

In a recent leadership survey by The Gallup Organization (Conchie, 2004), visioning is acknowledged as one of the key demands of effective leadership. Additionally, scholars of leadership and other related disciplines assert that strategic visioning is a critical aspect of the leadership process, organisational growth, and success over the longer term (Baum, Locke, & Kirkpatrick, 1998; Larwood, Falbe, Kriger, & Miesing, 1995; Lipton, 2003). Although the vast majority of leaders say it is one of the most important aspects of organisational leadership, research highlights that few truly understand and are comfortable with the strategic visioning process (Lipton, 2003).

Any new readers of strategic visioning would expect that for such an important aspect of leadership, the phenomenon would be well defined and agreed upon amongst scholars and practitioners. However, just as leadership is a much-contested area (Grint, 2002), there is no clearly accepted definition of strategic visioning (O'Brien & Meadows, 2000). At its core, the process of strategic visioning is about imagining *what is not present* and *what should be*; or, as Jonathan Swift (1667–1745) put it in his *Thoughts on Various Subjects*: "vision is the art of seeing the invisible." The key actors in strategic visioning need to consider not only the *what*—the content of strategic vision—but also the *where*, *when*, and *why* it should be achieved (Grint, 2000).

The need for strategic vision is central in leadership literature, with scholars frequently stating that it is a key aspect of effective leadership (Bass & Avolio, 1993;

Bennis & Nanus, 1985; Burns, 1978; Conger & Kanungo, 1988; Kotter, 1988; Nanus, 1992). In addition, eminent leadership scholars and those from other disciplines have identified "The potential of examining top level change processes through the construction and mobilisation of vision and purpose . . ." (Pettigrew, 1987, p. 653). Yet, strategic visioning is still little researched. Nevertheless, for organisations to be effective, their top management need to enhance their understanding of the visioning process (Korac-Kakabadse & Kakabadse, 1998).

> **❝ THE REASON FOR STRATEGIC VISIONING IS THAT IT CLEARLY ESTABLISHES BOTH A DIRECTION AND A DESTINATION. ❞**

The process of strategic visioning produces an artifact, which can take a variety of forms (vision statement, symbol, blueprint, etc.). However, it should be future-oriented, compelling, bold, aspiring and inspiring, yet believable and achievable (Levin, 2000). Wilson (1992, p. 18) integrates various definitions and perspectives: "Strategic vision is a coherent and powerful statement of what the business can and should be (n) years hence." The reason for strategic visioning is that it clearly establishes both a direction and a destination. It is needed "as the capstone and integrating mechanism for the elements of strategic planning—mission, philosophy, goals, objectives, strategy, action plans, organisation culture and structure" (Wilson, 1992, p. 18). Wilson concludes that strategic visioning is an activity that comes naturally to the born leader, but can be defined, laid out, learned, and practised by others. This definition aligns with the strategic leadership perspective and distinguishes strategic visioning from other leadership processes; thus, it provides a working basis for this research.

Strategic Leadership

Strategic leadership differs from other kinds of leadership in the magnitude of issues and the scale of complexity encountered (Adair, 2003). Finkelstein and Hambrick (1996, p. 6) defined strategic leadership, in that "it connotes management of an overall enterprise, not just a small unit; and it implies substantive decision-making responsibilities." The strategic leadership perspective focuses on executives who have overall responsibility for an organisation, their characteristics, what they do, how they do it, and in particular, how they affect organisational outcomes. These executives create meaning and purpose for the organisation (House & Aditya, 1997). In effect, strategic leadership translates as those responsible for determining the future of the organisation —the key actors in strategic visioning.

Hambrick and Mason (1984) argue that executives differ in their behaviours and choices; thereby, the organisation becomes a reflection of its top managers. This *upper echelons* perspective highlights that executives are likely to undertake strategic visioning in a variety of ways. For this research, strategic leadership, the strategic visioning process, and contextual influences are perceived to be intertwined. Westley and Mintzberg (1989) are supportive of this perspective, as they highlight that the concepts of strategy and leadership combine into that of strategic visioning, which is part style, process, content, and context. Therefore, the combination of the strategic leadership theoretical perspective, its antecedent—*upper echelons theory*—and contextual theories provide an underpinning theoretical framework for the development of this research.

The majority of previous studies have been primarily concerned with the content of strategic vision (Larwood et al., 1995) and its relationship to organisational growth (Baum et al., 1998). However, there has been little acknowledgement of the influence of the strategic leaders. In general, the extant literature answers the question *why* vision? There is much more literature about *what* constitutes a strategic vision than *how* to undertake strategic visioning (Wilson, 1992). Overall, there is a lack of depth in answering the question of *how* the strategic leaders and associated dynamics influence the strategic visioning process.

Research Approach

This explorative research serves to inform and advance academic and practitioner knowledge through the contribution of new knowledge about the strategic visioning process and the critical influences as interpreted by the strategic leaders themselves. A qualitative approach is adopted that involves semi-structured interviews with the strategic leaders of a variety of organisations. The interviews, on average, last one hour and forty-five minutes, during which time the strategic leader's strategic visioning experiences are explored and key influencing factors / strategic leadership dynamics are discussed.

Strategic leadership processes such as strategic visioning suffer the vagaries of political maneuvering, backstage activities, and other tactics as part of the process (Pettigrew & Whipp, 1991). Thus, strategic visioning research needs to adopt a philosophical stance that accommodates this type of activity and the researcher must employ a complementary research design. Strategic leaders tend to create shared meaning through what Pfeffer (1981) calls symbolic action. Accordingly, research within interpretive conceptions of the world seeks to discover and describe the meanings, interpretations, intentions, motives, experiences, and actions of individuals as social actors (Blaikie, 1993).

In a review of issues and challenges of studying strategic leadership, Leavy (1996, p. 435) argues for a more "dynamic and contextually-sensitive" approach. In addition, Morgan and Smircich (1980, p. 491) state that the appropriateness of a research approach "derives from the nature of the social phenomena to be explored." These comments combined with the strategic leadership theoretical framework and interpretivist philosophical paradigm provide the cornerstones for the research methodology. For these reasons, grounded theory, a qualitative research method that enables theory to be derived about a phenomenon from the data (Strauss & Corbin, 1990), is deemed most appropriate for this research.

In brief, this table shows the composition of the sample population for the U.K. study:

Total Sample Population	52 Strategic Leaders (All Main Board Directors)
Gender	3 Female 49 Male
Average Age	48 Years
Nationality/Origin	2 South African 2 Indian 3 American 45 British
Strategic Leadership Position	3 HR Directors of Global Corporations 2 Directors of Strategy 47 Key Leaders—CEO/Director General/Principal/ General
Sector	15 Public Sector 37 Private Sector (11 *FTSE 100* listed corporations)
Main Industry Clusters	5 Hi-tech (Biotech, Telecoms, Technology) 5 Educational Institutions 8 Insurance and Financial Services 8 Consulting/Business Services 26 Others

The influence of these basic demographics and interrelationships will be further examined in the final analysis. The researcher tried to involve as many female executives and those from diverse ethnic backgrounds as possible. Yet, even with this objective in mind, the sample population reflects the reality, and concurs with other leadership diversity research, that there are currently few female strategic leaders, and those from ethnic minorities are still the exception in U.K. organisations.

Findings Supporting the Strategic Leadership Perspective on Strategic Visioning

This section highlights some preliminary findings drawn from the early interviews that are consistent with the emerging analysis from the rest of the study. The researcher believes that these initial findings are worth sharing with leadership practitioners and scholars to garner much valued critical feedback. In general, these preliminary findings are supportive of the research positioning and the strategic leadership perspective. The following key relates to quotes from the research interviews:

R: Researcher   *SL: Strategic Leader*

The interviewees confirmed the lack of specific strategic visioning theory that could be applied by strategic leaders. Indeed, many highlighted that they would welcome the contribution of new knowledge:

"R: Did you feel in that reading, that it was clear what visioning and vision was about, and how to do it?

SL: No, a lot of it—I was experimenting. Some things worked and some things didn't."

Interview 6, Paragraphs 100–101

"R: Is that process rooted in any theory or any writing?

SL: No . . . but between this company having done this sort of work—the first project for them was about 1996—and for me having done this work since 1992/93, I think it's more based on our experience and we've taken the reading and used those as challenges . . . but I think the process that's involved is really based on learning of doing it as opposed to taking something out of a book. Now that may be bad or it may be effective, but it's just the way it's evolved."

Interview 3, Paragraphs 33–34

As per previous research (O'Brien & Meadows, 2000), no common definition of strategic visioning is found amongst the interviewees. In addition, the myriad of prevailing definitions confuses strategic leaders to the extent that many develop a *working definition* of strategic visioning. This is what makes sense to the strategic leaders in their particular situation and ultimately determines how the strategic visioning process is undertaken. One example of this:

"It's about creating a sense of purpose and direction in the group, it's about creating a sense of something to really aim for, a sense of urgency, the need to change, not to stand still but ultimately a sense of pride and people feeling valued."

Interview 6, Paragraphs 10–11

The interviewees highlighted that the strategic visioning process is much more than just an individualised phenomenon. For instance, when asked about the most influential level of context, the vast majority of interviewees identify the inner context around the strategic leadership group:

"Almost exclusively the team. Its 70–80 percent team dynamic . . . very often they are actually not used to their own team doing this sort of thing. When you say teams . . . there may be a fourth level which is individuals or it falls under teams, it doesn't matter but I would say that the team/individual dynamic is the biggest impact on which way it goes with the exception of something like September 11th . . . which completely shakes everything up."

Interview 3, Paragraphs 41–44

"R: If we now take that away from TECHSOFT and put it to your other experiences, is that the same generally or only rarely?

SL: Yes, generally. So how the actual process (strategic visioning) runs during the next two days is what's going on in that group there, it's the strongest influence."

Interview 2, Paragraphs 174–175

Group demography reflects similarity and dissimilarity among individuals, making it a meaningful perspective for understanding how the leadership process is affected by group dynamics (Korac-Kakabadse, Korac-Kakabadse, & Myers, 1998). Ten significantly influential demographic factors have been identified from research (Kakabadse & Kakabadse, 1999, p. 213): *tenure, location, size of organisation, configuration, specialisation, background, age, gender, ethnicity,* and *communication*. Some of these factors are the same as those presented as observable experiences within *upper echelons theory*. The relevance of these influencing factors to this study is emphasised by practitioners:

"Diversity has got to help vision and very homogeneous teams . . . white male, 45, big stomachs, balding, glasses, old school tie—forget it. You get Barings."

Interview 3, Paragraph 96

"Well they're aligned in their beliefs but we're very conscious not to get a team of 24 clones of me . . . that creative tension that confrontation produced over issues did lead to breakthroughs . . ."

Interview 6, Paragraph 65

One important aspect of group demography is *gender* and the composition of the strategic leadership group. The general indication from interviewees' interpretations seems to be that it could be a significant influencing factor. However, several were unable to distinguish this as a key influence due to the basic fact that there are too few women in strategic leadership positions:

". . . so I would certainly say that I have found that female executives are more open to the process of visioning."

Interview 4, Paragraph 43

". . . the difficult one with that—the reality is that most Boards don't have women—which is a fundamental failing in most Boards. If anything, having both genders in the room helps. It helps a lot."

Interview 3, Paragraphs 67–68

Research examining the relationship between the demography of top management teams and corporate strategic change suggests that top managers' cognitive perspectives, as reflected in a team's demographic characteristics, are linked to the team's propensity to change corporate strategy (Wiersema & Bantel, 1992). Strategic visioning is often considered as part of, or the umbrella for, changes in corporate strategy; thus, the executives' interpretations of the influence of top team demography and other strategic leadership dynamics provide key avenues for exploration. This strategic leadership dynamics perspective is supported by data from the interviews:

"I would use the word dynamics at the top team as opposed to process. So whether it's social integration or whether it's decision making, whether it's listening, whether it's roles or anything else, it's the whole dynamic that is fundamentally affected."

Interview 3, Paragraph 100

"The CEO wants his team and her team and him/her to be in control of the process but to be facilitated by someone who understands group dynamics as well as commercialism and vision . . ."

Interview 3, Paragraph 46

The choice of strategic visioning process is one of the key influencing dynamics highlighted in the research. This decision itself has potentially integrating or divisive effects upon the strategic leadership group:

"If one has got a top team that has largely independent roles, then do you need four strategic visioning processes or do you need one? Why are they a top team? What's the glue that glues them together?"

Interview 1, Paragraph 64

Discussion

Although the research is in progress, the researcher feels that significant considerations are already emerging that are worth bringing to the attention of leadership scholars and practitioners. In particular, some of the preliminary findings are discussed here with regard to implications for leadership theory and the study of strategic visioning/strategic leadership.

Strategic vision and visioning are central within several leadership perspectives—particularly *transformational* (Bass, 1985; Bass & Avolio, 1993; Burns, 1978), *visionary* (Bennis & Nanus, 1985; Nanus, 1992; Westley & Mintzberg, 1989), and *charismatic* (Conger & Kanungo, 1988; House, 1977). These perspectives, classified as *new leadership* theories (Boal & Hooijberg, 2001), can be considered subsets of strategic leadership with particular features seen as delimiters. For instance, charisma-building characteristics (attribution or impression management) are noticeably differentiated from transformational processes (bonding of individual and collective interest).

Strategic leadership is considered the least delimited and therefore broadest construct (Pawar & Eastman, 1997). Consequently, if any of the individual *new leadership* theories were to be used as the theoretical basis for research into strategic visioning, then it is inevitable that the phenomenon could only be viewed through the associated lens; for instance, the impression management or transformational process perspective. So, while leadership itself is a much-contested concept (Grint, 2002), it appears that in the absence of a truly integrative leadership theory, the strategic leadership perspective provides the most appropriate theoretical basis for research into the integrative phenomenon of strategic visioning.

It was apparent quite early on and confirmed throughout the study that the interviewees would make a distinction between *true* strategic leaders and others in the top management team. The interviewees clearly distinguish those who focus on not only the current situation, but also the longer-term view of where the organisation is going—these are considered the *true* strategic leaders. Usually numbering two or three of the upper echelon group, these strategic leaders are the key actors in strategic visioning and instrumental in how the process is undertaken. The ability of interviewees to distinguish strategic leaders from others confirms that practitioners are in accord with the strategic leadership perspective on strategic visioning.

As other strategic leadership researchers have found, gaining access to this elitist and protectionist population is very difficult. However, what became clear early in this research was the importance that participants attach to the strategic visioning phenomenon; this attachment itself "opened the doors." The strategic leaders acknowledge that they benefit from the interview, and many stated that it is a unique and rare opportunity for them to be able to reflect upon their strategic visioning experiences. Therefore, when researchers envisage engaging strategic leaders for future research, it is worth questioning whether the research agenda generates enough interest for participants to spare their precious time.

Leadership can be perceived as a social construct and as the process of making meaning (Drath & Palus, 1994), which is affected by visible and invisible leadership (Sorenson & Hickman, 2002) influences. In similar vein, interpretation is perceived to be a critical aspect of leadership (Pondy, 1978; Smircich & Morgan, 1982), and Grint (2000, p. 4) highlights that leadership itself is essentially "an interpretive affair." Therefore, the researcher argues that the interpretivist research philosophy primarily informs the choice of appropriate research methods. Conger (1998) highlights that previously quantitative based research methods have dominated the study of leadership. Nevertheless, Conger (1998) and Parry (1998) confirm the advantages of a qualitative study, such as grounded theory based research, for providing a richness of contextual data to illuminate a complex and context-sensitive leadership phenomenon such as strategic visioning.

Building new strategic visioning theory is challenging as it is a multi-level and multi-relational strategic leadership process and one-dimensional theories do not adequately explain this phenomenon. Although strategic leaders cannot fully know and control everything, they must know enough to maintain the integrity of strategic visioning and consequently of leadership itself. Therefore, multidimensional and holistic strategic visioning theory needs to be developed for assisting strategic leaders. This is unlikely to be achieved if study is isolated to the individual disciplines of leadership, strategy, change, etc. The development of *true* strategic visioning theory is likely to entail *creative transdisciplinarity* (Giri, 2002; Horlick-Jones & Sime, 2004) and a convergence between scholarship and practice of strategic leadership.

Improving Strategic Visioning Around the World

Strategic visioning makes significant demands on strategic leaders to work through the often-contending individual visions and through the group dynamics, while seeking to maintain the integrity of the right strategic vision for the organisation. Yet, one only needs to look in the *Sunday Times* (U.K.), or other broadsheet appointment sections, to discover what organisations are seeking in their leaders; generally, they ask for "leaders with vision." This signifies the prevalence of charismatic and visionary individuals being sought. This means that individuals with strong rhetoric and "a view" can be favoured. Collins and Porras (1991) confirm that although strategic visioning is a key element of visionary organisations that are successful over the longer term, there is disagreement as to whether a strong charismatic or visionary leader is essential to becoming a visionary organisation. Consequently, perhaps we should be seeking and developing those adept at strategic visioning—those able to *find the best way forward*, not just *bring a way forward*.

> " PERHAPS WE SHOULD BE SEEKING AND
> DEVELOPING THOSE ADEPT AT STRATEGIC "
> VISIONING—THOSE ABLE TO *FIND THE BEST WAY*
> *FORWARD*, NOT JUST *BRING A WAY FORWARD*.

Many scholars espouse the development of leaders as paramount to the ongoing development and success of organisations. In addition, leaders need to nurture the development of other leaders in the organisation (Bennis, 1999). Because of the inherent connection to past, present, and future leadership contexts, strategic visioning should be the foundation of leadership development efforts. However, many organisations embark on leadership development because they feel that they ought to be doing something to develop their leaders (Zenger, Ulrich, & Smallwood, 2000), regardless of strategic visioning. For future strategic leaders to undertake this critical aspect of leadership effectively, it is evident that strategic visioning education and experiential programmes need to be developed and implemented globally.

Recent corporate scandals not only highlight unethical leadership practices, but also the leadership's corrupt intentions for their organisations, which are often manifested in defective strategic vision. Consequently, the integrity of the strategic visioning process can also be suspect. By ignoring the morality aspects of strategic visioning, effectiveness is likely compromised and inauthentic leaders "mislead" by tending to promote their own self-interests above those of followers, employees, and other stakeholders (Ciulla, 2004). As a result, future leaders will have to conduct their strategic visioning within an ever more transparent environment, and subject to increasing scrutiny as new governance processes are established in the U.K., U.S., and other parts of the world. This "new order" increases pressure on leaders to justify the basis and the process of their strategic visioning.

To improve strategic leadership around the world, we need to better understand and consider the integrity of strategic visioning—for it is the vital process that facilitates strategic leaders to determine the best organisational futures. However, if wholly associated to individual CEOs, the critical issue is that strategic visioning is unlikely to outlast the incumbents. Consequently, the challenge for strategic leaders is to understand and effectively manage the dynamics of the strategic visioning process and produce a strategic vision that has an inherent level of integrity and consistency. In so doing, they will afford longevity of their organisations. Therefore, the researcher recommends a deeper examination of the strategic visioning processes adopted by strategic leaders, suggesting that *unexamined strategic visioning leads to development of limited futures.*

It is frequently stated that as humans, we are the only beings on this planet who have the power and ability to destroy ourselves and all other beings. However, little stated is the converse, that we are the only beings who have the power and ability to build a better world, if only we dared to imagine it and try to make it happen. This begins with strategic leaders daring and trying—this is the challenge of strategic visioning. For just consider the participants in this research, that combined body, their strategic visioning and resultant daily decisions affect all of our lives in some way or another. As one CEO of an *FTSE 100* corporation stated ". . . this vision and visioning stuff . . . it's about life and living!"

REFERENCES

Adair, J. (2003). *Effective strategic leadership*. London: Pan Books.

Bass, B. M. (1985). *Leadership and performance beyond expectations*. New York: Free Press.

Bass, B. M., & Avolio, B. J. (1993). Transformational leadership and organizational culture. *Public Administration Quarterly, 17*(1), 112–122.

Baum, J., Locke, E., & Kirkpatrick, S. (1998). A longitudinal study of the relation of vision and vision communication to venture growth in entrepreneurial firms. *Journal of Applied Psychology, 83*(1), 43–54.

Bennis, W. G. (1999, September). Recreating the company. *Executive Excellence*, p. 5.

Bennis, W. G., & Nanus, B. (1985). *Leaders: The strategies for taking charge*. New York: Harper & Row.

Blaikie, N. (1993). *Approaches to social enquiry*. U.K.: Polity Press.

Boal, K., & Hooijberg, R. (2001). Strategic leadership research: Moving on. *Leadership Quarterly, 11*(4), 515–549.

Burns, J. M. (1978). *Leadership*. New York: Harper & Row.

Ciulla, J. (2004). Ethics and leadership effectiveness. In J. Antonakis, A. T. Cianciolo, & R. J. Sternberg (Eds.), *The nature of leadership* (pp. 302–327). Thousand Oaks, CA: Sage.

Collins, J. C., & Porras, J. I. (1991). Organizational vision and visionary organizations. *California Management Review, 34*(1), 30–52.

Conchie, B. (2004, May). The seven demands of leadership. *Gallup Management Journal*. Retrieved from http://gmj.gallup.com/content/default.asp?ci=11614.

Conger, J. A. (1998). Qualitative research as the cornerstone methodology for understanding leadership. *Leadership Quarterly, 9*(1), 107–121.

Conger, J. A., & Kanungo, R. N. (1988). *Charismatic leadership: The elusive factor in organizational effectiveness*. San Francisco: Jossey-Bass.

Drath, W. H., & Palus, C. (1994). *Making common sense: Leadership as meaning-making in a community of practice*. Greensboro, NC: Center for Creative Leadership.

Finkelstein, S., & Hambrick, D. C. (1996). *Strategic leadership: Top executives and their effects on organisations*. St. Paul, MN: West Publishing Company.

Giri, A. K. (2002). The calling of a creative transdisciplinarity. *Futures, 34*, 103–115.

Grint, K. (2000). *The arts of leadership*. Oxford: Oxford University Press.

Grint, K. (2002). *What is leadership? From hydra to hybrid*. Paper presented at the Workshop on Leadership Research, European Institute for Advanced Studies in Management, Oxford, December 2002.

Hambrick, D., & Mason, P. (1984). Upper echelons: The organisation as a reflection of its top managers. *Academy of Management Review, 9*, 193–206.

Horlick-Jones, T., & Sime, J. (2004). Living on the border: Knowledge, risk and transdisciplinarity. *Futures, 36*, 441–456.

House, R. J. (1977). A 1976 theory of charismatic leadership. In J. G. Hunt & L. L. Larson (Eds.), *Leadership: The cutting edge* (pp. 189–207). Carbondale: Southern Illinois University Press.

House, R. J., & Aditya, R. (1997). The social scientific study of leadership: Quo vadis? *Journal of Management, 23*, 409–474.

Jaworski, J. (1996). *Synchronicity: The inner path of leadership*. San Francisco: Berrett-Koehler.

Kakabadse, A., & Kakabadse, N. (1999). *Essence of leadership*. UK: International Thomson Business.

Korac-Kakabadse, A., Korac-Kakabadse, N., & Myers, A. (1998). Demographics and leadership philosophy: Exploring gender differences. *Journal of Management Development, 17*(5), 351–388.

Korac-Kakabadse, N., & Kakabadse, A. P. (1998). Vision, visionary leadership and the visioning process: An overview. In A. Kakabadse, F. Nortier, & N. Abramovici (Eds.), *Success in sight: Visioning*. London: International Thomson Business Press.

Kotter, J. (1988). *The leadership factor*. New York: Free Press.

Larwood, L., Falbe, C. M., Kriger, M. P., & Miesing, P. (1995). Structure of organisational vision. *Academy of Management Journal, 38*, 740–769.

Leavy, B. (1996). On studying leadership in the strategy field. *Leadership Quarterly, 7*(4), 435–454.

Levin, I. M. (2000). Vision revisited: Telling the story of the future. *Journal of Applied Behavioural Science, 36*(1), 91–107.

Lipton, M. (2003). *Guiding growth: How vision keeps companies on course*. Boston: Harvard Business School Publishing.

Morgan, G., & Smircich, L. (1980). The case for qualitative research. *Academy of Management Review, 5*(4), 491–500.

Nanus, B. (1992). Visionary leadership: How to re-vision the future. *The Futurist, 26*(5), 20.

O'Brien, F., & Meadows, M. (2000). Corporate visioning: A survey of UK practice. *Journal of Operational Research Society*, 51.

Parry, K. (1998). Grounded theory and social process: A new direction for leadership research. *Leadership Quarterly, 9*(1), 85–105.

Pawar, B. S., & Eastman, K. (1997). The nature and implications of contextual influences on transformational leadership: A conceptual examination. *Academy of Management Review, 22*(1), 80–109.

Pettigrew, A. (1987). Context and action in the transformation of the firm. *Journal of Management Studies, 24*(6), 649–670.

Pettigrew, A., & Whipp, R. (1991). *Managing change for competitive success.* Oxford: Basil Blackwood.

Pfeffer, J. (1981). Management as symbolic action: The creation and maintenance of organizational paradigms. In L. Cummins & B. Shaw (Eds.), *Research in organizational behaviour* (Vol. 3). Greenwich, CT: JAI Press.

Pondy, L. R. (1978). Leadership is a language game. In M. W. McCall & M. M. Lombardo (Eds.), *Leadership: Where else can we go?* Durham, NC: Duke University Press.

Smircich, L., & Morgan, G. (1982). Leadership: The management of meaning. *Journal of Applied Behavioral Science, 18*, 257–273.

Sorenson, G., & Hickman, G. R. (2002). Invisible leadership: Acting on behalf of a common purpose. In C. Cherry & L. R. Matusak (Eds.), *Building leadership bridges 2002* (pp. 7–24). College Park, MD: James MacGregor Burns Academy of Leadership.

Strauss, A. L., & Corbin, J. M. (1990). *Basics of qualitative research: Grounded theory procedures and techniques.* Beverly Hills, CA: Sage.

Westley, F., & Mintzberg, H. (1989). Visionary leadership and strategic management. *Strategic Management Journal, 10,* 17–32.

Wiersema, M. F., & Bantel, K. A. (1992). Top management team demography and corporate strategic change. *Academy of Management Journal, 34*, 91–121.

Wilson, I. (1992). Realizing the power of strategic vision. *Long Range Planning, 25*(5), 18–28.

Zenger, J., Ulrich, D., & Smallwood, N. (2000). The new leadership development. *Training and Development, 54*(3), 22.

KULDIP REYATT is founder/director of Strategic Visioning Partners. He works across many business sectors with strategic leaders to improve their individual, group, and organisational performance. His work focuses on effective strategic leadership, visioning, and business transformation to deliver successful organisational futures. Clients have included divisions of UK/Global Banks, Global Property Services, European Power & Energy Trading, Energy Utilities, Public Services, Charities, Insurance, and Financial Services organisations. The practice is complemented by doctoral-level strategic leadership research into strategic visioning. Various aspects of the research have undergone external scholarly review with papers presented at U.K., European, and international leadership conferences. International partners are being sought for the next phase of the research programme, which will involve strategic leaders from across the globe. If you are interested, please contact Kuldip at kuldipreyattsvp@aol.com.

Leadership for Social Change: Cross-Cultural Development of Citizen Leaders

By Jan Secor and Marina Tyasto

MARGARET MEAD ONCE REMARKED, "NEVER DOUBT THAT A SMALL group of thoughtful, committed citizens can change the world. Indeed, it's the only thing that ever has." If Margaret Mead is right, bringing small groups of committed citizens together and giving them tools to facilitate thoughtful communication could result in significant social change. The authors discuss a Russian-American leadership development project based on this premise and suggest that cross-cultural experience is a powerful leadership development tool. We explore the question of how we can encourage positive social change given the complex nature of social forces in the modern world. We conclude with five specific suggestions for nurturing citizen leadership and creating the small groups that can change the world.

Background

The vast majority of literature and scholarship on leadership investigates the positional leader, a person whose position carries with it authority and the expectation of leadership. Positional leaders are CEOs, board members, elected officials, college presidents, celebrities, and pundits. However, another kind of leadership is practiced by the non-positional leader. Non-positional leaders—sometimes called citizen leaders—are the people who take on leadership without the position that accords them the authority and privilege of leadership. Often these leaders reluctantly step forward in a community or organization to solve a problem by calling it to the attention of the positional leaders. It is when they are ignored or rebuffed by these authorities that they become leaders by refusing to let the matter drop. As more people cluster around the cause, these individuals are pushed by their followers to become leaders.

Sometimes these citizen leaders become well known, such as Martin Luther King Jr. or Mahatma Gandhi. More often they labor with little or no recognition outside of a small circle of colleagues or friends. They persist because they believe in what they are doing, in the cause they champion. Frequently, they lack power because they belong to a social group that is not generally welcome in mainstream power circles. They may fight for social or economic justice in a society that does not see itself as unjust or unfair. They focus attention on truths that may cause pain and suffering.

For example, on December 1, 1955, tired after a long day of work, Rosa Parks sat down in a seat in the "whites only" section of a bus in Montgomery, Alabama. When the bus driver ordered her to give up her seat for a white man, she refused. When she continued to refuse to move to the back of the bus, she was arrested because her behavior was in violation of Montgomery's strict racial segregation laws. Three hundred eighty-one days later, when the U.S. Supreme Court ruled such segregation unconstitutional, the civil rights movement was in full swing across the Southern U.S. with lunch counter sit-ins, freedom rides, boycotts, and demonstrations. Martin Luther King Jr., pastor of the church Rosa Parks attended, had risen to national prominence. America was on its way to significant change.

Rosa Parks was not just an ordinary black woman who earned her living cleaning white folks' homes. She was a citizen leader. She was active in her church and highly respected in the black community. She had been teaching reading and writing and democratic values in "freedom schools" for many years. When Rosa Parks was arrested, her community clearly understood that this act was unjust. They reacted.

Citizen leadership is not limited to individuals. Leaders can be a group such as the "Committee of Soldiers' Mothers," originally organized in Russia during the war in Afghanistan. As the Soviet Union collapsed and the war in Chechniya heated up, service in the Russian Army, never easy, became very difficult. Therefore, these mothers spoke out against the war in Chechniya as they had the war in Afghanistan and the treatment of soldiers by the Army. Some of them went to Chechniya to visit injured soldiers. Some even brought their sons home from the battlefront. A trainload of mothers was stopped by the military and told that war is not women's business. But they persisted so that, while no one knows their names, everyone in Russia knows the "Committee of Soldiers' Mothers."

Citizen leaders like Rosa Parks and the "Committee of Soldiers' Mothers" exist in every community and society. Under some forms of government they are labeled dissenters or troublemakers and imprisoned or even executed. In other forms of government, they are encouraged or at least tolerated. In a democracy they should be encouraged, though that is not always the case, because citizen leaders ask a community to address issues and problems it would prefer to ignore. In fact, citizen leaders may struggle as much with those whose status they seek to improve as with officials or mainstream power figures. These very problems may prevent a community from creatively adapting to changing circumstances. If ignored, these problems can ultimately cause a society to decay and even collapse.

Richard A. Couto defines the citizen leader as one who facilitates organized and sustained action to bring about change that will permit continued or increased well-being for a group or community (1992). These people usually do not seek leadership. They seek instead to change a condition or solve a problem. When they begin, they expect to achieve their purpose quickly and return to private matters.

Ronald A. Heifetz, in his book *Leadership Without Easy Answers* (1994), describes leadership as mobilizing people to tackle tough problems, problems that are generally embedded in complicated interactive systems. If these problems had an obvious answer, then only a technician would be needed to implement the solution. But most social problems do not have easy answers because at the heart of these problems are competing values—jobs versus health, freedom versus safety, current needs versus long-term consequences, and so on—that require leaders to perform adaptive work. This adaptive work always involves clarifying competing values and purposes as well as facing the painful trade-offs and adjustments required to move toward solutions that work for everybody involved.

" THERE MAY BE ADVANTAGES TO LEADING WITHOUT AUTHORITY BECAUSE ONE MAY BE ABLE TO RAISE DIFFICULT QUESTIONS MORE DIRECTLY. "

People tend to look to leadership for rescue in times of crisis. According to Jean Lipman-Blumen (2005), this is an important element in the allure of toxic leaders. Toxic leaders promise to rescue us from a crisis they may have magnified all out of proportion. A non-toxic leader does not rescue people from problems they can learn to solve. Instead, she manages the environment to foster learning. Leadership does not require status or authority. In fact, sometimes there may be advantages to leading without authority because one may be able to raise difficult questions more directly. Leadership does not confer privilege or power, as the leader should be the servant of the group's purpose as well as a higher purpose. Leading with authority provides resources to do certain things. Leading without authority simply requires different strategies. The challenges for the leader remain the same: How can I identify an adaptive challenge, keep attention focused on the real issue, regulate stress to keep it within a productive range, and take action to promote social learning so that a new equilibrium is reached? (Heifetz, 1994).

Whenever adaptive work is required, the citizen leader becomes especially valuable to the community, sparking debate and keeping the pressure up until the community begins to tackle the tough issue presented. This is a difficult proposition because the identifier of a distressing problem may come to be seen as the source of the distress. A major challenge for the citizen leader is to draw attention and then to deflect it to the questions and issues that need to be faced. If the leader or the group becomes the issue, the purpose of mobilizing people to do adaptive work is defeated.

> **“** **A MAJOR CHALLENGE FOR THE CITIZEN LEADER IS TO DRAW ATTENTION AND THEN TO DEFLECT IT TO THE QUESTIONS AND ISSUES THAT NEED TO BE FACED.** **”**

Thus, the first step of the citizen leader is to learn as much as possible about the issue and to educate the supporters. The leader has to define a context for any action, including defiant acts. The audience for the act needs to readily comprehend the purpose of unusual or defiant behavior so that it focuses less on the behavior itself and more on its meaning. For any defiant act there are at least three audiences: the authorities being challenged, the supporters standing behind the leader, and the uninvolved spectators. In the long run, it is the spectators whose attitudes and behaviors will determine the outcome of the confrontation between the authorities and the challengers. As their attitudes change, they may either switch allegiance, thereby increasing the ranks of supporters, and/or bring pressure to bear on the authorities to change public policy (Couto, 1992; Heifetz, 1994; Loeb, 1999).

To illustrate these principles, the next section describes how citizen leaders in the U.S. were able to engage emerging, citizen leaders in Siberia to help them address complex, adaptive work necessitated by the collapse of the Soviet Union. Russian women in particular were disadvantaged as a social structure based on values of equality gave way to unfettered capitalism. The social support structures collapsed leaving women responsible for family welfare without the tools they had used previously. At the same time American women were struggling with the challenges and opportunities of globalization, as jobs were outsourced and companies began to utilize a global supply chain. Within this rapidly changing environment, Women of Vision, a small, nonprofit organization based in Tacoma, Washington, sought to address the leadership issues faced by both Russian and American women who are citizen leaders.

The Connective Leadership Project

Women of Vision was formed in 1988 by a group of experienced citizen leaders who wanted to focus attention on local women's concerns through a countywide conference in Tacoma, Washington. While in the final planning stages for that conference, the organizers of the 1990 Goodwill Games in Seattle asked the group to organize a Soviet-American women's issues conference. Women of Vision organized not only the 1990 Goodwill Games conference but also traveled to the Soviet Union in 1991 for a follow-up conference in Mahachkala, a city on the Caspian Sea.

By 1997 Women of Vision had hosted several groups of Russian women, primarily from Novosibirsk. We felt we were basically acquainted and wanted to move beyond sponsoring another cultural exchange. The Office of Citizen Exchanges of the U.S. government advertised a grant program for women's leadership development in Russia outside of Moscow, which seemed a likely source of support for our vision. It became the Connective Leadership Project, incorporating a number of concepts from Jean Lipmen-Blumen's work (1996). The project's lead designers were both experienced leaders as well as leadership scholars in their respective countries. We set out to plan the project together rather than simply to offer courses about American leadership in Russia.

The Connective Leadership Project was designed to connect women across Siberia with each other and with American women who shared a concern for improving the status of women and their families worldwide. Leadership studies led us to understand that we all face constant change, which requires us to respond in the same manner as a living organism must adapt to changes in its environment or face the prospect that it will die out. Organizations and societies, too, must change and adapt to the changes in their environment. Leadership then is responsible for providing an environment and a structure in which this adaptive change can take place. One important part of the work of adaptive change is the exchange of information. When information is available from a diverse collection of resources, more options are presented for innovative change. Under globalization, cross-cultural understanding is essential. Therefore, we began to explore leadership in a cross-cultural environment.

Project Goals

Our first goal was to create a truly joint project even though the funding would come primarily from the U.S. government. This was achieved by offering a two-way exchange with Americans visiting three cities in Siberia and Russians visiting three cities in western Washington. We also earmarked funds for interpretation and translation so that we could select candidates who seemed appropriate regardless of language skills. We maintained a very broad focus on skill development rather than specific, issue-oriented content, understanding that women in both countries would pursue different issues or perhaps the same issues in different ways.

In 1997–1998, Russia was well into the transition to a market economy and was moving toward democratic governance. Women were suffering much of the burden of the transition as social support systems collapsed, employment practices changed, and problems such as alcoholism and violence in the family increased. On the other hand, women were not represented in decision-making bodies in numbers large enough to have an impact. The numbers of women elected to office had fallen considerably from levels during the Soviet period. In this environment, the first Leadership Development Institute we held in Russia discussed leadership, small business development, domestic violence, and life-skills training for youth.

** WE LEARNED FIRSTHAND THAT ADAPTIVE WORK REQUIRES LEARNING AT THE EMOTIONAL AS WELL AS THE INTELLECTUAL LEVEL.**

Russian practice was based almost exclusively on lecture and printed materials. We chose to introduce American practices of experiential learning, participatory exercises, and small-group discussion. By planning and implementing this institute with American and Siberian leaders, we demonstrated shared leadership, the use of metaphor, and the importance of personal relationships. Because none of the Americans spoke Russian and very few of the Russians spoke English, the interpreters became the key to the success of the program.

A second goal of the project was to create something that would continue beyond the year of the project and involve many more people than could participate in the actual exchange. We accomplished these ripple effects by holding large conference-type gatherings in each city we visited in Russia and by involving homestay families and multiple agency hosts in Washington. Wherever possible we included time for informal interaction among Russians and Americans to strengthen relationships. The project became the catalyst for dozens of friendships and projects that continue in various forms to this day.

The 1998 exchange was followed by more leadership exchanges in 1999, 2000, and 2001. The network was expanded from Novosibirsk, Gorno Altaisk, and Irkutsk to Tomsk, Krasnoyarsk, Ulan Ude, and many smaller communities across eastern and western Siberia. In 2004 the project was extended into the Khabarovsk region, Primorsky Krai, and Sakhalin Island, drawing two-thirds of the land area of Russia together in a web of connections among citizen leaders for the betterment of women and their families. We created forms of cross-cultural learning as we moved across this vast territory on trains, buses, and even boats. Our leadership institute in motion included conversations, storytelling, songs of each culture, games, feasts, stopping at special places, and visiting one another's families.

We learned firsthand that adaptive work requires learning at the emotional as well as the intellectual level. Logical argument is rarely sufficient; all parties involved must sort through the old and fashion the new, which requires dealing with habit, tradition, and pride. This risky work can be accomplished more easily in the context of friendship, in small affinity groups where trust can be established and confidentiality preserved. By placing project participants under the stress of traveling through an unfamiliar culture, the Connective Leadership Project created opportunities for learning at the emotional as well as the intellectual level and fostered in these citizen leaders the capacity to adapt to change. These are important because, according to Heifetz,

> . . . [t]he long-term challenge of leadership is to develop people's adaptive capacity for tackling an ongoing series of hard problems. The point is not to foster dependency but to counteract the inappropriate dependency on authority that distress tends to produce in adaptive situations. (1994, p. 247)

Our experience demonstrates that international travel and work in the cross-cultural situation rapidly develops adaptive capacity in individuals.

A third goal of the project was teaching the specific skills our experience deemed necessary for the citizen leader. In every phase of the project, we held workshops in listening, conflict resolution, asking effective questions, facilitating discussion, framing an issue, and cross-cultural communication. We worked on the skills of critical thinking, including the capacity for brainstorming and recognizing possibilities as well as "both/and" thinking. This kind of thinking entertains several ideas simultaneously and builds bridges between them instead of widening divides by hardening opposing positions. These are skills that can be taught but are never fully learned, a critical understanding that is essential for all participants—and leaders— to grasp.

Perhaps empowering participants to use their voices has been more important to the success of the project than teaching specific skills. It doesn't really matter how astute an analysis is if it is not applied to the problem. It is one thing to understand the changes that need to be made in a given situation but quite another to speak out or act in favor of those changes. For example, when project participants in the Novosibirsk region began to create hotlines, crisis centers, and shelters for women who were victims of domestic violence the authorities, including the leaders of some women's organizations, said that domestic violence was strictly an American problem not existing to any significant extent in Russia. By coordinating their efforts across Siberia through networks and coalitions, the project participants soon had not only enough evidence to verify the existence of the problem but used their voices to make domestic violence one of the hottest women's issues in Russia. Currently, the Russian government is beginning to offer counseling and other services to victims of domestic violence, the American problem that didn't exist in Russia.

In stimulating citizen leadership we must take our eyes off the leader as authority figure, solver of problems, maker of meaning, and creator of vision. Instead we must look toward developing interactive systems in which every citizen will lead. Where citizen participation is not an elective, but a given. Where citizens take responsibility for solving the tough problems in their neighborhoods, places of business or work, their city, region, nation, and the world. To achieve these objectives women in particular must speak out because they are prone to saying what is expected, to suppressing their voices both in public and in private. Gloria Steinem (1992) identifies a convergence of the contemporary movements for political rights and personal growth, urging the establishment of a network of small groups that both nurture their members and take political action. The 1970s American women's movement indeed was born in small, self-managed groups where women's voices were valued.

> **" IN STIMULATING CITIZEN LEADERSHIP WE MUST "**
> **TAKE OUR EYES OFF THE LEADER AS AUTHORITY**
> **FIGURE, SOLVER OF PROBLEMS, MAKER OF**
> **MEANING, AND CREATOR OF VISION.**

Successful Techniques

As the Connective Leadership Project evolved from 1997–2004, we introduced several techniques that would help women understand themselves and each other, identify areas of common ground where they could work together, and build action plans that were highly likely to be implemented. Chief among the techniques were the future search conference and open space technology.

The *future search conference* is a strategic planning method developed by Marvin Weisbord and Sandra Janoff in the course of their work as corporate consultants (1995). The success of this method with diverse groups focused on complex problems makes it equally applicable for community issues. Future search conferences have been held around the world to look at problems ranging from education in South Africa to housing in Santa Cruz, California. The idea is to bring together people who would not otherwise be likely to talk to one another about particular issues.

The future search method looks at past and present trends affecting an issue, then envisions an ideal future and develops action plans to achieve the ideal. The goal is to identify common ground rather than to identify problems; to create a picture of the desired outcome rather than lists of what "they" should do. Evidence from hundreds of future search conferences confirms that follow-up on future search action plans is better than follow-up on plans generated through other strategic planning methods (Weisbord & Janoff, 1995). In the Connective Leadership Project the future search conference became our starting point for establishing relationships, identifying common ground, and defining strategies for collaboration. Since we introduced the method, Marina has facilitated at least thirteen future search conferences in several regions of Russia.

We also used *open space technology*, which was developed by Harrison Owen (1997) because he found the conversations held during coffee breaks to be more fruitful than official conference sessions. Open space provides a minimal structure through which a group of any size can organize itself to discuss whatever topics are of most importance to its members. In the Connective Leadership Project we have used it with groups of 6–10 people as well as with groups of 20–100. Because women step forward to take responsibility for leading the break-out sessions and reporting the results back to the whole group, it provides excellent training for citizen leaders. Since open space does not require many supplies or very much time, dozens of open space sessions have been facilitated for all kinds of groups and organizations within and beyond the Project. Both of us belong to international networks of future search and open space facilitators that provide daily opportunities to communicate online with colleagues learning from this unlimited source of wisdom.

Emerging Model for Social Change

So, how do we build these interactive systems of citizen leaders that will tackle the tough problems of society? We suggest here a five-step process.

The first step is to ask certain questions: Whose voices have been silenced? Who is not included? Why? What can they tell us? What else can they tell us? How can we work in alliance with them? What common ground do we share? Where do we disagree? How can we respect our disagreements while moving forward on our common ground? These questions identify faulty assumptions made by the mainstream such as "if you loan money to very poor people they won't pay it back." Muhammad Yunus (1999) proved that assumption wrong through building the Grameen Bank in Bangladesh, which serves the poorest of the poor and maintains a 97–98 percent repayment rate. His ideas now have become mainstream as the World Bank and U.S. AID sponsor micro-lending programs around the world. Yunus has moved on to building a cell phone network in rural Bangladesh.

Dropping the assumption that we, as leaders, know what "they" think, what "they" will do, what "they" need, and listening to the voices of people on the margins—poor people, tribal people, street people, homosexuals, women—is the critical second step. When Wilma Mankiller as Chief of the Cherokee Nation went to a very poor village in Oklahoma to ask them what they needed from their tribal government to improve life in the village, she was very surprised at the answer. They wanted help in building a monument in the center of the village. She had expected they would ask for a water and sewer system, a low-income housing project, or something of the like. But Wilma Mankiller was willing to abandon her assumptions and to listen. So the tribal government helped the people build their monument, then the people went ahead to build new houses and a water and sewer system because at last they had a sense of identity and pride in their village and trusted that the tribal government would listen to them (Steinem, 1992).

In the third step we open our eyes to the possibilities that are all around us. Social justice requires social change. Social change is ongoing. In other words, we will never achieve perfect justice. The best we can hope to achieve is movement toward justice. Just as life is the journey, not the destination, social change is the process, not the product. Individually, we are living organisms that grow, adapting to the circumstances in which we find ourselves. Society is a set of interdependent, living organisms that grows and changes before our very eyes. We can influence the direction of its growth and guide its adaptations but we cannot escape the consequences of its changes. We cannot isolate ourselves. For example, we are not immune to the lack of social justice even though we are not the direct targets of injustice. Just as an oil spill washes up on a distant beach or polluted air creates acid rain in distant forests, poverty, ignorance, disease, and injustice injure people without regard for who caused the results.

Once we open our eyes, we will see an overwhelming array of possibilities. The problem becomes choosing an effective path, which again involves listening to the community so that we can help people do the adaptive work that will move them toward needed change. As Heifetz puts it, "social systems must learn their way forward" (Heifetz, 1994, p. 87). It is up to leaders to provide opportunities for the system to learn, to adapt to reality even when reality is harsh. In 1983 when William Ruckelshaus was head of the U.S. Environmental Protection Agency (EPA), he was faced with a decision about what to do with a large copper smelter in Tacoma, Washington, that was emitting toxic levels of arsenic over Puget Sound. Instead of providing an answer that would either shut down the plant or require the plant owner to install costly emissions controls, Ruckelshaus turned the decision over to the community. Company and community representatives met in often-heated debate with representatives of the EPA until they finally hashed out a plan together. The plant closed and the community rallied around the workers and helped them retrain for new jobs. Ruckelshaus helped the community do the adaptive work necessary to solve its own problem (Heifetz, 1994).

❝ WE ARE ONE INTERWOVEN, INTERCONNECTED WEB OF LIFE. WHAT WE EACH DO MATTERS. ❞

The idea of giving over leadership to communities leads to the important fourth step in building civil society: we must accept responsibility for ourselves, our families, our society, our government, and our planet. We are one interwoven, interconnected web of life. What we each do matters. It can be overwhelming to feel the weight of the world on our shoulders. Fortunately, while each of us bears this responsibility, none of us bears it alone. We all live in communities and systems that can support our efforts, especially when citizen leaders are empowered so that many problems are solved by self-organizing, community-based groups. Meeting in open space provides opportunities to step from pessimism at the enormity of the problems to optimism that together we can do a lot to make our lives better.

And, finally, in the fifth step in this process, we can reach out and form small circles with others who share our understanding of the web of life and the importance of social justice. These circles support us as we grow, adapt, change, and seek justice. In her circles Marina, having learned the technique from Birgitt Williams, uses the ceremony of the Medicine Wheel, which connects a person to a community as well as to the universe (Arrien, 1992). These circles work best as small groups (10–15 people) who gather regularly to share their struggles and mark their achievements through shared leadership, discussion, ceremony, eating, listening, singing, and working together. "In my life I have belonged to many circles. I have organized several. I have joined others. Yet, for over 30 years now, I have not been without at least one" (Secor, 2004). Next, it is important to bring these circles or their representatives together in larger gatherings to form networks. Throughout the Connective Leadership Project, we began each major network gathering by blending water from all the localities represented in the room. This tied us together for our meeting while reminding us of the circles we represented. The networks begin to form connections with other networks working on related issues at a regional, national, or international level.

> ❝ GRADUALLY, A SOCIAL MOVEMENT GROWS WITH ENOUGH STRENGTH TO BRING ABOUT MAJOR CHANGE BUT NOT WITHOUT THE SMALL CIRCLES OF CITIZEN LEADERS THAT FORM ITS CORE. ❞

Conclusion

Leadership theory is beginning to recognize that leadership is not necessarily the ideas and actions of an individual but instead may be the processes we use to define our goals and move toward them. By making the circle the organizing image in our minds, a prison of lines and limits will gradually disappear (Steinem, 1992). Sitting in the circle we share our wisdom, we contribute our passion and take our responsibility as we choose our path. As these circles reach out to other circles they form a network, a web that grows and changes, spiraling through time and space asking questions, listening without judgment, opening to all that is possible, accepting responsibility, and interconnecting with new circles, networks, and webs. Gradually, a social movement grows with enough strength to bring about major change but not without the small circles of citizen leaders that form its core.

REFERENCES

Arrien, A. (1992). *The four-fold way: Walking the paths of the warrior, teacher, healer and visionary.* New York: HarperCollins.

Couto, R. A. (1992). "Defining a citizen leader." In J. T. Wren (1995), *The leader's companion: Insights on leadership through the ages.* New York: The Free Press.

Heifetz, R. (1994). *Leadership without easy answers.* Cambridge, MA: Harvard University Press.

Lipman-Blumen, J. (1996). *The connective edge: Leading in an interdependent world.* San Francisco: Jossey-Bass.

Lipman-Blumen, J. (2005). *The allure of toxic leaders: Why we follow destructive bosses and corrupt politicians—and how we can survive them.* New York: Oxford University Press.

Loeb, P. R. (1999). *Soul of a citizen: Living with conviction in a cynical time.* New York: St. Martin's Press.

Owen, H. (1997). *Expanding our now: The story of open space technology.* San Francisco: Berrett-Koehler.

Secor, J. H. (2004). *Building civil society.* Keynote address presented July 7, 2004, at the International Women's Forum, Irkutsk, Russia.

Steinem, G. (1992). *Revolution from within: A book of self-esteem.* Boston: Little, Brown, and Company.

Weisbord, M. R., & Janoff, S. (1995). *Future search: An action guide to finding common ground in organizations and communities.* San Francisco: Berrett-Koehler.

Yunus, M. (with Alan Jolis). (1999). *Banker to the poor: Micro-lending and the battle against world poverty.* New York: Public Affairs.

JAN SECOR, Ed.D., in addition to completing a doctorate focused on community leadership, has more than thirty years of practical experience as a community leader and social change agent. Through Women of Vision, an NGO based in Tacoma, Washington, Jan has participated in the global women's movement since 1990. She represented Women of Vision at the United Nations Fourth World Conference on Women in Beijing. She designed and led the *Connective Leadership Project* with Marina Tyasto. She was a Fulbright Scholar in 1999–2000 at the Siberian Academy for Public Administration working to create a Leadership Development Institute. Prior to her work with Russians, she was a program planner in the employment and training system and a social activist for human rights in the U.S. Currently, she is retired.

TYASTO MARINA VICTOROVNA is a sociologist and currently heads the Department of International Relations at the Siberian Academy for Public Administration, Novosibirsk, Russia. Marina has nearly twenty years of experience in citizen diplomacy and cross-cultural communication and nearly fifteen years of experience in gender conflict resolution, women's leadership development, NGO management training, and participatory methods of organization and community development. She is a trainer, consultant, and facilitator on leadership and management, effective communication, social partnerships, conflict resolution, negotiation skills, etc. Among her many projects, Marina designed and led the *Connective Leadership Project* with Jan Secor. Prior to her international work, Marina was an assistant professor in the Department of Philosophy, Novosibirsk State University.

Learning Journals: An Underutilized Tool in Leadership Education

By John J. Sherlock and Grant Morgan

LEADERSHIP EDUCATORS WORLDWIDE FACE A SPECIAL PEDAGOGI-cal challenge as they endeavor to help their students grow in their understanding of leadership. Leadership research has shown that individuals develop as leaders through experience (Kouzes & Posner, 2002; McCall, 2004). Most university programs in leadership are unable to offer extensive field experiences and, thus, have tended to utilize the more traditional pedagogical approaches of textbook reading, class lectures, paper assignments, and the like. It has been suggested by authors such as McCall (2004) that "the primary source of learning to lead, to the extent that leadership can be learned, is experience" (p. 127). While it can be a powerful teacher, the experience alone does not equate with learning. As Dewey (1933) pointed out long ago, not all experiences result in learning.

What increases the capacity for learning from experience is reflection on that experience, and this is particularly true for leadership development. Reflection, and specifically critical reflection, is believed to be at the core of leadership development (Densten & Gray, 2001). Unlike thinking, which is natural, reflection can be learned and developed (Dewey, 1933). This paper asserts that the use of learning journals can be a valuable tool for leadership educators in developing the reflective practice of their students. Further, this development has enormous potential for the students' ultimate leadership influence in society, irrespective of their geography or work sector.

Following a discussion of the literature regarding reflection and reflective practice, the pedagogy of the learning journal assignment is discussed with specific linkages to the development of reflective practice. The practical aspects of the learning journal assignment, including communicating expectations and grading, are explored. Finally, the impact the journal assignment can have on student learning and on leadership development is presented.

Reflection and Learning

Many scholars on reflection (Kolb, 1984; Mezirow, 1990; Schon, 1983) were influenced by the concepts asserted by John Dewey (1933). Dewey saw reflective thinking as distinct from other forms of thought because it involves a state of doubt or perplexity in which thinking originates, and then a subsequent searching to find material that will resolve the doubt. He adds that reflection is the "active, persistent, and careful consideration of any belief or supposed form of knowledge in the light of the grounds that support it and the further conclusions to which it tends" (p. 9). Boud, Keogh, and Walker (1985) have described reflection as "those intellectual and affective activities in which individuals engage to explore their experiences in order to lead to new understandings and appreciation" (p. 19). Doyle and Young (2000) explain reflection as a process of disengaging from or stepping back from an experience and taking time to deliberately and carefully review it, think about it, and construct meaning from it. Learning results from this process when one determines the meaning of the experience and draws inferences from it. Boyd and Fayles (1983) define reflection as "the process of internally examining and exploring an issue of concern, triggered by an experience, which creates and clarifies meaning in terms of self and which results in a changed conceptual perspective" (p. 100). One can see from these definitions that reflection is a process, and the product of that process is meaning having been made of experience. In demonstrating this point, Smith (2001) provides examples of the benefits that can result from reflecting on experience.

Reasons why we reflect:

Natural element of learning, gain insight and understanding, foresee consequences, solve problems, justify action, achieve control, improve decisions, increase options, clarification, detect errors, forced to do it, seek "truth," explore mindsets, identify "right" problems, challenge norms, gain new perspectives, self insight, self development, personal mastery, overcome resistance, apportion blame, explore responsibility, increase self confidence, get new ideas, part of thinking, conflict resolution, negotiation, cultural expectations, be more successful, enhance performance, gain multiple viewpoints, intuitive element in adaptation, gain an edge, uncover discrepant reasoning, shift blame (distancing), make the tacit explicit. (Smith, 2001)

Dewey (1933) believed that thinking was natural but that reflection needed to be learned. Attitudes play an important role in acquiring reflective skill. Dewey stressed the importance of cultivating the attitudes of open-mindedness, enthusiasm, and responsibility. In suggesting responsibility as an attitude, Dewey (1933) was referring to the need to consider and accept the consequences of one's reflections. He also claimed that reflection benefits individuals by giving them more control over experience, thereby increasing the value of experience. Schon's (1987) work on developing reflective practice builds on Dewey's ideas concerning the nature of reflection. Schon claimed that the technical rationality of the epistemology taught in schools ought to be combined with reflection. Mezirow (1990) makes a distinction between reflection and introspection. He does not regard introspection as reflective because it involves no attempt to re-examine, critique, or test the validity of prior knowledge. Further, he subdivides critical reflection into three categories—content, process, and premise reflection. Content reflection focuses on *what* one perceives, thinks, feels, or acts upon. Process reflection focuses on one's method or manner for *how* one thinks. Premise reflection (a higher level of reflection) focuses on *questioning* the very presuppositions of fundamental beliefs. Learning resulting from critical reflection may be marked by affective, cognitive, and behavioral changes (Scanlon & Chernomas, 1997).

❝ **REFLECTION BENEFITS INDIVIDUALS BY GIVING THEM MORE CONTROL OVER EXPERIENCE, THEREBY INCREASING THE VALUE OF EXPERIENCE.** **❞**

Journaling and the Development of Reflective Practice

Asking students to keep a learning journal is synonymous with asking them to be reflective. Moon (2000) contends that individuals reflect on something in order to consider it in more detail. Langer (2002) states that journal writing represents a formal tool for developing reflective thinking, noting that the literature offers evidence that students, regardless of the course topic, improve their learning by keeping journals. In addition to learning, Rainer (1978) used journal activities to enhance a sense of perspective that over time affected student attitudes and behavior. It should be noted here that no universally accepted description of a learning journal exists, but it is important to stress what the learning journal is not. It is not a personal diary, scrapbook, or course log. According to Boud (2001), in terms of learning, the journal is both a place where events and experiences are recorded and the forum by which they are processed and re-formed. Journaling provides an environment in which one can express his or her struggles, challenges, thoughts, feelings, etc. Beyond this concept, journaling exercises can vary greatly.

Journals have also been shown to be a technique for enhancing reflective thinking and facilitating self-discovery (Fisher, 1996; Huber, 1998; Taggart &

Wilson, 1998; Varner & Peck, 2003). Working with prior experience is a way of making sense of experiences, recognizing the learning that results, and building a foundation for new experiences that will provoke new learning (Boud, 2001). One of four critical lenses that Brookfield (1995) suggests can assist in the reflective process in teacher training is student autobiography, which has many similarities with journaling. Densten and Gray (2001) apply this lens to the leadership development context specifically. They state that student autobiographies (journals) encourage students to record how they perceive actions and experiences. They assert that in the journal exercise students take experiences that are tacit in nature and make them explicit by recording them in journal entries, which form the foundations for further learning. Loughran (1996) posits that students should gain a deeper understanding of the learning episodes they experience through deliberately reviewing one's thoughts and action in light of reflection. Varner and Peck's (2003) seven-year study of the journal assignment used in an MBA program supports these views, finding that the majority of students did claim their learning had been enhanced through the journal assignment.

Journaling contributes to how we challenge ourselves with new approaches to thinking as well. Mezirow (1991) argues that we are trapped comfortably inside our own meaning schemes and perspectives, which suggests that teachers have difficulty encouraging students to reflect on practices that challenge the students' fundamental beliefs (Densten & Gray, 2001). Lukinsky (1990) states that keeping a journal may help adults (and, by extrapolation, college students) break habitual modes of thinking and change life direction through reflective withdrawal and reentry. He goes on to say that journal writing is a promising aid to the ongoing effort to bring together the inner and outer parts of our lives. Additionally, Lukinsky suggests that the journal is a "tool for connecting thought, feeling, and action—a synthesizing tool that works from the inside out and the outside in" (1990, p. 214).

Assessment Considerations for Learning Journals

Educators already appreciate the importance of being clear with students regarding assignment expectations. The learning journal assignment is typically presented at the beginning of a semester and is due at the end. There is considerable variability in the journaling assignment depending on a number of factors, such as course objectives, educator's teaching style, and the like. The guidelines for using a learning journal can vary, but it is important to mention again that the journal is not meant to serve as a personal diary, scrapbook, or course log. Students often have a heightened sensitivity regarding the use and assessment of a journal. Barclay's (1996) study of 100 graduate students found that over 90 percent indicated that they would have preferred more information at the outset about the assessment criteria. Boud et al. (1985) note that the more journal writing moves into the realm of critical reflection, the more it is necessary to consider the very personal nature of journal information.

One issue regarding assessment is how much a journal assignment should count toward the final grade. Loo (2002) weighted the journal in their case study as 5 percent of the final grade. The authors have typically assigned either 15 or 20 percent of a student's grade to the journal assignment. Journal writing can be read and responded to without being given a grade. In some courses, educators grant automatic credit to students who complete a journal-writing requirement (Fenwick, 2001). It is beyond the scope of this paper to discuss the ongoing debate within education regarding what grade weighting might be necessary for students to take an assignment seriously.

> ❝ **REFLECTION INVOLVES A FOCUS ON UNCERTAINTY, PERPLEXING EVENTS, AND EXPLORATION WITHOUT NECESSARILY KNOWING WHERE IT WILL LEAD.** ❞

There is a risk that assessment can alter the ownership of the journal if it is perceived that the journal's content is to be written for the educator rather than the learners themselves (Barclay, 1996). When considering the use of learning journals, one must take into account certain factors that inhibit reflection. Boud (2001) notes that one possible factor is having any outside reader of the journal. He suggests that the expectation of an external audience profoundly shapes what we write or allow ourselves to consider. Brookfield (1995) has been outspoken in his view that journals should not be viewed or individually graded by the educator. Boud et al. (1985) notes that keeping journals private, away from the eyes of others, can be a useful principle to adopt in courses. They note that reflection involves a focus on uncertainty, perplexing events, and exploration without necessarily knowing where it will lead. They add that it is in the interest of learning that writers express their doubts, reveal their lack of understanding, and focus on what they do not know. They go so far as to tell students that "unless they feel sufficiently free to write things in their journals that they would be embarrassed" for others to read, then they are probably not using their journals sufficiently well for them to be good examples of reflection (p. 16).

Where time limitations or the personal nature of the journal writing prohibit the reading of the whole text by an educator, the student might select and submit a few passages for assessment. The learner then controls disclosure and vulnerability of personal writing. Alternatively, the student may prepare and submit a few reflective pages summarizing the journal or its process for assessment. The summary might note themes appearing throughout the journal, as well as turning points and critical incidents in their development. The summary might also present reflection and include quotes selected by the writer. Learners who have completed this sort of summary often remark that the synthesizing process is almost as valuable as the journal writing itself (Fenwick, 2001).

Fenwick and Parsons (2000) offer the following criteria for approaching assessment: overall fluency (i.e., thoroughness and variety of topics addressed), evidence of thoughtful reflection exploring various required issues/readings, evidence of connection making (going beyond narrations of personal experience), evidence of growth, evidence of critical thinking and questioning. Other possibilities are full credit for completing the assignment (no review), students turn in sample entries of their choosing, students turn in a synthesis of learning journal experience, etc. Regardless of the assessment technique that is selected or not selected, what is important to remember is that the technique may influence the students' journaling practice. The criteria to be used by an educator should be based on the purpose and context of the learning journal assignment. Thus, while there is no consensus regarding the grading of journals, there is an imperative for educators to appreciate that, by giving the journal assignment, they have inserted themselves into a potentially intense, personal process of reflection, and they must be absolutely clear about their purposes and rationale.

Using journals in education is not simply a matter of inserting the assignment into the curriculum. As with any assignment, the learning journal should be aligned with learning objectives. In keeping with the learning objectives, possible journal entry questions could be:

- What did you see, feel, think that prompted you to write?
- What is the fundamental likeness of this issue, problem, concern, feeling, etc., to others?
- What is the fundamental difference?
- Why is it significant to you?
- What unconscious assumptions may you be applying in this situation?
- What struck you as a really significant issue in class this week?
- What are you learning about the issue right now?
- What are you learning about yourself?

As one can see from the questions above, the journal exercise has great potential to develop the reflective practice of those who truly engage in the assignment.

Reflective Practice in Leadership Development

Leadership development in the contemporary context requires learners to become adept at shaping and fulfilling not only their own aims but also those of others involved in the leadership relationship (Kaagan, 1999). According to Drath and Palus (1994), leadership involves finding meaning and making sense within a community. It can be understood as a process that develops over time as a shared experience within the context of a community. Meaning has both cognitive and emotional components that allow a person to know (in a sense of understanding) a representation of the way things are and the way things ought to be, i.e., a world view (Drath & Palus, 1994).

> " **REFLECTIVE PRACTICE PLAYS A PIVOTAL ROLE IN CONSTRUCTING MEANING FROM EXPERIENCE, AND SUCH PRACTICES CAN BE LEARNED AND SHARPENED.** "

Making meaning involves the recognition that we are continually challenged to see data become information, information become knowledge, knowledge become wisdom, and wisdom become meaningful thought and action (Komives, Lucas, & McMahan, 1998). The process by which data become thought and action helps explain how experiential learning occurs. The most appropriate means of developing one's leadership is an area of debate, but a significant number of scholars and practitioners are advocates for experiential learning. Bolman and Deal (1994) and Clarke and Clarke (1994) have pressed for greater attention to experiential forms of leadership development. The roots of experiential learning are heavily tied to the work of John Dewey (1938). Dewey's *Experience and Education* is a seminal piece that "set the stage for most of the expert commentary on experiential learning" (Kaagan, 1999, p. 12). Dewey (1938) states that "every experience enacted and undergone, modifies the one who acts and undergoes, while this modification affects, whether we wish it or not, the quality of subsequent experiences" (p. 35). In leadership development, teachers may encourage students to draw on past experience to critically evaluate common or established leadership behaviors (Densten & Gray, 2001). The lessons learned from past experiences contain an element of depth and richness that other development techniques lack.

McCall (2004) states, "the primary source of learning to lead, to the extent that leadership can be learned, is experience" (p. 127). He also acknowledges that not all experiences are the same, and that different individuals benefit differentially from a given experience based on previous experiences, what they know and do not know, and whether their own styles and context around the situation promote learning. As one gains experience, the impact on his or her learning depends largely on the context and individual. It then becomes crucial in leadership development that one learns to recognize the contextual factors and reflect on his or her understanding and reaction to maximize learning. Most development experiences entail facing adversity, going into the unknown, and struggling with the unfamiliar (McCall, 2004). McCall suggests that the categorical experiences that emerge as being particularly important are challenging assignments, exposure to other people, hardships, and personal events.

Important to remember is that experience does not always equate to learning. Development as a result of experience presents a challenge in the form of giving the right experiences to people who will learn from them and then provide support that will help them learn what the experiences offer (McCall, 2004). The ability to reflect critically about one's self and experience is an essential element of the development process (Huber, 1998). Experience alone can shape a person, but taking a much deeper, reflective view of the experience allows for more valuable meaning and development opportunities.

Conclusion

In developing one's leadership, learning from experience through reflection is vital irrespective of context. In leadership development, the most important person to understand may be one's self, which suggests the crucial role of reflection (Komives, Lucas, & McMahan, 1998). McCall (2004) asserts that to make effective use of experience to develop talent, we need a better understanding of the learning process as it plays out and of how to help people make the most of the experiences they have.

Reflective practice plays a pivotal role in constructing meaning from experience, and such practices can be learned and sharpened. Reflection sheds light into the learning process and can influence leadership development in a way that spans borders, sectors, classrooms, or culture. Because learning journals place ownership with the learner, national and cultural boundaries are eliminated due to the personalization of the activity. Reflection occurs at the individual level and is thus beneficial to leadership development in any cultural setting. While there is no consensus on the most appropriate means of developing one's ability to reflect critically, it is our belief that the learning journal presents an exciting and promising way of meeting that challenge.

REFERENCES

Barclay, J. (1996). Learning from experience with learning logs. *Journal of Management Development, 15*(6), 28–43.

Bolman, L., & Deal, T. (1994). Looking for leadership: Another search party's report. *Educational Administration Quarterly, 30*(1), 77–96.

Boud, D. (2001). Using journal writing to enhance reflective practice. *New Directions for Adult and Continuing Education, 90,* 9–17.

Boud, D., Keogh, R., & Walker, D. (1985). Promoting reflection in learning: A model. In D. Boud, R. Keogh, & D. Walker (Eds.), *Reflection: Turning experience into learning* (pp. 18–40). London: Kogan Page.

Boyd, F. M., & Fayles, A. W. (1983). Reflective learning: Key to learning from experience. *Journal of Humanistic Psychology, 23*(2), 99–117.

Brookfield, S. (1995). *Becoming a critically reflective teacher.* San Francisco: Jossey-Bass.

Clarke, K., & Clarke, M. (1994). *Choosing to lead.* Greensboro, NC: Center for Creative Leadership.

Dewey, J. (1933). *How we think.* Boston: DC Heath.

Dewey, J. (1938). *Experience and education.* London: Macmillan.

Densten, I., & Gray, J. (2001). Leadership development and reflection: What is the connection? *The International Journal of Educational Management, 15*(3), 119–124.

Doyle, W., & Young, J. D. (2000). Management development: Making the most of experience and reflection. *The Canadian Manager, 25*(3), 18–23.

Drath, W. H., & Palus, C. (1994). *Making common sense: Leadership as meaning-making in a community of practice.* Greensboro, NC: Center for Creative Leadership.

Fenwick, T. J. (2001). Responding to journals in a learning process. *New Directions for Adult and Continuing Education, 90,* 37–47.

Fenwick, T., & Parsons, J. (2000). *The art of evaluation: A handbook for educators and trainers.* Toronto: Thompson.

Fisher, D. (1996). Using journals in the social psychology class: Helping students apply course concepts to life experiences. *Teaching Sociology, 24*(2), 157–165.

Huber, N. S. (1998). *Leading from within: Developing personal direction.* Melbourne, FL: Krieger Publishing Company.

Kaagan, S. (1999). *Leadership games: Experiential learning for organizational development.* Thousand Oaks, CA: Sage.

Kolb, D. A. (1984). *Experiential learning.* Paramus, NJ: Prentice-Hall.

Komives, S., Lucas, N., & McMahan, T. (1998). *Exploring leadership for college students who want to make a difference.* San Francisco: Jossey-Bass.

Kouzes, J., & Posner, B. (2002). *The leadership challenge* (3rd ed.). San Francisco: Jossey-Bass.

Langer, A. (2002). Reflecting on practice: Using learning journals in higher and continuing education. *Teaching in Higher Education, 7*(3), 337–351.

Loo, R. (2002). Journaling: A learning tool for project management training and team-building. *Project Management Institute 2002, 33*(4), 61–66.

Loughran, J. (1996). *Developing reflective practice: Learning about teaching and learning through modeling.* London: Falmer Press.

Lukinsky, J. (1990). Reflective withdrawal through journal writing. In J. Mezirow (Ed.), *Fostering critical reflection in adulthood: A guide to transformative and emancipatory learning* (pp. 213–234). San Francisco: Jossey-Bass.

McCall, M. (2004). Leadership development through experience. *Academy of Management Executive, 18*(3), 127–130.

Mezirow, J. (1990). *Fostering critical reflection in adulthood: A guide to transformative and emancipatory learning.* San Francisco: Jossey-Bass.

Mezirow, J. (1991). *Transformative dimensions of adult learning.* San Francisco: Jossey-Bass.

Moon, J. (2000). *Learning journals: A handbook for academics, students, and professional development.* London: Kogan Page Limited.

Rainer, T. (1978). *The new diary: How to use a journal for self-guidance and extended creativity.* Los Angeles: JP Tarcher.

Scanlon, J. M., & Chernomas, W. M. (1997). Developing the reflective teacher. *Journal of Advanced Nursing, 25*(5), 1138–1143.

Schon, D. A. (1983). *The reflective practitioner: How professionals think in action.* New York: Basic Books.

Schon, D. A. (1987). *Educating the reflective practitioner.* San Francisco: Jossey-Bass.

Smith, P. (2001). Action learning and reflective practice in project environments that are related to leadership development. *Management Learning, 32*(1), 31–48.

Taggart, G. L., & Wilson, A. P. (1998). *Promoting reflective thinking in teachers.* Thousand Oaks, CA: Corwin Press.

Varner, D., & Peck, S. R. (2003). Learning from learning journals: The benefits and challenges of using learning journal assignments. *Journal of Management Education, 27*(1), 52–77.

JOHN J. SHERLOCK is an assistant professor and director of the master's program in human resources at Western Carolina University. He earned his Ed.D. in human resource development from George Washington University. His research interests include leadership development, adult learning, and spirituality. His research has appeared in journals including *Advances in Developing Human Resources, Journal of Association Leadership,* and *Journal of Counseling & Development.*

GRANT MORGAN recently earned his M.S. degree in human resources from Western Carolina University. His research has been presented at the Organizational Behavior Teachers' Conference and published in *FORUM* magazine.

Political Charisma in a Globalized World[1]

By Blanca A. Deusdad

THE WORD "CHARISMA" MEANS DIFFERENT THINGS TO DIFFERENT people. It is broadly used to describe different phenomena such as politics, religions, the arts, and even to refer to places. The word is used with a hint of personal fascination to illustrate exceptional and extremely popular events, particularly those which no one knows why they are so successful and appealing. The term "charisma" has become a useful word that expresses the reasons for public success. It is also used as a simplistic historical concept to explain social events.[2] It is possible to say that there is a banalization of the term, especially in the mass media, where virtually everything can be considered charismatic.

Charisma is a characteristic of political leadership that increases the success of a political leader and his or her number of adepts. Charisma is not necessarily an ethical leadership based on values and morality. A charismatic leader can use his or her appeal in order to have more followers without taking into account a morality of means and ends. The aim of this paper is to analyze political charisma in a globalized world focusing on Western democracies after World War II. First, I attempt to provide a clarifying definition of the term. I will also make references to some examples of non-democratic charisma such as Osama Bin Laden. I will then go on to examine the concept of charisma as used in classical sociological theory. After this first analysis, there are still some important questions about the nature of charisma in Western democracies, such as: How has the process of globalization changed its configuration? What is the influence of mass media in the construction of charisma? Can we talk about a globalized charisma and a mediatic charisma? Is there a charisma of gender? In the main, this paper will argue that political charisma has been redefined in Western democracies in recent times.

Historical analyses often do not give sufficient emphasis to political leadership in helping us understand the process of historical decision-making and how populations have been convinced and controlled to act in a determined way. Charisma cannot be omitted, and it's understandable how some political actions are accepted by populations and how some irrational attitudes, such as dying for a religious and political cause, could take place in our societies.

It would not be possible to grasp the concept of charismatic leadership in modern societies without taking into account the actual social context and the process of globalization. In modern societies decisions made in one part of the world can have an effect in different parts of the planet. For instance, the policies of the President of the United States often have an impact on China, the Middle East, or Europe. Probably, if we were to conduct a survey, European citizens would be more interested in having the right to give their opinion about the American President rather than vote in the European Parliamentary elections or for the European Constitution because of the impact he has on their lives.

The Concept of Charisma

The concept of charisma in Greek denotes charm, grace, pleasure, glee, festivity, gift, favor, merit, and also veneration. In Latin, *Charisma –atis* signifies divine grace or gift: a favor that God concedes to humans. That term is used also in French. In English, the quality in question is called magnetism. If we examine the word, it is very closely related to concepts like cheerfulness and liveliness but also to other terms associated with personality like genuineness, originality, and uniqueness. The term charisma was originally used in the context of religion, but we can find in our societies different kinds of charisma: religious charisma as shown by the late Pope, John Paul II, or Mother Teresa of Calcutta; the charisma of artists like Madonna or Prince or of athletes like Michael Jordan or Pelé; and, finally, political charisma, which is the subject of this analysis. However, the different charismatic spheres are not completely separate, and we can find, for instance, religious elements in political charisma.

The concept of charisma is related to the concept of "sacred," with "extraordinary" people who have the gift of being mediators between the divinity and human beings,[3] who transmit God's message. In a broader sense the concept is related to the notion of *maná, virtue,* or *asabiya*[4]. This last term, *asabiya*, means a personal quality, exclusive to the member of the original community, capable of transmitting wisdom, gift, and divine grace to the people of their own community.

The term charisma also has a religious origin. It is possible to describe Jesus Christ as a charismatic figure surrounded by his disciples and followers. Jesus is seen as an extraordinary figure who has supernatural powers, and miracles are attributed to him. At the same time the primitive church has been considered charismatic, too. The figure of the prophet, the *nabi*, in Hebrew means "one who has been called or who calls." The prophet is seen to tell the truth and transmit the wisdom of God to the community.

Another aspect of religion, apart from the prophets, that is related to charisma is the movement of Charismatic Renovation, which Catholics embraced in 1967 in the United States. The Charismatic Renovation has been spread around the world and is considered one of the great movements among the "born again." I will not delve deeply into these charismatic movements; my point is simply to remind the reader of the many forms that charisma can take, and the multiple ends toward which it can be employed.

Furthermore, in the Catholic Church one finds charisma attributed to monks or nuns who, for instance, have founded a religious order. A nun, Paula Montal, for example, created the order of Escolapias. Her followers believed she had "good charisma."[5] Another such example is the enormous popularity of Father Paisios of Mount Athos in Greece to whom many miracles are attributed.[6] Religious charisma is an emotional way to attract followers who find meaning in their lives and a guide in the charismatic figure. It can be through emotive acts such as charitable events, which produce manifestations of collective effervescence. There is a kind of falling in love with the person who guides them. In politics, a similar phenomenon is observed among Marxist leaders. The leader convinces, touches, and converts the followers to his or her ideology.[7]

Charisma in Modernity

In an age when we are immersed in the process of secularization, the emergence of forms of elemental religious and political charisma appears as a response to social complexity. Furthermore, the tendency to individualism and introspection implies the felt need among many for professional or spiritual guidance in order to understand themselves and the world. On the one hand, paradoxically, charismatic religions act as an alternative to the crisis of the ideologies of the nineteenth century such as communism, fascism, or anarchism and to the crisis of traditional religions, too.[8] Charismatic religion creates community and ties upon which people rely in front of a complex, dangerous, and unknown world. On the other hand, not only is charisma related to huge multitudes or demonstrations, it is present in small communities, small groups directed by a leader in a relation of comradeship.

The charisma of the artist converts him into an idol who the followers would like to emulate. Through his or her image the followers will transform their everyday routine by participating in concerts or listening to the artist's music. The fans will shout and cry in front of their hero. The myth in modern societies is transmitted through the cinema and the television, where "extraordinary" images are shown. The mass media construct a figure with a charismatic aura, who every teenager wants to be like and who people adore. This form of charisma is less dangerous than others, such as political or religious, because it is a relationship through music and the arts. However, it can imply cultural changes, as in the case of the Beatles or Punk groups, as an expression of a youth and countercultural movement.

Political charisma has its tradition in the hero who has superhuman qualities and performs exceptional acts. The martyr is one who is capable of giving even his life for the political cause and whose sacrifice is often in the name of a political, social, military, or religious ideal. Political charisma cannot be understood without considering the multitude of followers and adepts that the leader has. The leader's appeals to the population are proof of his or her influence or power; at the same time, it is a form of legitimacy. One example is the call of President Felipe González to vote for NATO membership in the Spanish Referendum of 1986 when a great percentage of the population was against it. Recently, Jacques Chirac made appeals on a TV program asking for the French people to vote in support of the European Constitution. This was after surveys showed that about 54 percent of the French were against the EU constitution.[9] Another example is the radio talks of American presidents every Saturday, such as Ronald Reagan made during his presidency in order to explain to the nation the political situation and to make appeals to some political issue.[10]

" CHARISMA IS SOMETIMES PERCEIVED AS A BREATH OF FRESH AIR, A HOPE FOR A BETTER FUTURE ... "

All these are manifestations of charismatic relations. Charisma is a way to legitimize the political leader, his policies, and the political system, democracy or new supranational structures such as the European Union, and it is used in moments of crisis and in order to legitimate policies and political actions. However, the real legitimacy of the political leader is not in the manifestation of support but in the ballots.[11]

Moreover, charisma is sometimes perceived as a breath of fresh air, a hope for a better future, in the face of social injustices and the need for social reforms in a lot of communities, and especially in Third World nations. Charisma can be perceived as a force that is transmitted among the population and that can generate changes. One such example is that of the Brazilian President "Lula" (Luiz Inácio da Silva) who, when he emerged as a leader, created a lot of expectations and hopes not only in his country but also among the Western left. Nonetheless, these great expectations must be followed by transformational measures, which generate changes and benefits such as the possibility of owning their "fabelas."

As is the case of nationalism, charisma covers this space of emotion in politics and legitimizes changes and attitudes. Moreover, nationalism often increases charisma and charisma has the potential to reinforce the nationalistic message. Furthermore, the charismatic relation implies that there is a recognition of some qualities of the leader and a trust in him or her.[12] People tend to become more daring regarding changes when they accept leaders' political views and values. The charismatic leader has the power to connect with the audience to seduce and to penetrate their collective mind and try to give answers to the inquietudes, wishes, and uneasiness.

Proposed Definition

The spheres of charisma that I have described are not completely delimited and we can find influences of the three spheres—religious, political, and artistic—mixed in a certain way together. In other words, in political events we can find aspects of religion and the use of artists at political meetings or celebrations, and vice versa. I propose a definition of political charisma in a globalized world, which includes aspects of manufactured charisma:

> Political charisma refers to places, objects, or individuals endowed with an aura, perceived as almost divine, whose characteristics and actions are interpreted as exceptional by the community which falls within their sphere of influence. In the case of charismatic individuals, or leaders, although the leader can convert the followers to his or her ideas, this conversion would be facilitated by a shared identity or shared values, especially in a globalized world. Charismatic places, objects, or individuals become charismatic because of their relation to a recognized tradition and at the same time because of their "genuineness" and innovative ability to face new and old challenges. Moreover, charisma acts as a cultural catalyst. Charisma is a synthesis of values and identity symbols of a culture and the moods and aspirations of the community. The charismatic leader is capable of expressing these moods and aspirations and so of guiding the followers of communicating and of implementing new and revolutionary ideas. The leader may embody some representative qualities which encourage identification between him/her and the community that trusts in him/her and arouses to her or his appeals. The mass media help to construct and to expand the charismatic aura at the same time as they diffuse the message and the image of the charismatic leader.

Charisma as a Revolutionary Source

The crucial author in social theory who defined the concept of charisma was Max Weber.[13] He derived the concept from the theorists of religion, Rudolf Sohm (1841–1917) and Ernst Troelsch (1865–1923), who used the term to describe the process of transformations of religious sects.[14] Weber distinguished between three classes of authority: rational, traditional, and charismatic. In reality, we do not find them in a pure state and we can find a mix of the three types of legitimacy. For Weber charisma is a revolutionary force that establishes a new order and awakens irrational feelings among followers. Charismatic leaders are exceptional and not very frequent. They are considered to have extraordinary characteristics. According to Weber, charisma cannot be learned; it can only be awakened or tested as a natural characteristic of the personality.

Despite his important and seminal work on charisma, Weber's definition is not sufficient to understand the dynamics of charisma in the present context and especially after World War II. The use of mass media and the diffusion of new technologies, such as the Internet, at the end of the twentieth century have completely changed the way charisma is constructed and perceived by populations. The domain of charisma has been spread around the world and national borders have become less relevant. Furthermore, the changes in social context and the development of Western democracies have promoted a kind of charisma that is more attenuated and more based on pleasant and attractive relations rather than on irrational and despairing feelings among followers.[15]

The concept of political charisma is very closely related to the concept of political leadership and the personal characteristics of the leader, such as astuteness, political intelligence, discernment, versatility, ambiguity, and sometimes overact.[16] The image makers and political advisors underline in each leader his or her best characteristics in order to make him or her appealing and charismatic.[17] For instance, President George Bush's advisors in the 2004 campaign highlighted his human face. They knew Bush was not an excellent speaker, but he had a very appealing human face.[18]

Even though Émile Durkheim has never mentioned the concept of charisma, he has analyzed two phenomena that are closely related: the *collective effervescence* and the *moral authority*. The collective effervescence reflects those "cathartic" moments in rituals, when crowds converge and express together an emotive and enthusiastic feeling. By moral authority, Durkheim understands an authority that is followed not because of the leader's wisdom but because of his or her physical energy that is present and can be felt.[19]

The Psychological Approach

Psychologists have analyzed the relation between leaders and followers. Le Bon emphasized the idea of the loss of critical attitude in the middle of the crowd. The followers are happy without thinking. The mass becomes a collective soul and the fact that they act collectively makes them braver than an individual alone. The mass are motivated by emotion, and in order to control them the leader has to make short and repetitive sentences. Le Bon does not talk about charisma, but he develops the concept of prestige. He distinguishes between acquired prestige, which is linked to one's place in society, and personal prestige, which is a characteristic that a few people have and which consists of magnetism and personal appeal.

Freud is the other theorist who talks about the transformation of the individual in the crowd, and considers that followers come under the suggestion of the leader. For Freud the leader is a hypnotist capable of generating suggestion. He talks about the concept of "primitive soul" and its capacity to act unconsciously. In the mass the individual transcends the limits of self and becomes abandoned. He adopts the ideal of the mass that is ruled by the leader. In the crowd individuals act in an imitative reaction and the mass gives them strength and the feeling of being unbeatable. All individuals can be the same in the horde and there is one that is stronger and superior to others: the leader. Freud's analysis also underlines that irrational attitudes can be ambivalent. They can go between love and hate, which was not observed by Weber.[20]

It is possible to see manifestations of this kind of enthusiastic and despairing charisma in societies where their culture allows them to express free emotion and where political systems are less stable. Two examples of this were the aroused and irrational crowds that carried away the bodies of Yasser Arafat in Ramallah and former Lebanese Prime Minister Rafik Hariri.[21]

Edward Shils' Approach

The other classical author who was fascinated by the concept of charisma and convinced of its importance was Edward Shils. In his classical definition, Shils considered that the attribution of charisma is in the process of order-creating. Charisma is an element that gives order and centrality to society. Shils asserts that there is a need for order in societies and in some individuals. He considers that this "perception of the central" is accompanied by the "attribution of sacred." Charisma is the essence of the center because it connects it with the "central value system." Shils' approach is one of the most useful in order to analyze charisma in democracies.

Other important contemporary authors who have underlined the importance of charisma in Western societies are Charles Lindholm who, in his excellent book, describes the classical philosophical, psychological, and sociological approaches to the concept and, at the same time, tries to understand the behaviors of people like Jim Jones and the phenomenon of collective suicide.[22] He attributes one of the reasons for the increase of charisma in modern societies to the loss of traditional ties such as family and neighborhood relations, and an increase in the feeling of vacuity. The charismatic relations permit people to transcend the limits of the self and feel part of a new group.

Liah Greenfeld also observed that the increase of anomie in our societies reinforces charismatic relations.[23] Greenfeld observes that charisma is manifested in the delivery of the message and that it acts as a lubricant to the political discourse.[24] The image and the way that the message is delivered become especially important in democracies. To control the nonverbal language such as gestures, posture and dress is important in order to make the speech and the speaker more attractive. Salvador Giner contends that in modern societies, as we manufacture books and everything, charisma is also manufactured. It is a mediated product of our society which becomes effective by using all the resorts of mass media: a lovely image, good manners in front of TV cameras, a pleasant voice, and an elegant suit.[25] Nonetheless, aspects of the discourse such as nationalism and populist appeals also increase the charisma of the leader. The passion of the leader and the emotional relations that he or she awakens amplify his or her charismatic appeal.[26]

Political Charisma: The Effects of Globalization

The process of globalization has interconnected social and economic relations from distant parts of the world at the end of the twentieth century. Globalization implies economical, cultural, political, as well as environmental interconnections around the world which make national borders irrelevant.[27] The way that politics are presented and affect people's behavior has changed considerably with the use of TV and, lately, with networks like the Internet. The use of mass media increases the effect of globalization. On the one hand, TV diffuses the message of political leaders and amplifies their importance and the domain of their message. Before mass media, the people could hardly see leaders more than once in their lives, whereas now they are present every day through TV. He, more frequently than she, becomes familiar and popular. The "aura" of deference that emanated from his infrequent appearances, as it was highlighted by Walter Benjamin when he wrote about the masterpieces of art, is transformed in a mediated extraordinariness.[28] The modern aura is constructed because the political figure is retransmitted by TV, which gives to the leader a special importance and an aura of magnificence. Nonetheless, there are political figures, such as monarchs, who are not seen very often and conserve this aura of deference and glory.

At the same time, TV has increased the domain of charisma. A political leader can be seen almost at the same time all over the world and have followers and detractors far from his or her borders. To share the same national identity with the leader is an aspect that gives charisma, but it is not the only one and it is not indispensable. In order to be successful, politicians have to learn how to present themselves and act in front of TV cameras. Their discourse becomes more attenuated because it is not delivered for a great mass of public; it is expressed to be heard in every house. Therefore, the political activities are thought in terms of mass media discourse and timing. The political advisor chooses the piece of the speech that is going to be retransmitted and political acts take place in a time chosen in order to be shown on the evening news.

The new technologies, such as the Internet, have increased the way that people are interconnected around a leader or a social event. A mass of people can communicate without being present. Web sites, emails, and mobile messages create a new way of immediate and effective communication that is also used for revolutionary purposes. Globalization has developed increasing differences between countries. We find people who understand and can control by themselves the world where they live and individuals who, in front of the confusion, trust and rely completely on leaders and charismatic relations.

There are still forms of antidemocratic charisma such as in communist countries like North Korea or Cuba, where charisma is reinforced by the propaganda of the regime. There is even a cult of the personality of the leader who is seen as a god. An example is the commemoration of the 63rd birthday of Kim Jong Il in North Korea in February 2005. The case of Fidel Castro proves the routinization of a genuine charismatic leader who was formed in the revolutionary processes in South America and in Cuban revolution. After that, he became premier and head of the government in 1959.

An example of bad leadership is the charisma of Osama Bin Laden. His domain is completely globalized. He wishes to appeal to all Islamic believers around the world and his image is spread by *Al-Jazira*, Western TV, and the Internet. His "pleasant" face does not correspond with the evil image of a terrorist who acts without piety. His face of "goodness" is meant to attract Arab populations by means of his appeals on videos shown on TV all over the world. This constructed innocent image contrasts rather starkly with his terrorist attacks. It is said in the Arab countries that the real brain of Al Qaeda is Ayman al Zawahiri, and that Bin Laden's role is limited to being the public face of Al Qaeda and to providing financial support to the organization, which might be the most important. Furthermore, Bin Laden's charisma is incremented by his Islamic nationalistic appeals and also his religious fundamentalism, which even asks its followers to give their lives in the terrorist attacks.

An antidemocratic charisma can be considered an unethical leadership. I am not going to enter into the polemic as to whether it is effective, but the argument that such a leadership is looking out for the good of its followers is weak and even wrong because the means that it uses are simply unethical, such as large-scale attacks against innocent civilians and the immolation of young terrorists. As we could see in the terrorist attack in London on July 7, 2005, it might be a charismatic relation among these suicide terrorists and some imams and leaders. The kamikazes rely on them and found in these relations and actions an identity and a sense of their lives.

Political Charisma in Western Democracies

The complexity of globalized societies and the need for continued adaptation and understanding has left much of the population relying on political leaders' decisions and acts. Nonetheless, in democracies, there is a section of the population that is more demanding of leaders and that does not accept their leadership if they do not share the same kind of values and outlook.[29]

As I argued before, charisma in democracies appears more attenuated. The influence of mass media in the construction of charisma has made some scholars talk about "pseudocharisma." They emphasize the mask that covers the real political personality. The fakeness or unauthenticity can be the charisma of modern politicians.[30] Politicians have always covered their feelings in front of big audiences. What is different in democracies and in the globalized world is the way charisma is constructed through the mass media. The relation among leader and followers is mediated by TV, and there is an emphasis on the scenography and scenic elements of politics.

What is the rational action connected to charisma in Western democracies? The way that charisma is expressed is more attenuated and demanding from the followers. Thus, charisma is more based in rational achievements such as shared values, goals, and the demand for accountability. Nonetheless, these aspects lead to a trust in the leader in some of his or her politics and policies. The political leader gives meaning to the followers; after that, they can accept to be transported in a charismatic relation. In his Weberian approach, Michael Bernard underlines that when rational-legal elements predominate over charismatic: democracy exists. What he does not mention in his study is the influence of the social context, especially in democratic transitions where there is an emergence of charismatic leaders who implement the new political system.[31]

The charismatic manifestations in democracies are established in more concrete spaces, such as electoral campaigns, electoral debates, or meetings where candidates are acclaimed by their followers who show their support in an emotive, enthusiastic, and exciting way. However, there is a tendency to overrationalize where the attitudes become more critical toward the political leader. Furthermore, the moments of being carried away and arousal are delimited and controlled in planned spaces. The public scenographies are prepared in detail to receive the candidate and to create an emotive entourage.

In democracies, instead of propaganda we find what is called political marketing.[32] The difference in democratic regimes is based on the plurality of candidates and political options; during the political campaign, all of them can sell their political program and goals. They try to be the most attractive in a transparent competition.

Moreover, in democracies, there is no cult of the leader and he or she is not considered a superhuman, a god, and a father figure as in communist regimes. Nonetheless, in democratic transition there can be a paternalist relation with the president as a form of relating to the leader which is carried over from fascist or communist regimes. I found this element in the figure of Jordi Pujol as president of the Regional government of Catalonia in Spain (Generalitat of Catalonia), who was in power from 1980 to 2003. Even though he was representing a Catalan nationalist party, he could be situated in the center of the political spectrum and had the votes from emigrants of other parts of Spain that lived in Catalonia. His nationalism and defense of the economic budget for the Generalitat increased his charisma and his popularity. To his political figure has also been associated a kind of messianic leadership due to the fact that from his youth he was defending the ideal of a democratic Catalan nation. Furthermore, he solved "the problem of succession," nominating (even before his retirement in 2003) Artur Mas as new candidate of Convergència Democràtica de Catalunya, his political party, which was founded in 1974.

The case of President Ronald Reagan is an example of the control of the mass media. On the one hand, he knew how to perform in front of the cameras; on the other hand, what was shown on TV was carefully selected by his press advisors. The public image of Reagan was very successful, not only because of his career as an actor, where he created his image of an American hero, but also because he knew how to transmit an image of optimism and joy. His political performance was excellent; he always introduced an anecdote and told stories about what he wanted to say, entertaining the audience. He made people laugh even in some dramatic situations, as in his assassination attempt in 1981, when he said, "I hope the doctor is a Republican." His political behavior in front of the cameras connected tremendously with the American people. He liked to speak in public and was not shy if he did not know something.

Most scholars will agree that he was a "great communicator" and an excellent political performer.[33] Reagan learned nonverbal language: how to look to the camera, how to move in an appropriate way. He controlled his public image and knew how he was being seen by the public in every moment. He could be very elegant and also casual according to the occasion. As I mentioned before, he also liked to speak in public and to joke with the audience. His speeches were almost pedagogical. He presented his ideas and the way decisions and political activities were made with a lot of clarity and simplicity.

I submit below a possible typology of charisma in democratic societies. I have made two big subdivisions of types classifying charisma into democratic or antidemocratic regimes in order to better analyze the phenomenon.

ANTIDEMOCRATIC DICTATORIAL CHARISMA	AUTHORITATIVE BROKEN OFF (RADICAL) PERSONAL MESSIANIC MEDIATED POPULIST MODERNIZING MULTITUDES[36]
DEMOCRATIC CHARISMA	BROKEN OFF (RADICAL) PLURALISTIC CONSENSUAL AUTHORITATIVE PERSONAL MESSIANIC MEDIATED MODERNIZING MULTITUDES

Conclusions

In this paper I have tried to examine the concept of charisma, and to analyze the manifestations of political charisma in Western democracies and in a context of globalization. It seems that in democracies charisma is more attenuated and less irrational; nonetheless, there can be forms of charisma related to extreme movements of right and left, such as xenophobic and ultranationalist parties like Front National of Jean Marie Le Pen in France. Charisma is now constructed differently, and while its manifestation in democracies is present, it is more attenuated. It can appear in every part of the world and can have a globalized effect. It can go beyond nation states. As a result of the process of globalization, charisma does not have to be limited to one region or one nation state and can appear anywhere.

In the actual social context, charisma appears as a multipolar element that has different centers around the planet and acts in a global world. Osama Bin Laden is an example of antidemocratic charisma, "the evil," which has no relation to a nation state and acts in a global and mediated world as a supernatural and omnipresent power. Nobody knows his whereabouts, but he is present and threatening. On the other side of the coin, there is the charisma of a democratic leader such as Tony Blair who, after the terrorist attack in London on July 7, 2005, appears as a world leader talking to the world audience in the G8 summit. This political speech became very important in the face of a situation of shock and crisis.

The new forms of construction and manifestation of charisma in a globalized world are expressed through mass media. Television has constructed a new form of charisma and has helped in its diffusion and globalization. It has broadened the domain of charisma. A good politician in the modern world has to know how to act in front of the cameras. In order to be successful, his or her discourse has to be clear and pedagogical. Politicians' speeches can become so simplistic, repetitive, or even meaningless that they can be appealing to the population but could be considered ethically incorrect. The good political leader is one who can explain his or her political decisions in a social context in a didactic way; in other words, who makes the complexity understandable. In a democracy, charismatic women act in the same stenography as men and use all the attractive elements (clothes, makeup, or a stylish haircut) as a way of being more attractive and seductive. Nonetheless, there is a kind of genuine charisma among revolutionary women, such as Aung San Suu Kyi, Rigoberta Menchú, or Phoolan Devi based above all on their heroic deeds.

Political charisma is a double-edged sword: it can be a way of misleading and increasing irrational attitudes, but it can be a way of rallying populations around a leader and increasing the social cohesion. Nonetheless, followers have to behave in an active way, demanding to share the same kind of values and attitudes as the leader. The art of the politician is to convince the multitudes about his or her ideas and better policies. It is necessary to find innovative and imaginative ways for elites and populations to relate in order to succeed in social policies and politics and to submit leaders to accountability. In this sense, charisma is a sort of veil that covers the politician's acts and makes people forgive political responsibilities.

NOTES

1. I want to thank The Institute for the Advancement of Social Sciences, and especially its director Professor Liah Greenfeld, for encouraging me and for aid to do this paper; and Professor Salvador Giner at the University of Barcelona. I am also very grateful to Dr. Jonathan Eastwood, Dr. Joseph Fernando, and Dr. Nikolas Prevelakis who have helped me with the text and have given me interesting comments. This paper has been made with the financial support of DURSI (Department of Universities, Research and Information Society) of Generalitat of Catalonia (Spain).

2. See Tal Howard. "Charisma and History: The Case of Münster, Westphalia, 1534-1535." *Essays in History, 35*, 1993.

3. See Franco Ferrarotti. *Una fe sin dogmas*. Barcelona: Ediciones Península, 1993, p. 227. This idea of the messenger of God is in one of the Dialogues of Plato "Ion." Plato. *Ion dialogo platonico*. Madrid, 1901.

4. According to Durkheim, *maná* is the same as *wakan* among Sioux or *orenda* among Iroquois. Émile Durkheim. *The Elementary Forms of Religious Life*. Oxford: Oxford University Press, 2001.
Maná is also a concept described by Marcel Mauss. It is a word common among all the languages of Melanesia and Polynesia and is a very meaningful word. *Maná* is what gives people a magic value, religious and

even social. Thus, it is related with shamans and with magic things. It is a magic quality that can be transmitted. Marcel Mauss. *Sociología y Antropología.* Madrid: Editorial Tecnos, 1979, pp. 122–133.

The *asabiya* is a word described by Ibn Haldun, an Arabic historian of the 14th century. In his *Universal History,* he refers to the agnatic group. The *asabiya* is a distinction attributed to a few families and which is compulsory if you have to rule. For instance, a foreigner has not the same status and he could never have it. However, the *asabiya* promotes solidarity. Attitudes of luxury and slovenliness bring about the loss of it. It is possible to say that the *asabiya* promotes a kind of social cohesion and redistribution. Ibn Haldun. *Introducción a la Historia Universal.* Mexico: Fondo de Cultura Económico, 1977.

5. See Rosalía Haro Savater. *El carisma de Paula Montal: Fidelidad y dinamismo, coordenadas para una lectura actualizada.* Roma, Zaragoza: Edelvives, 1995.

6. Interview with Dr. Nikolas Prevelakis and Fr. Methodios Alexiou at The Institute for the Advancement of Social Sciences, Boston University, MA, Thursday, March 17, at 6 P.M. In Spain, there has appeared recently a priest, "Pare Jony," who sings rock in favor of the poor people of the world and even has made a video clip. His fundraising will be for a Foundation which has his name.

7. The idea of converting into an ideology, to a new idea in a political faith in a state of enthusiasm with disposition to the sacrifice has been pointed out and analyzed by Alessandro Pizzorno. *Le radici della politica assoluta, e altri ssagi.* Feltrinelli: Milano, 1993. Also, Cavalli exposes the same idea: the "metanoia" in Luciano Cavalli. *Carisma. La qualità straordinaria del leader.* Bari: Laterza, 1995.

8. See Luciano Cavalli. *Carisma. La qualità straordinaria del leader.* Bari: Laterza, 1995.

9. See "Chirac goes on TV to promote Europe's Constitution." *New York Times.* April 15, 2005, p. A3.

10. See Fred L. Israel (Compiled). *Ronald Reagan's Weekly Radio Addresses. The President Speaks to America.*Wilmington: Scholarly Resources Inc., 1987, Vol.1, 274 pp.

11. See "Charismatic legitimation is the process of creating loyalty for the new state through the personal influence of the charismatic leader." Claude Ake. "Charismatic Legitimation and Political Integration." *Comparative Studies in Society and History, 9*(1), 1966, 1.

12. For the concept of "trust" see Robert C. Solomon, "Ethical Leadership, Emotions, and Trust: Beyond 'Charisma,'" in Joanne B. Ciulla, Ed., *Ethics, the Heart of Leadership.* Westport: Praeger, 2004.

13. For Weber definition see Max Weber. *Economy and Society.* 2 vols. Los Angeles: University of California, 1979, 1469 pp.

14. See Franco Ferrarotti. *Una fe sin dogmas.* Ediciones Península: Barcelona, 1993, 247 pp.

15. See Ronald M. Glassman and William H. Swatos, Eds., *Charisma, History and Social Structure.* New York: Greenwood Press, 1986, 240 pp.

16. This concept of political characteristics is analyzed by Alistair Cole. *François Mitterrand, a Study in Political Leadership:* London and New York: Routledge, 1997.

17. See Dan Nimmo. "Political Image Makers and the Mass Media." *The Annals of the American Academy of Political and Social Science, AAPSS.* No. 427 (September 1976): 33–44.

18. Information in a lecture of Mark McKinnon at the Institute of Politics at the Kennedy School of Government, Harvard University, April 21, 2005.

19. Émile Durkheim. *The Elementary Forms of Religious Life.* Oxford: Oxford University Press, 2001 [1912], p. 155.

20. See Charles Lindholm. *Charisma.* Cambridge, MA: Basil Blackwell, 1990, p. 360.

21. He was assassinated in Beirut February 14, 2005.

22. See Charles Lindholm. *Charisma*. Cambridge, MA: Basil Blackwell, 1990.

23. Interview with Liah Greenfeld in September 2004.

24. Ibid.

25. See Salvador Giner. *Carisma y Razón: la estructura moral de la sociedad moderna*. Madrid: Alianza Editorial, 2003, 262 pp.

26. See Robert C. Solomon. "Ethical Leadership, Emotions, and Trust: Beyond 'Charisma,'" in Joanne B. Ciulla, Ed., *Ethics, the Heart of Leadership*. Westport: Praeger, 2004, p. 83.

27. See Manfred B. Steger. *Globalization. A Very Short Introduction*. Oxford: Oxford University Press, 2003, p. 7.

28. See Walter Benjamin. *L'obra d'art a l'època de la seva reproductibilitat tècnica*. Barcelona: Edicions 62, 1983. [1936]. (Clàssics del pensament modern, 9). See also José Luís Brea. *Las auras frías*. Barcelona: Anagrama, 1991. (Colección Argumentos, 121).

29. See Jane M. Howell and Boas Shamir. "The Role of Followers in the Charismatic Leadership Process: Relationships and Their Consequences." *Academy of Management Review, 30*(1), 2005, 96–112.

30. See Ronald M. Glassman and William H. Swatos, Eds., *Charisma, History and Social Structure*. New York: Greenwood Press, 1986, 240 pp.

31. See Joel Poldolny, Rakesh Khurana, and Marya Hill-Popper. "Revisiting the Meaning of Leadership." HBD Working Paper. February 15, 2005. See also Michael Benhard. "Charismatic Leadership and Democratization: A Weberian Perspective." Program on Central and Eastern Europe Working Papers Series #43. Harvard University, p. 13.
One example of that is the case in Spain of the President Adolfo Suárez (1976–81) and his implementation of "Ley de Reforma Política" with a Referendum. Furthermore, the political figures of the Spanish President Felipe González (1982–96) and Jordi Pujol (1980–03), President of the Regional Government of Catalonia.

32. Propaganda was first found among the Greeks who used popular parties, theatre, and music, and where the poor people could assist for free. After the 4th century B.C. it's possible to talk about a global propaganda in all Greece. The Romans also used propaganda to expose the feats of the Empire as well as the cult to the Emperor.
The *New Deal* was the first period of the *New Politics* when the word "propaganda" ceased to be used and instead appeared the concept of "political marketing." The word propaganda was refused because of its connotations of manipulation and falsification committed by Goebbels, "Propaganda Staffel," and the lessons of Pavlov used by Stalin. Political marketing consists in the promotion and diffusion of the candidates. Instead of selling a product we sell candidates. Political marketing presents the candidate to the public as the best option in front of the other candidatures. His or her qualities are promoted and a professional and efficient image is sold. See Jacques Ellul. *Histoire de la propaganda*. Francia: Press Universitaire de France, 1967. (Que sais-je?), 127 pp. See also Philippe J. Maarek. *Marketing político y comunicación. Claves para una buena información política*. Barcelona: Paidós, 1997. (Paidós Comunicación, 88), 281 pp.

33. In many books about Reagan's life there are references to Reagan's capacity to communicate. He is known as "the great communicator." There is even a book with this title. I also have to say that this book is an example of the construction of the public image, with a lot of chosen and nice pictures about his life idealizing the character. See Frederick J. Ryan, Ed. *Ronald Reagan. The Great Communicator*. New York: Perennial, 1995, 175 pp. Reagan also has other books about his life, including, *Where's the Rest of Me?* (New York: Duell, Sloan and Pearce, 1965) and *An American Life* (New York: Simon & Schuster, 1990).

34. I use the term multitudes instead of mass following Salvador Giner's analysis. This author criticizes the use of the concept of mass because it does not imply a well-defined ideological or scientific reference into the

social theory. Furthermore, its meaning expresses the anguish and fear which has produced in the theorist the new forms of modern societies rather than a description of social reality. See Salvador Giner. *Mass Society*. London: Martin Robertson, 1976, 288 pp.

REFERENCES

Aberbach, D. (1996). *Charisma in politics, religion and the media. Private trauma, public ideals.* London: McMillan Press.

Ake, C. (1966). Charismatic legitimation and political integration. *Comparative Studies in Society and History, 9*(1).

Benhard, M. Charismatic leadership and democratization: A Weberian perspective. *Program on Central and Eastern Europe Working Papers.* Series #43. Harvard University.

Benjamin, W. (1983/1936). *L'obra d'art a l'època de la seva reproductibilitat tècnica.* Barcelona: Edicions 62. (Clàssics del pensament modern, 9).

Brea, J. L. (1991). *Las auras frías.* Barcelona: Anagrama. (Colección Argumentos, 121).

Burns, J. M. (1978). *Leadership.* New York: Perennial.

Burns, J. M. (2003). *Transforming leadership.* New York: Grove Press.

Cannon, L. (2003). *Governor Reagan. His rise to power.* New York: Public Affairs.

Carlyle, T. (1985/1841). *Los héroes.* Barcelona: Iberia.

Cavalli, L. (1992). *Governo del leader e regime dei partiti.* Bologna: Universale Paperbacks Il Mulino.

Cavalli, L. (1995). *Carisma. La qualità straordinaria del leader.* Bari: Laterza.

Colacello, B. (2004). *Ronnie & Nancy. Their path to the White House 1911 to 1980.* New York: Warner Brooks.

Cole, A. (1997). *François Mitterrand, a study in political leadership.* London and New York: Routledge.

Conger, J. A. (1989). *Le charismatic leader: Behind the mystique of exceptional leadership.* San Francisco: Jossey-Bass.

Corcoran, P. E. (1979). *Political language and rhetoric.* Queensland: University of Queensland Press.

Dallek, R. (1984). *Ronald Reagan. The politics of symbolism.* Cambridge, MA: Harvard University Press.

Durkheim, É. (2001/1912). *The elementary forms of religious life.* Oxford: Oxford University Press.

Eisenstadt, S. N. (Ed.). (1968). *On charisma and institution building.* Chicago: University of Chicago Press.

Ellul, J. (1967). *Histoire de la propaganda.* Francia: Press Universitaire de France.

Ferrarotti, F. (1993). *Una fe sin dogmas.* Barcelona: Ediciones Península.

Francis, L. J., & Turton, D. W. (2002). A charismatic clergy more satisfied with their ministry? *Mental Health, Religion & Culture, 5*(2), 135–142.

Freud, S. (1968/1912–13). *Totem y tabú.* Madrid: Alianza Editorial.

Freud, S. (1924/1921). *Psicología de las masas y análisis del yo.* Madrid: Biblioteca Nueva. (Obras completas del profesor).

Gergen, D. (2003). Stubborn kind of fellow. *Compass. A Journal of Leadership, 1*(1).

Giner, S. (1976). *Mass society.* London: Martin Robertson.

Giner, S. (1997). La iluminación carismática de la razón. *International Review of Sociology, 7*(3).

Giner, S. (2003). *Carisma y razón: la estructura moral de la sociedad moderna*. Madrid: Alianza Editorial.

Glassman, R. M., & Swatos, W. H. (Eds.). *Charisma, history and social structure*. New York: Greenwood Press.

Guibernau, M. (1999). *Nacions sense estat: nacionalisme i diversitat en l'era global*. Barcelona: Columna. (Columna assaig, 21).

Guibernau, M. (2002). *Nacionalisme català. Franquisme, transició i democràcia*. Barcelona: Pòrtic. (Visions, 5).

Greenfeld, L. (1992). *Nationalism: Five roads to modernity*. Cambridge: Harvard University Press.

Greenfeld, L. (1985). Reflections on the two charismas. *The British Journal of Sociology, 36*(1), 117–132.

Haro Savater, R. (1995). *El carisma de Paula Montal: fidelidad y dinamismo, coordenadas para una lectura actualizada*. Roma, Zaragoza: Edelvives.

Hebrard, M. (1991). *Les charismatiques*. Paris: Éditions du Cerf.

Howard, T. (1993). Charisma and history: The case of Münster, Westphalia, 1534–1535. *Essays in History, 35*.

Howell, J. M., & Shamir, B. (2005). The role of followers in the charismatic leadership process: Relationships and their consequences. *Academy of Management Review, 30*(1), 96–112.

Ibn Haldun. (1977). *Introducción a la historia universal*. Mexico: Fondo de Cultura Económico.

Israel, F. L. (1987). (Compiled). *Ronald Reagan's weekly radio addresses. The President speaks to America*. Vol. 1. Wilmington: Scholarly Resources Inc.

Kellerman, B. (2004). *Bad leadership. What it is, how it happens, why it matters*. Boston, MA: Harvard Business School Press.

Le Bon, G. (1995/1896). *Psicología de las masas*. Madrid: Ediciones Morata.

Lindholm, C. (1990). *Charisma*. Cambridge, MA: Basil Blackwell.

Lindholm, C. (2002). Culture, charisma, and consciousness: The case of the Rajneeshee. *Ethos, 30*(4), 357–375.

Maarek, P. J. (1997). *Marketing político y comunicación. Claves para una buena información política*. Barcelona: Paidós. (Paidós Comunicación, 88).

Mauss, M. (1979). *Sociología y antropología*. Madrid: Editorial Tecnos.

Nimmo, D. (1976, September). Political image makers and the mass media. *The Annals of the American Academy of Political and Social Science, AAPSS, 427*, 33–44.

Pizzorno, A. (1993). *Le radici della politica assoluta, e altri ssagi*. Milano: Feltrinelli.

Plato. (1901). *Ion dialogo platonico*. Madrid.

Poldolny, J., Khurana, R., & Hill-Popper, M. (2005). *Revisiting the meaning of leadership*. HBD Working Paper.

Reagan, R. (1965). *Where's the rest of me?* New York: Duell, Sloan and Pearce.

Reagan, R. (1990). *An American life*. New York: Simon & Schuster.

Ryan, F. J. (Ed.). (1995). *Ronald Reagan. The great communicator*. New York: Perennial.

Savater, R. H. (1995). *El carisma de Paula Montal: Fidelidad y dinamismo, coordenadas para una lectura actualizada*. Roma, Zaragoza: Edelvives.

Shils, E. (1965). Charisma, order, and status. *American Sociological Review, 2*, 199–213.

Solomon, R. C. (2004). Ethical leadership, emotions, and trust: Beyond 'charisma.' In J. B. Ciulla (Ed.), *Ethics, the heart of leadership*. Westport: Praeger

Steger, M. B. (2003). *Globalization. A very short introduction*. Oxford: Oxford University Press.

Weber, M. (1979). *Economy and society*. 2 vols. Los Angeles: University of California.

Westlake, M. (Ed.). (2000). *Leaders of transition*. New York: St. Martin's Press.

Willner, A. R. (1968). *Charismatic political leadership: A theory*. Princeton: Princeton University Press.

BLANCA DEUSDAD is a visiting scholar at Boston University. She earned her Ph.D. from the Department of Social Theory at Barcelona University and earned her degree in geography and history from the same institution in the Department of Social Anthropology. She has written several articles about popular culture and has received and been nominated for several distinguished fellowships. Her recent research has been focused on the study of charisma and politics and the development of the concept of political charisma through the social theory. Her next project, which is the topic of her chapter in this volume, will elaborate on the political comparisons she makes in Western societies. Blanca can be contacted at bdeusdad@xtec.net.

Leadership in German and U.K. Organisations

By Grace McCarthy

INDUSTRIALISATION AND INTERNATIONALISATION OF BUSINESS, INternational consultancies, and publications together with institutions such as the European Union, have had a modifying effect on leadership practices in some countries, to the point where some believe that convergence is taking place. The author has carried out research in Germany and the U.K. to determine whether convergence has taken place or whether there are still differences in German and U.K. organisations in how leadership is exercised. Based on her research, she derived two models of leadership, a traditional German model and a U.K. model. The models look broadly similar but differ subtly in many respects.

Literature Review

Problems in mergers, e.g., Daimler-Benz and Chrysler, have been attributed to cultural differences by several authors including Shelton et al. (2003), Nguyen and Kleiner (2003), and Levy (2001). Hofstede (quoted in Hoppe, 2004) argued that the "dramatically poor success record" of transnational mergers, acquisitions, and alliances is due to a lack of understanding and recognition of national cultural differences, particularly among senior decision-makers. Referring to cross-border mergers, Schneider and Littrell (2003) warned: "Failure on the part of organizational executives to expect, consider, plan for, and deal with cross-cultural issues in management constitutes culpable negligence."

The International Labor Organization (ILO, 2001) claimed that two-thirds of mergers and acquisitions fail to reach their objectives, and that the difficulties of blending cultural and other human factors are often underestimated.

Apart from mergers and acquisitions, there are many other forms of international collaboration, each of which has its own challenges. Expatriate assignments often fail, with a cost both to the organisation and the individual (Cassiday, 2003). Marx (1999) reported that in addition to more managers working on short-term international assignments than previously, there are even more managers who work in international teams from their home base. Many supply chains are international, leading to relations between customers and suppliers in different countries. International collaboration is also part of many research projects, in particular European funded projects. Mayrhofer (2000) described the difficulties experienced in an international research project on human resource management.

Although previous Anglo-German studies have highlighted differences in how leadership is exercised in both countries (e.g., Ebster-Grosz & Pugh, 1996; Stewart et al., 1994; Warner & Campbell, 1993), not all researchers accept the impact of national culture, arguing that the common pressures of industrialisation force organisations to adopt the same attitudes and behaviors (e.g., Rodrigues & Kaplan, 1998; Zink, 1997). Heinrich Von Pierer, CEO of Siemens (cited in Javidan, 2002), argued that the cultural similarities between global industries were very high. Eales-White (cited in Van Maurik, 2001) argued that there was a large core of common views on leadership that transcend culture, race, or status. Convergence is aided by international institutions, e.g., EU, GATT, OECD, and developments in technology and industrial organisation. Paulson et al. (2002) found that a common management model was developing in the EU. However, according to Engwall et al. (2001) there are also counteracting forces such as organisational inertia and national differences, for example in education.

The GLOBE project, a major international research project on the cultural influences on leadership carried out by 170 researchers in 62 cultures (Javidan & House, 2001) concluded that "the fact that the business world is becoming increasingly global does not mean that cultural differences are disappearing or diminishing." Bird and Stevens (2003) agreed, claiming that while national cultures might be experiencing some erosion, they were not being erased. Kanter (1991) concluded from a survey of 11,678 managers in 25 countries that the idea of a corporate global village where a common culture of management unified the practice of business around the world was more dream than reality. Beer (2003) also argued that "the more commercially integrated the world becomes, the more we revert to our tribal cultural inheritance and national way of thinking."

The organisational context has been seen by some, e.g., Bennett (1999), as more significant than national culture. However, Libermann and Torbiorn (2000) found that even in a single multinational corporation, with a common corporate culture, management practices varied substantially across matched countries. Functional culture, e.g., the culture of engineers, has been used to fill some cultural gaps, according to Chevrier (2003), but she cautioned that "the federating power of occupational cultures should not be overestimated." Claus (2003) interviewed fifty HR experts from fourteen European countries and reported consensus that while management practices at the top level of organisations might be converging due to teamwork and interactions with colleagues from abroad, there would be little change at the blue-collar level for the next decade

Begley and Boyd (2003) argued that there were three drivers for U.S. multinationals to export their corporate culture to their subsidiaries: effectiveness through worldwide systems, efficiency through cost consolidation, and ethnocentric assumptions. Trompenaars and Hampden-Turner (1999) commented that much model managerial behavior owes its origins to observations of business practice in Anglo-Saxon or U.S. studies, is often ethnocentric, and the practices listed do not transfer to other countries or other types of organisation. Kets de Vries and Florent-Treacy (1999) argued that the value Americans place on individualism and on participatory management is often in opposition to leadership practices in other parts of the world. McKenna (1998) suggested that while American multinationals dominated industrial development across the world, it did not follow that the universalistic American perspective on leadership would translate easily into other societies and cultures.

66 **THE VALUE AMERICANS PLACE ON INDIVIDUALISM AND ON PARTICIPATORY MANAGEMENT IS OFTEN IN OPPOSITION TO LEADERSHIP PRACTICES IN OTHER PARTS OF THE WORLD.** **99**

Hoecklin (1994) observed that there was great cultural diversity even within Europe, despite the small distances separating cultures. Wilderum et al. (1997) suggested that although Europeans shared a number of fundamental values, national or regional cultural diversity is likely to persist. Brodbeck et al. (2000) proposed that "Since European cultures are diverse and are unlikely to merge in the near future, the ability to build conceptual bridges between cultures will remain a key competence for cross-cultural leadership, not only in Europe, but also worldwide."

Schneider and Barsoux (2003) noted that recent trends in the U.S. and Europe toward participative management and empowerment were leading to a change in the role of the leader from boss to coach, from directing and controlling to facilitating and developing. However, they warned that notions of empowerment and the leader as coach might not easily transfer. Eberwein and Tholen (1993) warned that one model could not simply be introduced into another cultural circle, which had led to failure, for example, when West German practices had been introduced into East Germany. Instead, they recommended adapting relevant elements and training managers for the future.

Lawrence (1998) challenged the tendency to assume that differences will lessen over time. Despite increasing international contacts over the last fifty years, he affirmed that differences have not lessened. He accepted, however, that convergence might occur with increasing competition or changes brought about to the business system by the EU. Hofstede (1996) affirmed categorically that convergence of management would never come. Hofstede (2001) argued that national cultures are extremely stable over time and that correlations in his data in the 1970s and 1990s had not altered.

It appears from the above that despite strong pressures for convergence such as globalisation and common institutions, differences in leadership practices still exist between countries. The research reported here focused on two European countries, with much common heritage and many common institutions. Despite all they share, differences were still found in leadership practices.

Methodology

There were three stages in the research—document analysis, survey, and interviews. The initial stage was a document analysis of award submissions based on the European Foundation for Quality Management Excellence Model. The EFQM Excellence Model (EFQM, 2003) consists of nine criteria, one of which is leadership. Applicants describe their approach to leadership and how their approach is deployed. The submissions included ten European documents from the U.K., nine European documents from Germany, ten national documents from the U.K., and two national documents from Germany. All thirty-one had been submitted for verification by external assessors. As organisations know that assessors may visit them to verify their submission, they are unlikely to include practices that they do not deploy. They are, however, likely to describe themselves in a positive light. Applicants included both public and private organisations and both large and small organisations.

The practices identified were used as the basis for the postal survey. The survey was mailed to 150 organisations in Germany and 150 organisations in the U.K., in automotive, pharmaceutical, and service industries as well as EFQM members in Germany and the U.K., British Quality Foundation members in the U.K., and Deutsche Gesellschaft für Qualität members in Germany. In addition, surveys were mailed to ten EFQM assessors in each country. The purpose of the survey was to understand whether the practices identified in the EFQM award submissions were common in organisations in both countries, whether or not they were familiar with the Excellence Model, and also to assess whether these practices were perceived as good practice. The assessors' views were ascertained in order to provide a check on the organisations' self-perceptions. An overall response rate of 20 percent was obtained.

A series of sixteen interviews in a multinational organisation was then undertaken in Germany and the U.K. The interviews were held with senior-level leaders such as the European Managing Director and the Senior Vice President of Sales and Marketing, with functional pairs such as Human Resources and Finance in Germany and the U.K., and with people lower in the organisational hierarchy such as Customer Service Representatives and Personal Assistants. An American and an Italian who had worked for the company in Germany and the U.K. were also interviewed to gain an external perspective.

The interviews provided a rich understanding not only of the differences as experienced by people in daily contact with people from another country, but also the effect these differences had on working relationships.

Leadership Themes

Six themes were identified in the award submissions and subsequently verified in the surveys and interviews.

Theme 1—"Self-management" refers to aspects of leadership which the leader undertakes whether or not he has people reporting to him. The practices included under this heading relate to feedback on leadership performance, targets, peer support and job rotation, leaders as role models.

Theme 2—"People management" refers to how leaders manage their team members. It includes practices relating to communication, target setting, empowerment, recognition, socialising outside work, and single status organisations.

Theme 3—"People development" relates to how leaders develop their team members, for example by coaching and mentoring, or providing opportunities for training, learning, promotion, and cross-functional collaboration.

Theme 4—"Strategy" relates to the strategic role of the leader, for example defining mission, vision, values and goals, reviewing and communicating strategy.

Theme 5—"External relations" refers to aspects of the leader's role outside their own organisation. It includes involvement with customers, recognition of suppliers, collaboration with customers and suppliers, and involvement with local community.

Theme 6—"Excellence" refers to the role of the leader in innovation and improvement. It includes support for and participation in improvement, acting on suggestions, promoting excellence, organisational self-assessment, use of other models (e.g., Balanced Scorecard, Chartermark, and Investors in People).

Research Findings

The findings of this research have been reported elsewhere (McCarthy 2003, 2004) but are summarised here. Many aspects of leadership were common between the two countries, particularly relating to strategy, quality management and customers, while involvement with suppliers was more common among German organisational leaders than U.K. There were more differences in practices relating to managing and developing people and self-management. Empowerment featured more in U.K. organisations. Team recognition was more common in Germany and individual recognition in the U.K., consistent with Hofstede (2001). Setting personal targets and using employee feedback were more usual in the U.K., although team targets were used in Germany. Encouraging future leaders was more common in the U.K. Forms of employee communication varied, with U.K. organisations generally opting for team briefings and German organisations using site-wide meetings. Organisations in both countries used Internet, email, voicemail and newsletters to supplement face-to-face meetings.

Leadership Models—Same but Different
The findings suggest differences in the way leadership is perceived and practised in the U.K. and in Germany, particularly before the recent changes in Germany noted by some interviewees. Two models of leadership which incorporate the leadership practices identified in each country were developed by the author. The German model is presented in Figure 1 (see page 172) and the U.K. model in Figure 2 (see page 173).

Traditional Model of Leadership in Germany
The traditional view of leadership in Germany described by interviewees is shown in Figure 1. The leader communicates organisational goals to employees as was found in award submissions, survey responses, and interviews. German leaders meet customers. This may result in opportunities for innovation or improvement. For instance, a detailed understanding of customer specifications may lead to new products, and may result in improved business results (Van der Wiele et al., 2002). Involvement with suppliers and the local community was found in the survey responses. Feedback on leadership performance tends to come from superiors.

The leader defines tasks for his or her team members, giving detailed instructions, although team members' suggestions may be incorporated. As Stewart (1994) pointed out, the leader is able to give this detailed guidance because he or she is an expert in the area the leader manages. German leaders cannot do this when their team members work in different countries as they lack the requisite local knowledge. Interviewees described how their leader keeps in touch with team members throughout the process. Team members follow defined processes. There is little recognition for completed tasks, according to interviewees. Team members are self-motivated and are satisfied when they do their jobs well. Opportunities for promotion and development are organised in a systematic way in German companies, again, according to interviewees, not something they expect their supervisor to arrange.

When both team leader and team members are expecting to operate in this way, morale can be high and team members perceive their leaders positively. High employee morale leads to additional benefits in terms of customer satisfaction and business results according to Whiteley (1991).

This has been termed the traditional German model of leadership here as interviewees and the literature (Orth, 1997; Otto, 2003) highlighted recent changes in Germany. However, the 2003 Excellence Barometer (Prudent, 2003) found that technical ability was still valued far above people management or commercial skills in German leaders.

U.K. Model of Leadership

The U.K. model described by interviewees is somewhat different as shown in Figure 2. The leader involves the team in developing the strategy and the leader and team agree on objectives, a process which the U.K. interviewees valued highly. Lim (1997) found that in the U.K., visioning was part of the process of gaining group commitment, and that identifying common goals motivated the team to higher achievement. Handy (1985) also identified allowing others to contribute to the vision as a way of gaining their commitment to it. U.K. interviewees described how they gained an understanding of business priorities and where their contribution fitted in. They were able to make useful suggestions for improvements and innovation and make day-to-day decisions. They had some freedom in defining their own jobs and in carrying out their jobs. They did not expect their manager to be hands-on but rather to have a personal, encouraging, and motivating approach. Team members gave feedback to leaders on their performance. Leaders and team members were involved with customers, which could result in innovation opportunities, e.g., for as yet unspecified products to meet customers' needs.

The leader recognised and rewarded successful achievements. The leader was influential in arranging opportunities for promotion or development. Again, if both team members and team leaders are expecting to operate in this way, employee morale will be high and employees will perceive their leaders positively. As with the German model, high employee morale can lead to customer satisfaction and good business results. Ugboro and Obeng (2000) found a positive relationship between top management leadership, employee empowerment and job satisfaction, and between job satisfaction and customer satisfaction.

Discussion

The models shown in Figures 1 and 2 are very similar, especially in their opening and closing steps. The themes identified in this research are relevant in Germany and the U.K. and can result in high employee and customer satisfaction and positive business results in both countries. The similarities can fool people into thinking that German and U.K. leaders behave in the same way. However, as one interviewee warned, "we may all look the same but we are not the same." The two models differ in the detail as the themes are enacted in different ways, e.g., involvement in objectives, defining team roles, deciding how to carry out tasks, recognition, involvement in improvement. It is these differences which can cause conflicts between German and U.K. team leaders and team members.

> **" THE SIMILARITIES CAN FOOL PEOPLE INTO THINKING THAT GERMAN AND U.K. LEADERS BEHAVE IN THE SAME WAY. "**

The U.K. model in Figure 2 is in line with Kotter's (1988) view of leadership, which included creating a vision, developing a strategy, motivating a group of people to achieve the strategy. The traditional German model is task-focused and consistent with Kotter's view of management summarised as organising and controlling. Most people have both a leadership role and a management role according to Lim (1995), and it should be possible for leaders to deploy both roles as appropriate. Zenger et al. (1991) suggest that directing, one-on-one management, and a focus on one's own department are suited to a rigidly traditional workplace, but that today's more progressive workplace needs to encourage teamwork, get people to generate and implement their own ideas, initiate change, and champion cross-functional improvements.

The similarities between the two models of leadership presented in Figures 1 and 2 can lead to difficulties as people may be unaware of the differences that exist. People are used to their managers behaving according to the traditional model in their country. When instead leaders behave in the way that is normal for their own culture rather than their team members' culture, team members can feel lost, frustrated, or demotivated.

German interviewees managed by U.K. leaders missed the detailed hands-on guidance they were used to. They found U.K. managers too subtle in their feedback

Figure 1
Traditional German Leadership Model

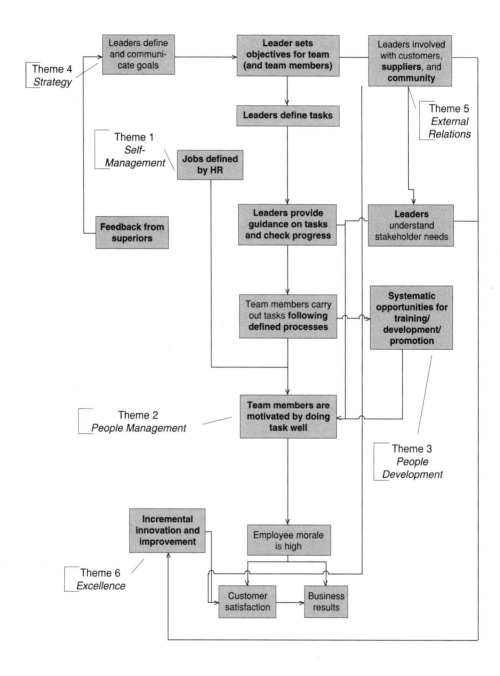

Steps in **bold** differ from the U.K. model shown in Figure 2.

Figure 2
U.K. Leadership Model

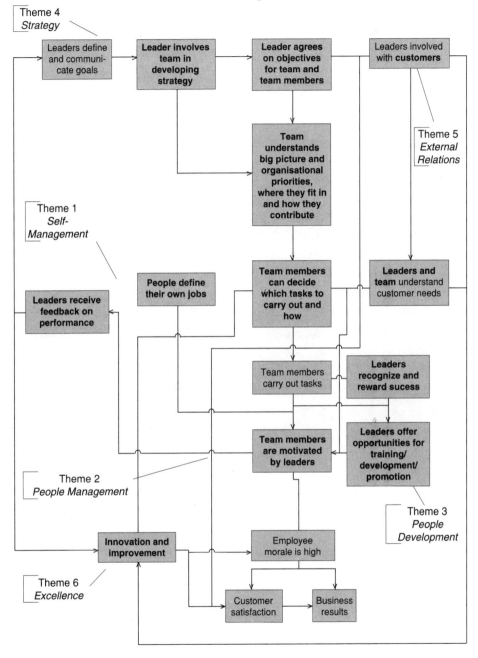

Steps in **bold** differ from the German model shown in Figure 1.

and too vague in communicating objectives. They complained that communication often lacked depth of content, with more emphasis on style and presentation. The German HR interviewee spoke of the difficulties experienced by German employees when the new U.K. boss did not adopt the symbols they associated with power. They were confused as to who was the real leader and looked to German executives who had the traditional trappings and the style they expected. Interviewees noted that with time, people were beginning to regard the U.K. leader as a good leader with a different way of doing things.

U.K. interviewees managed by German leaders resented being micro-managed, as they saw it. They missed the freedom to define their own roles, to decide which tasks to carry out and how. They missed being involved in setting objectives, and receiving feedback, recognition, and reward as well as giving feedback to their team leaders.

Leaders may go against the norms in the country in which they are operating but need to be aware when doing so of the expectations of their team members. Den Hartog (1999) found that going against the norms occasionally may increase the attribution of charisma to the leader. Gupta and Govindarajan (2002) warned that while costly mistakes had been made by companies ignoring heterogeneity across cultures and markets, equally costly mistakes were made by companies dealing with such heterogeneity by becoming its prisoner. This suggests that leaders need to understand the norms in the countries where they operate or have team members, but also need to understand when deviation from the norm may be advantageous.

Both U.K. and German organisations can appreciate each other's strengths and learn from each other. Making changes, however, is not easy. A systematic way of introducing changes was used by German interviewees, although this was sometimes seen as slow and bureaucratic by U.K. interviewees. An individualised approach to motivation was used by U.K. interviewees as a way to encourage their team members to change toward the values and behaviors that the organisation had defined as key, e.g., for their team members to allow more empowerment and less control of their own teams. Change is possible but it takes time.

Conclusions

The intention here is not to assess whether leadership in one country is "better" or more effective than the other. However, it is hoped that greater understanding will increase sensitivity to the differences that do exist and that matter to people, even if they seem trivial to those working at headquarters.

A great deal of effort is expended in mergers and acquisitions in ensuring that a new company will succeed. However, much of this effort is devoted to financial and market analysis, while the failure of many mergers is due to cultural factors according, for example, to Shelton et al. (2003) and ILO (2001). Language lessons are not enough. It is crucial for organisations to understand that there are many differences in how leadership is exercised even within Europe. Organisations should define what they expect of their leaders, which values are core for the entire organisation, and which can vary in importance or in implementation at local levels. Leaders of multicultural teams need to understand what their team members expect and to be sensitive in introducing necessary changes.

The research reported here provides a snapshot of leadership differences in Germany and the U.K. at a particular point in time. It was noted that changes were taking place in Germany, and it may be that differences will lessen over time. However, at present, there are still differences, and those working with Anglo-German teams need to be aware of them.

REFERENCES

Beer, L. A. (2003). The gas pedal and the brake . . . toward a global balance of diverging cultural determinants in managerial mindsets. *Thunderbird International Business Review, 45*(3), 255–273.

Begley, T. M., & Boyd, D. P. (2003). Why don't they like us overseas? Organizing US business practices to manage culture clash. *Organizational Dynamics, 32*(4), 357–371.

Bennett, R. (1999). The relative effects of situational practices and culturally influenced values/beliefs on work attitudes. *International Journal of Commerce and Management, 9*(1/2), 84–102.

Bird, A., & Stevens, M. J. (2003). Toward an emergent global culture and the effects of globalization on obsolescing national cultures. *Journal of International Management, 147*, pp. 395–407.

Brodbeck, F. C., Frese, M., et al. (2000). Cultural variation of leadership prototypes across 22 European countries. *Journal of Occupational and Organizational Psychology, 73*(1), 1–29.

Cassiday, P. A. (2003). Leadership in international settings: Lessons learned. In C. Cherrey, J. J. Gardiner, & N. Huber (Eds.), *Building leadership bridges 2003* (pp. 43–57). College Park, MD: International Leadership Association.

Chevrier, S. (2003). Cross-cultural management in multinational project groups. *Journal of World Business, 38*(2), 141–149.

Claus, L. (2003). Similarities and differences in human resource management in the European Union. *Thunderbird International Business Review, 45*(6), 720–755.

den Hartog, D. N. (1999). Culture specific and cross culturally generalizable implicit leadership theories. *Leadership Quarterly, 10*(2), 219–256.

Eberwein, W., & Tholen, J. (1993). *Euro-manager or splendid isolation? International management—an Anglo-German comparison.* Berlin: Walter de Gruyter.

Ebster-Grosz, D., & Pugh, D. S. (1996). *Anglo-German business collaboration: Pitfalls and potentials.* Anglo-German Foundation/Palgrave Series. Hampshire, UK: Palgrave Press.

EFQM. (2003). *EFQM Excellence Model.* Brussels: Author.

Engwall, L., Alvarez, J.-L., et al. (2001). *CEMP, The Creation of European Management Practice. Final Report.* Uppsala, Sweden: University of Uppsala.

Gupta, V., & Govindarajan, V. (2002). Cultivating a global mindset. *Academy of Management Executive, 16*(1), 116–126.

Handy, C. B. (1985). *Understanding organisations*. London: Penguin Books Ltd.

Hoecklin, L. (1994). *Managing cultural differences*. Workingham, England: Addison-Wesley.

Hofstede, G. (1996). Cultural relativity of organisational practices and theory. In A. Inkeles & M. Sasaki (Eds.), *Comparing nations and cultures: Readings in a cross-disciplinary perspective.* Lebanon, IN: Prentice Hall.

Hofstede, G. (2001). *Culture's consequences: Comparing values, behaviors, institutions, and organizations across nations*. Thousand Oaks, CA: Sage.

Hoppe, M. H. (2004). An interview with Geert Hofstede. *Academy of Management Executive, 18*(1), 75–79.

ILO. (2001). Financial sector workforce hit by mergers and acquisitions. "Human Factor" is key element in success rates for merged companies. ILO. 2004.

Javidan, M. (2002). Siemens CEO Heinrich von Pierer on cross-border acquisitions. *Academy of Management Executive, 16*(1), 13–15.

Javidan, M., & House, R. (2001). Cultural acumen for the global manager: Lessons from Project GLOBE. *Organizational Dynamics, 29*(4), 289–305.

Kanter, R. M. (1991). Transcending business boundaries: 12,000 world managers view change. *Harvard Business Review, 69*(3), 151–164.

Kets de Vries, M. R., & Florent-Treacy, E. (1999). *AuthentiZotic organizations: Global leadership from A to Z*. Fontainebleau, France: INSEAD.

Kotter, J. P. (1988). *The leadership factor*. New York: Free Press.

Lawrence, P. (1998). *Issues in European Business*. Macmillan.

Levy, A. (2001, April). Cross-border mergers: Promises unfulfilled. *Bloomberg Markets*, pp. 37–45.

Libermann, L., & Torbiorn, I. (2000). Variances in staff-related management practices at eight European country subsidiaries of a global firm. *International Journal of Human Resource Management, 11*(1), 37–59.

Lim, B. S. H. (1995). *Management competencies and transformational leadership*. Manchester School of Management. Manchester, UMIST.

Lim, B. S. H. (1997). Transformational leadership in the UK management culture. *Leadership & Organization Development Journal, 18*(6), 283–289.

Marx, E. (1999). *Breaking through culture shock*. London: Nicholas Brealey.

Mayrhofer, W. (2000). Market, bureaucracy, and clan in the Cranfield Network on European Human Resource Management (Cranet-E). In C. Brewster, W. Mayrhofer, & M. Morley (Eds.), *New challenges for European human resource management* (pp. 290–312). Palgrave Macmillan.

McCarthy, G. (2003). *Leadership practices in Germany and the UK*. IHRM 2003, Limerick, Ireland.

McCarthy, G. (2004). *Leadership practices in German and UK organisations*. Manchester School of Management. Manchester, UMIST.

McKenna, S. (1998). Cross-cultural attitudes towards leadership dimensions. *Leadership & Organization Development Journal, 19*(2), 106–112.

Nguyen, H., & Kleiner, B. H. (2003). The effective management of mergers. *Leadership & Organization Development Journal, 24*(8), 447–454.

Orth, W.-F. (1997, November). Rollenwechsel. *Druckwelt*, pp. 36–37.

Otto, B. (2003). Den Blick für das Ganze schärfen. *Quality Engineering, 2003*(11), 10–13.

Paulson, S. K., Steagall, J. W., et al. (2002). Management trends in the EU: Three case studies. *European Business Review, 14*(6), 409–415.

Prudent, C. (2003). Was Firmen an die Spitze bringt. *Impulse*, pp. 18–25.

Rodrigues, C. A., & Kaplan, E. (1998). The country's uncertainty avoidance measure as a predictor of the degree of formalisation applied by organisation in it: Propositions for the European Union countries. *Management Research News, 21*(10), 34–45.

Schneider, J., & Littrell, R. F. (2003). Leadership preferences of German and English managers. *Journal of Management Development, 22*(2), 130–148.

Schneider, S. C., & Barsoux, J.-L. (2003). *Managing across cultures.* Harlow: Prentice Hall.

Shelton, C. D., Hall, R. F., et al. (2003). When cultures collide: The challenge of global integration. *European Business Review, 15*(5), 312–323.

Stewart, R., Barsoux, J.-L., et al. (1994). *Managing in Britain and Germany.* New York: St. Martin's Press.

Trompenaars, F., & Hampden-Turner, C. (1999). *Riding the waves of culture, understanding cultural diversity in business.* London: Nicholas Brealey.

Ugboro, I. O., & Obeng, K. (2000). Top management leadership, employee empowerment, job satisfaction, and customer satisfaction in TQM organizations: An empirical study. *Journal of Quality Management, 5*(2), 247–263.

Van der Wiele, A., Boselie, P., et al. (2002). Empirical evidence for the relationship between customer satisfaction and business performance. *Managing Service Quality, 12*(3), 184–193.

Van Maurik, J. (2001). *Writers on leadership.* London: Penguin Books Ltd.

Warner, M., & Campbell, A. (1993). German management. In D. J. Hickson (Ed.), *Management in Western Europe: Society, culture and organization in 12 nations.* Berlin: Walter de Gruyter.

Whiteley, R. C. (1991). *The customer driven company: Moving from talk to action.* New York: Perseus Books.

Wilderum, C., Glunk, U., et al. (1997). European management as a construct. *International Journal of Management and Organisation, 26*(3), 3–12.

Zenger, J. J., Musselwhite, E., et al. (1991, October). Leadership in a team environment. *Training and Development,* pp. 46–52.

Zink, K. J. (1997). *Successful TQM—Inside stories from European Quality Award winners.* Aldershot, UK: Gower.

GRACE MCCARTHY, at the time of writing this paper, was a researcher at Manchester University, working on both European and U.K.-funded projects. Her research interests include leadership, multinational teams, business excellence, and innovation. Grace spent several years in industry in a variety of roles, including librarian, business excellence, internal communications, and European Director of Customer Service for a major telecommunications equipment supplier. She thus combines real-world experience with academic rigour in exploring significant themes in management today. Grace has now moved to Australia where new challenges await.